Sindu Sreebhavan is a leading mindset coach, management consultant, design thinker, entrepreneur, speaker and author. Sindu specialises in guiding individuals and teams to expand their innovation potential by developing their growth mindset and innovative mindset so that they can discover their own infinite potential and maximize that. She has worked as a management consultant advising world-leading corporations around the world on innovative business practices and cutting-edge technology. Her clients include Honeywell Aerospace, HP, SAP, A*star, Sony, and Schering-Plough. Passionate about youth development, Sindu is the founder of International Youth Leadership and Innovation Forum (IYLIF) where she brings youth from around the world in dialogues with educators, parents, and industry thought leaders to reimagine youth development and education.

Sindu is the author of *Infinite Possibilities: Unlock Your Real Potential with the Secret Recipes of Superachievers, 30-Day Gratitude System, Great Growth Mindset Challenges* , co-author of *Breakthrough: Secrets of growth, happiness and bouncebacks from women around the world*. She has created numerous resources on building growth mindset, self-leadership, innovation potential and resilience in both adults and children.

Sindu is the recipient of the Exceptional Woman of Excellence award at Women Economic Forum (WEF) and is a graduate of Oxford University's Saïd Business School, National University of Singapore and UCLA Anderson School of Management. Science Centre Singapore featured her as a maker to look forward to in the book they published on the occasion of SG50, Singapore's 50th anniversary of independence.

ADVANCE PRAISE FOR *UNLOCK YOUR HIDDEN POTENTIAL*

'One of the most important books of our times! This is the book that is right for today-and for tomorrow. As we equip ourselves to match with the rapid changes of the new industrial revolution, we need logical and practical solutions to transform ourselves and the world around us. In *Unlock Your Hidden Potential*, Sindu Sreebhavan brings together the power of storytelling and research, and take us through the process of unravelling our hidden potential and expand it. The Three Gates framework provides us with a smooth blueprint on how to boldly set our purpose and fearlessly pursue it, to climb the ladder of success. A lot of thought has gone into this book on the emotional challenges faced by people in applying various strategies of self-leadership, and that makes it practical and relatable for people who really want to find the next best in their personal, professional and social life.'

—Pascal Bornet, AI & Automation Evangelist,
author of *Intelligent Automation*

'*Unlock Your Hidden Potential* is an exhilarating read! This wonderful book will help you recognize your potential, then clarify steps you must take to realize your potential. With a brilliant Three Gates Framework, Sindu Sreebhavan guides you through each phase of personal expansion. With fascinating studies, stories, and anecdotes, you will enjoy this journey of personal and professional transformation your—for you and those you love and care about.'

—Ron Kaufman, New York Times bestselling
author of *Uplifting Service*

'I first met Sindu when she was organising a global forum for the youth from around the world. Invited as a speaker, I was impressed by her sincerity, drive and resourcefulness in pulling-off a global event right here in Singapore.

'It is hence with good credibility that Sindu puts forth the Three Gates Framework. It is not just a theoretical framework, she has experimented with it in her own career and picked the components from a wide array of leaders and professionals she has worked with.

'This book is not a narrow list of tips though. It also pulls you out to the space, to the domain of micro animals, and pulls the threads together through real life examples. A great read to refresh, rejuvenate and rewire ourselves to achieve our full potential, no matter the stage of career or life we might be at.'

—Vivek Kumar, Chairman, Asia-Pacific Advisory Board, Global CMO Council Member, Digital Committee, Singapore Institute of Directors, Lifelong Fellow, Institute of Directors, India

'Fear is a monster of the mind that locks up our potential. Only by achieving self-knowledge, self-respect and self-insights, we become authentic about who we are and what we can do. In *Unlock Your Hidden Potential*, Sindu has presented the ways for us to discover and re-imagine ourselves, by affirming our strengths based on lived experiences and re-skilling our mindsets to excel. We all lead from where we are, and learn what to sharpen, and how, to build forward better.'

—Claire Chiang, Co-founder, Banyan Tree Holdings

'Sindu's book *Unlock Your Hidden Potential* provides a useful compass and pathway using the Three Gates Framework. It leads you on a journey to understand yourself, how to work collaboratively and finally how to be a change maker. This book would be a useful tool for anyone who wants to understand their potential and purpose and apply themselves to it. I congratulate Sindu in putting this together to help those seeking clarity of purpose and fulfilment.'

—Thambyrajah T, COO, Singapore Indian Development Board (SINDA)

'Sindu has filled every single page of this book with interesting anecdotes. With the Three Gates framework, Unlock Your Hidden Potential will help you identify your hidden potential, and tell you why and how to unlock the same. A must read, this book is a perfect gift for someone you care about.'

—Deepshikha Kumar, Founder and CEO, SpeakIn

'This book is a must-read for those who want to elevate their game in their personal and professional lives to find growth and success. Infused with easy-to-follow strategies, research findings and real-life stories, in *Unlock Your Hidden Potential*, Sindu Sreebhavan provides a gripping narrative on why it is necessary for us to unlock our hidden potential in the age of IR4.0, and how this can be achieved. The Three Gates Framework gives us the perfect strategies to expand our potential, at every phase in our life, making it a compelling read for everyone, irrespective of whether you are starting your professional life or a career veteran looking for more.'

—Michael Henry, CTO at CYFIRMA, Member at Forbes Technology Council

'*Unlock Your Hidden Potential* is a must-read for anybody who wants to raise themselves to greater success. It reminds us that success and leadership are about the value we create when we invest in ourselves and unearth our own "super powers". The Three Gates framework outfits you with the techniques to discover your innate potential and apply that in your life to manifest those superpowers to touch lives significantly.'

—Dr Timothy Low, CEO & Board Member of
Farrer Park Hospital, Singapore,
Healthcare Investment Consultant for
Pavilion Capital (Temasek Group),
author of *The Triangulation of Success*

'Industrial Revolution 4.0 has triggered unprecedented disruptions to organisations and individuals, in terms of jobs, tasks, skills and personal lives. *Unlock Your Hidden Potential* is a timely and useful guide in this era. It is also a time for reflection, to reimagine and refresh one's future where they are now, who they want to be in the midst of these uncertain times of change. Therefore, the analogy of using the Three Gates—personal, people and universal is most apt and the Secret Codes and Drivers to "unlock" these gates are most useful to realise one's inner potential, discover the beauty in you and kindle a spark in realising the beauty of the world you are in.'

—Dr Koh Tat Suan, CEO at Ori9in, Co-founder at
Workdough, Former Director at SkillFuture

Unlock Your Hidden Potential

Sindu Sreebhavan

PENGUIN BOOKS

An imprint of Penguin Random House

PENGUIN BOOKS

USA | Canada | UK | Ireland | Australia
New Zealand | India | South Africa | China | Southeast Asia

Penguin Books is part of the Penguin Random House group of companies
whose addresses can be found at global.penguinrandomhouse.com

Published by Penguin Random House SEA Pte Ltd
9, Changi South Street 3, Level 08-01,
Singapore 486361

First published in Penguin Books by Penguin Random House SEA 2022

10 9 8 7 6 5 4 3 2 1

ISBN 9789815017731

Typeset in Garamond by MAP Systems, Bangalore, India

www.penguin.sg

To my children Advaith and Aditi
without whom I wouldn't have learned many marvelous lessons
and experienced many marvelous adventures I cherish.

Contents

Introduction

The Crash

'Ten . . . Nine . . . Eight . . . Seven . . . Six . . . Five . . . Four . . .
Three . . . Two . . . One . . . Zero . . . Lift Off'

It was a cold night in Cape Canaveral in the east coast of Florida on 22 February 2019. All eyes and ears were on the Beresheet spacecraft. After all it was not just a space mission, it was a small country's bid to be among the mighty fours to succeed in a moon mission. Till then only four other countries had accomplished a soft touch down on the moon's surface. It was not just that—it was also the world's first private lunar lander. It was the dream of three engineers, Yariv Bash, Kfir Damari, and Yonatan Winetraub who dared to make their moon dreams a reality. This was a mission anticipated to make many first moments in history.

In Yahud, Israel, about 6,500 miles away from Cape Canaveral, a group of scientists and engineers were working on the last-minute details to ensure the successful launch of the Beresheet from Cape Canaveral. It was not just the people in the control room that anxiously watched this historic spacecraft launch, but the entire space community and millions of space enthusiasts across the world were also excitedly watching it. They cheered after watching a successful launch.

After a seven-week voyage through the void of space, as the spacecraft reached the vicinity of the moon, it was ushered in by the gravitational pull of the moon. Beresheet positioned itself into an elliptical orbit fifteen kilometres above the moon's surface. Back on earth, inside the control room, the launch team who had been working on this project for the past several years were excitedly waiting for the final touchdown. Outside the control room, hundreds of people, who wanted to be a part of this historical moment, were eagerly waiting to watch the grand touchdown that was being telecasted live.

The first part of the landing went as per plan. There were loud cheers all around. Now it was the time to move onto the second part—to land on the Sea of Serenity, a colourful landscape on the moon formed by ancient volcanic eruptions. As people on earth excitedly watched the unfolding of the events through the signals from the lander on their computers, suddenly, the display screen went blank, and the signals stopped coming in. The scientists leapt into action on tenterhooks, to re-establish the connection. The tension in the room was palpable. To everyone's relief, when the signals started coming in again after a few minutes, this time the applause in the control room was even louder. But the celebration didn't last long. Shortly the display went blank again and they lost the connection with Beresheet once again. Despite their best efforts, the scientists could not bring it back to life. Then the horrible truth sank in—Beresheet did make it to the moon, but it didn't make a soft touch down as planned and they lost their chance to be part of the mighty fours this time.

Beresheet was designed to capture high-resolution photos of the moon. It was even expected to send selfies, and on the way to the moon, it did send a selfie with the Earth in the background. However, after that, it went out of control and crashed on the moon. To witness their mission perish was a major shock for the team. Years of work became a heap of moon junk. It looked like a disaster. But was it really a disaster?

Incidentally, there is a surprising tale of survivors here. Who are those survivors? Before we dive into the lesson, let us 'visit' the crash site.

Part 1

The Three Gates

Chapter 1

A sprinkle of water for your hidden potential

Who can possibly survive a shock as devastating as a lunar crash we discussed in the Introduction? What are these folks made of? What makes them imperishable?

Once the Beresheet team accepted the fact that they couldn't bring the spacecraft back to life, they started investigating the crash. They were desperate to find what was left of the craft. The Beresheet carried a digital time capsule, the size of a DVD, of our planet in it to the moon. It contained thirty million pages of information in digital form, human DNA samples, children's drawings and at the last minute, the team introduced some 'astronauts', thousands of tardigrades, also into the disc.

Tardigrades are cute little plump creatures, also known as water bears or moss piglets, that are all of one millimetre in size. These critters have this swoon-worthy smooth skin and they look so unreal that people may mistake them for a toy if they were larger. You can find them anywhere and everywhere on earth. Tardigrades are known as the toughest animals in the known universe. They surprised the zoologists when they subjected these tiny critters to shocks after shocks, testing their limits of perishability. They took them to some of the highest altitudes and then to some of the deepest trenches on earth, they boiled them to unbearably high temperatures and then froze them to extremely low temperatures, they put them in bone-crushing high-pressure spots and then at floatingly low pressure, they kept them in a vacuum and then exposed them to very high radiation levels. Though tiny, tardigrades managed to survive all these shocks. The interesting fact is, that they can remain alive without oxygen and water as well. It sounds like they don't have limits when it comes to surviving shocks to remain imperishable. Tardigrades' tiny frame definitely conceals the enormous potential it hides within, just like some people whose external appearance does not give any trace of the enormous inner strength they possess.

After conducting extensive probes, it came as no surprise to the Beresheet team that though the spacecraft perished, the time capsule and the tardigrades in it most likely had survived. In the same way that the tardigrades survived the crash, you might know or have heard of people or organizations who have emerged triumphant after a series of disturbances, much to the admiration and jealousy of others. Others may call them smart or lucky, but it goes much beyond that. This may thus beg the question: just like tardigrades, how do individuals, groups or organizations emerge victorious despite facing disruptions? This has something to do with unlocking the Three Gates to our hidden potential. In this book, you will learn why it is essential for you to unlock the Three Gates with the Secret Codes to uncover the potential hidden within you.

Your potential is all about your limitless behaviour

What makes certain people and organizations invincible in the face of shocks? This is something similar to what tardigrades do. A tardigrade is ever observant of its circumstances. When faced with shocks and unfavourable situations, tardigrades acknowledge and accept the reality of the situation. It brings its metabolic processes to a halt and dries out to about three per cent of its normal body water content. This state is called the 'tun' state and they can continue in that state for decades and possibly for centuries. The interesting fact is that tardigrades can come out of the tun state and thrive again. In order to come out of the tun state what it needs is just a sprinkle of water. These droplets of water kickstart the metabolic process and the tardigrade recoups itself and gets back to the state of action and growth.

There is a great similarity between the tardigrades and people who come out triumphant from shocks. These people also acknowledge and accept their reality and unlock their hidden potential to adapt and blossom. However, there is a huge upswing in what these people do compared to tardigrades—they find their own sprinkle of water. They don't collapse on the outset of a shock; they turn into their tun state. But they don't remain idle there, instead, they unlock their hidden potential and make use of it to come out of their tun state swiftly. However, what keeps them apart from people and organizations that perish in shock is what they do during and after the tun. These are people who have carefully nurtured themselves in such a way that they use certain strategies and processes to unlock their hidden potential and make use of it to emerge triumphant, no matter how bad their situation is.

We come across many people who lose hope at the onset of facing disappointments. Many a skilled professional have lost their belief in themselves after losing an interview, many an executive got stuck in their career because they were unaware of the enormous potential inside themselves to rise to the occasion, many brilliant students have lost their inner strength to persevere upon not getting the desired results and many creative geniuses have lost their confidence when people don't believe in their creative expressions. Is it because of the lack of inspiration and motivation? That could be a reason, but just with superficial inspiration and motivation, people don't transform. What if they develop their internal resources in such a way that upon facing these challenges, they are able to use those internal resources to strive toward success on the next try? It is those who identify and cultivate those internal resources with the right tools and practices that ultimately transform. And, it is in such instances that inspiration and motivation positively aid transformation.

Tardigrade is a perfect metaphor for those individuals and corporations who are positioned on a definite path to strive, thrive and grow in today's world which is being influenced and shaped by the nine meta-trends. Before we learn what they do to survive and thrive in an increasingly disruptive world, let us first take a look at the meta-trends that are currently shaping our world.

The meta-trends we need to watch out for

Historically, meta-trends precede major disruptions and deep shocks. It's the *meta trends* that lead to *mega trends* and *multidimensional disruptions*. People and organizations that learn to detect these trends early and decide to evolve are rewarded in the end. Others are more likely to succumb to failure in spite of their popularity and mastery of their work.

Have you ever seen someone with a Blackberry? Heads of states, CEOs and busy professionals carried Blackberry phones in the mid-2000s. In the corporate world, it was also a symbol of showing how important a person is in an organization. At one point there were 80 million Blackberry users around the world. In spite of its stature and popularity in the corporate world, Blackberry failed to innovate itself, ignoring many meta-trends predicting the onset of smartphones, changing customer tastes and evolving corporate culture.

What were the reasons for Blackberry's fall? In the early 2000s, many organizations hailed the 'Bring Your Own Device' (BYOD) policy, allowing the use of personal mobile phones in accessing the organization's information, along with company-provided devices. Before BYOD, Blackberries were primarily purchased by enterprises for their executives to serve the same purpose. But Blackberry didn't seem to consider BYOD as a threat to their existence. Blackberry also failed to grasp the rate at which smartphones were stealing the hearts and minds of people across the world. In the end, despite its popularity, high reputation and large market penetration, unfortunately, it had to perish. If Blackberry hadn't ignored the meta-trends and instead innovated itself, it was at the right place to accelerate its growth and presence and become the market leader.

It's not just the organizations that suffer when they ignore meta-trends, individuals do so too. In 2010, when the subprime economic crisis was snowballing, though many experts in the financial industry kept warning about the upcoming crash, when the shock finally happened, it came as a surprise for many who could have paid attention to the obvious meta-trends and made course corrections early on. The cracks were so deep that many corporate giants collapsed, and many more organizations had to pull the plug on their highly anticipated projects. More than a decade later, some are still gasping for air and a sprinkle of water. While there are people who perish failing to notice the meta-trends, there are also people who evolve themselves by observing the meta-trends and developing the behaviours and skills needed to survive the disruptions that the meta-trends foreshadow. We can learn a lot from history because history has a tendency to repeat itself. It is important to watch the meta-trends and stay prepared for the disruptions of the future.

But what could possibly disrupt the future?

If you look back on history, you will easily observe that every Industrial Revolution directly or indirectly influences the way we live and work. With drones delivering parcels, self-driving cars, online banking, and virtual holidays, we are experiencing colossal changes in the way we live and experience life in today's technology-driven interconnected world. We currently live in the Imagination Age in which we make use of our imagination and creativity to innovate and create economical value. What makes it possible is the rapid technological advancements, which are collectively known by various names such as the Fourth Industrial Revolution, IR4.0, 4IR and Industry 4.0.

We are already in an era of relentless change and perpetual turmoil. Structured unemployment, economic downturns, epidemics, changes in societal patterns, global uncertainties, interminable competitions, forced isolation, turbulent relationships, and the list goes on. Our minds are not wired for this scale of change and uncertainty. The only solution here is to train and rewire our brains to adapt and grow.

Let's look at the nine most compelling meta-trends that we need to be ready for.

1. Globalization and Localization

After decades of globalization and the dominance of capitalistic ideologies like free trade, we are seeing a surge of nationalism and localization, such as Brexit. The nationalistic sentiments force transition from global interdependence to local self-reliance. There are several reasons contributing to the growing trend of localization.

Since the 1990s, the focus of many businesses had been to outsource certain functions of their businesses, such as IT and manufacturing, overseas. These decisions were influenced by economic, political and climatic factors. This introduced a new wave of economic developments in many developing countries and extensive supply chain networks around the world. But the recent developments point to a reversal of this trend.

According to a 2020 report from Bank of America Global Research, more than 3,000 companies across America, Europe and

Asia Pacific, which constitutes a market cap of USD twenty-two trillion, are planning or have already announced their plan to shift a portion of their current supply chains from their current location. The increasing labour costs in developing countries, escalating political tension in the free trade agreements, disquieting national security concerns, growing anticipation of more epidemics and soaring calls for reducing carbon footprint are some of the main factors triggering these relocations. Moreover, the Covid-19 pandemic brought the necessity of local self-reliance to attention and is accelerating the pace of localization.

While localization efforts are on the rise, it is interesting to notice the globalization trends in some totally unexpected areas. There is an increasing number of job advertisements with the location of work 'anywhere'. What it means is that a person living in South America can work remotely for an organization in Singapore. This trend of globalization of remote manpower is going to accelerate as people and organizations have discovered the freedom, productivity and cost savings of working from home. The growing trend of the gig economy too adds fuel to the growth of this global pool. Now an employer has the access to the best talent based anywhere in the globe without having to worry about expat packages, visa processing and relocation costs.

The world is going to be a playground for people who are willing to work seamlessly with people who are different from them. Self-management, emotional management, value systems, collaboration skills and lifelong learning determine the growth, success and imperishability of individuals in the midst of these changing paradigms.

2. Rapidly evolving silver economy

Recently I asked an audience, 'Do you know how many Singaporeans are above the age of 100?' Someone said ten. In fact, it's over 1,000, that's one in 5,000 among a population of five million. In 2020, the median age of people in Singapore was 42.2 years, which is the oldest in Southeast Asia. Southeast Asia has a median average age of 30.2 years while the global average is thirty-one years. The global life expectancy in 1950 was forty years.

In many parts of the world, the birth rate is rapidly decreasing, but due to lifestyle changes and advancements in healthcare, life expectancy is increasing. By 2050, it will rise to eighty years. According to a study by World Economic Forum, sixteen per cent of Asia's population will be over sixty-five by 2040. This has a direct impact on the working-age population. Consider the case of the current working population in China. Those who were born in the cities are most probably the only grandchild of two sets of grandparents. This means that these people are the only ones available to support their parents and grandparents. In an ageing world where the percentage of the working age population is getting lesser and lesser, those who are working will have to provide support for more people.

At the same time, we have started seeing the extension of the retirement age in many countries. We will also see a gradual increase in the involvement of the silver generation, who are popularly known as senior citizens, in the day-to-day functioning of society. Currently there are phones, dating websites and modelling agencies just for seniors. They also come with huge spending powers. In the age of the ageing population, we can anticipate many more changes in infrastructure, entertainment, medical and other sectors. This gives rise to technological advancements in these areas as well.

Silver economy is the businesses catered to the needs of the silver generation. It introduces new challenges, opportunities and competition in the business and job markets. In such a business environment, your age has little influence compared to the experience you are bringing in. Irrespective of age, this economy commands advancing lifelong learning, collaboration and emotional intelligence skills for a more inclusive and healthier lifestyle for all generations to live safely.

3. Relentless demand for equality in humanity

In our interconnected world, diversity is much wider than gender, race, religion and ethnicity. Organizations are fast discovering more areas of diversity than just political beliefs, gender identity, sexual orientation and physical and mental abilities. Are we able to meet this relentless demand for equality in humanity? Is it beneficial? Is it possible?

Many studies on diversity point to the fact that diversity drives innovation and hence provides an edge over competitors. Singapore is a great example of that. This Southeast Asian city ranks high internationally in various socioeconomic and living standard indicators. One of the striking features of Singapore is the HDB flats around the island. These are the public housing estates developed by the Housing Development Board of Singapore. HDB buildings in each neighbourhood come with their own common design, colours and amenities. Singapore applied carefully designed diversity measures for bringing people of diverse ethnic identities together, through policies such as allocating housing based on the national percentage distribution of various ethnicities in these estates. This ensures that people of various ethnic identities get a chance to know each other's culture and customs, while using the common amenities and nearby facilities, as a community. As per the Hamilton Project, there is a direct effect of high-skilled immigration on innovation. Singapore is a shining example in facilitating the possibility of a diverse highly skilled workforce.

When it comes to becoming a role model for best case practices on diversity and inclusion, Southeast Asian countries have a lot to contribute to the other parts of the world. A country that is fast becoming a role model for the number of women CEOs, as well as women on boards, is Vietnam. On the global front, we have seen the remarkable power of #metoo and #blacklivesmatter movements.

A study by Boston Consulting Group found that by increasing diversity in the leadership team, companies can boost their innovation and financial performance. Apart from these points, most of the other meta-trends we discuss here also point to the importance of diversity and inclusion. A Harvard Business Review report points out that an increase of zero to thirty per cent increase in women on boards translated to a one-percentage-point increase in net margin. This is about a fifteen per cent increase in profit for a typical organization. Female leaders bring in traits such as flexibility in understanding, less dictatorial approach and empathy in the boardroom as well as in the workplace.

Corporations and countries are taking various measures to introduce more diversity in the upper ranks and boardrooms. Norway, which was the first country to introduce such quotas, necessitates that publicly listed companies should have at least forty per cent female representation on their boards. Many other countries have introduced minimum quotas for the number of women board members.

However, in spite of this evidence, we don't see enough diversity and inclusion in the workplace. The reasons for that are the thoughts and attitudes we developed based on age-old practices. Understanding diversity and consciously practicing inclusion is increasingly imperative to remain a valued contributor to your workplace and community. And to practice it, we need to cultivate self-awareness and socio-emotional leadership. Those who carefully cultivate and exercise these skills are the ones who are going to emerge victorious from personal and global uncertainties.

4. Multi-generational work environment

I have been fortunate to work with people of various age groups through my speaking, consulting, training and entrepreneurial ventures. This experience helped me get greater insights into various generations, their working styles and preferences. The varying working styles of different generations is blatantly apparent when I conduct design thinking consultation and workshops to help people and organizations to be more innovative. We observe younger children getting excited about trying new challenges while the older generations play safe as they do not want to 'look stupid' when they try and fail. However, the world is looking for innovators – people who can come up with ideas to solve challenging problems and are confident enough to try out those ideas.

Millennials entering the workplace was a huge awakening for the world. That is when the world saw a major shift in thinking, working and attitudes in a generation, and organizations are still spending millions of dollars to create a sustainable working environment on account of this. However, it is high time to realize the fact that the next generation, Gen Zs, has already entered the workforce, with yet a new set of work ethics. By 2025, Gen Zs, the generation born between 1996 and 2005, will become a force to be reckoned with in Asia, representing a quarter of the Asian population.

As children, Gen Zs have seen their parents and the world going through challenging economic and political transitions. Many of them had the first-hand opportunity to see different familial structures, experience diversity and learn about various challenges faced by our planet and humanity since young. Compared to Millennials, Gen Zs are more pragmatic and are inclined toward finding the balance between their core values and financial returns. They are the first true digital natives, having grown up in the age of personalised devices, which have made them choosy when it comes to their materialistic pursuits. Having undertaken many big and small projects at school compared to previous generations, they are more forthcoming when it comes to trying out challenges, and that positions them in a better place to be more innovative compared to previous generations.

If you take a look at today's workplace, with the extension of retirement age in many countries, you will see many Gen X, Millennials, young Gen Zs, and even Baby Boomers. In such an environment with differences in thinking and working, to work productively and amicably, it is essential for each generation to understand the thinking and working styles of other generations and cultivate tolerance and flexibility. In order to thrive and stay happy in such an environment, skills such as self-awareness, social awareness, emotional intelligence, and effective communication are essential.

5. Rising chorus for revolution in education

Anything that doesn't innovate itself to stay relevant in time becomes unusable, just as we have seen in the case of Blackberry. Unfortunately, that is the case with our current education systems. Over a century old, these systems struggle to make it relevant to people who are using them. Education has become a battlefield that takes up the entire time, energy and efforts of a student's day. Yet it fails to prepare the students to be proficient and confident to take on the future world of incessant shocks. We need to re-imagine education as a lifestyle where we can choose and adopt the style to upgrade our knowledge, behaviours and mindset, staying close to reality as close as possible, to increase our chance to withstand the shocks and disruptions.

I have had the opportunity to be part of influencing youth education in many ways, including organizing events with international participation to re-imagine education and developing and delivering courses to students and teachers on various 21st century skills, innovation, mindset and learning skills. While students at school are busy learning how to multiply, divide and memorize the flora and fauna of faraway countries, they are missing out on discovering their own hidden potential to grow and flourish.

In one instance, a teenager who was in our learning skill development workshop at As Many Minds told me, 'I don't revise my lessons in advance. Anyway, I forget what I learn by the time of the exam. So I have to spend time revising again. Then, why waste time now? I will study closer to the exam'. Needless to say that her strategy didn't help her much. As the children are burdened with more and more things to learn, the mere management of their studies and other activities has become a challenge for them. This results in anxiety, stress and poor lifestyle choices among the youth. Since uncertainties and changes are going to be constant companions of their future, it is crucial for them to develop the right mindset and learn how to be productive before they learn subjects and languages.

During Covid-19, our education world was suddenly forced to adopt an online learning model and realized that the current systems are so far off from what we want to achieve from education. In the next decade or so, what we are going to witness is not a reform, but a revolution in education. We will see collaborative and co-creative learning in a student-driven learning environment, where students from across the world will have the opportunity to attend classes from the best in the world online.

In 2021, for the first time in its ninety-two-year-old history, *Time* magazine picked fifteen-year-old Gitanjali Rao as the *Kid of the year*, a barometer for the rising leaders of America's youngest generation from among 5,000 US-based nominees. Rao was selected for the social impact she made with her invention and leadership, in areas as diverse as diagnosing addiction to morphine Epione and detecting lead in water. The borders of education systems are slowly becoming invisible and we will see more innovations coming out from schools. In the innovation-driven world, we will need to be fully prepared to invite students to our workplace to contribute and witness more competition in the workplace from all age groups.

Ten years ago while I was waiting to watch my son's elementary school performance, I mentioned to a fellow mom that I enrolled in a new course. She looked at me with admiration and said, 'It is amazing that you are still studying at this age.' Oh boy, did I feel ancient? Many among us still entertain the concept of 'studying age', which we need to wipe out like a pest from the past. The concept of studying age puts out many people's fire to reinvent themselves. As technology and innovation are advancing at an unprecedented pace, adults also need to cultivate lifelong learning to stay in the game. Just like we do the hardware and software upgrades of our gadgets, we need to make periodic upgrades to our knowledge, skillsets and mindset a norm, to remain resourceful and relevant.

Nevertheless, to prepare yourself to acquire new skills and knowledge, the availability of courses in the relevant area is just the background. What is more important is your initiative to take learning as a lifestyle and approach each unachievable target as a challenge. Learning to boost willpower and productivity is of utmost importance here.

6. Era of working together with robots

When Sophia the humanoid social robot became a citizen of Saudi Arabia in 2016, the media celebrated it. Sophia went on to give interviews on the world's top talk shows and gave her expert opinion on many topics. Did you notice that we don't even call Sophia 'it' though it is a robot? We use the appropriate gender pronouns to address 'her'.

But Sophia was just a start. It is predicted that by 2025, we will be riding in self-driving cars and other autonomous vehicles. Every task for which we can list the exact steps will be fulfilled by Artificial Intelligence, automation, Internet of

Things and robots. There was no exaggeration when projecting the corporate situation thirty years ahead, way back in 2017, Jack Ma said, '*Time* magazine cover for the best CEO of the year will very likely be a robot. It remembers better than you, it counts faster than you, and it won't be angry with competitors'. But, even before that happens, we will have human CEOs with an AI counterpart where the human CEO's role would be more to inject emotions and empathy into the analytical decisions proposed by the AI. So having a robot co-worker will no longer remain a thing of fiction in the future.

Internet-related technologies contribute to ten per cent of US GDP today. However, sixty-three per cent of CEOs believe that AI has a bigger impact than the internet. AI is sure to bring in more jobs, technologies and functions that are not yet created. These new technologies will demand new skills, efficient learning and faster adaptation. Some people might deny it, and some may run away to seclusion from all these developments, but some will stay alert and tackle this new era with confidence and determination.

In the past several decades, the corporate world was thinking in terms of business, logic and formal interaction, leaving human emotions aside, but now they have realized that human emotions are a much-needed asset in business too. Understanding emotions is currently considered the final frontier for artificial intelligence. Deciphering our own emotions and that of others is one of the areas that would be of immense value to increase our success in the workplace as well as in society.

Practicing and championing emotional intelligence and empathy with the right mindset is a prerequisite to remain imperishable as we prepare to co-work and co-create with our AI counterparts.

7. The mental health predicament

Researchers observe that when a pandemic strikes, there is another pandemic in the making—mental health crisis. Reports from all over the world indicate that people are suffering psychologically due to the Covid-19 pandemic. Studies reveal that this is not a temporary situation and that if this mental health crisis is not handled timely, we will be suffering from its impact for a very long time.

Even before Covid-19, the mental health crisis was at an all-time high. Covid-19 just escalated the mental health crisis. At the same time, Covid-19 helped to bring this stigmatized illness into the open. For instance, one in seven people experience a mental health disorder at some point in their life in Singapore. British anthropologist Robin Dunbar came up with the Dunbar number to indicate how many people can a person form stable relationships with. In his book *Friends: Understanding the Power of our Most Important Relationships*, he writes that on average the number of close friends a person can maintain is five and if you include pretty close friends, the number is fifteen. This shows that we are likely to see more than two people close to us suffering from mental health. However, what is more alarming is more than seventy-five per cent of the sufferers do not get professional help.

In general, any disruption has the potential to affect mental health. Mental health is not a taboo subject anymore, and hence understanding, preventing and treating mental health issues should be of utmost importance. We need to have a healthy self-identity and self-awareness and develop self-care practices to keep our minds healthy and to identify whether we need support.

8. Gig economy

Some twenty years ago, when I joined a new organization, what they offered me was a contractor role. Singapore was just coming out of the Asian Financial Crisis and employers were cautious about their financial commitments. While I was happy about my new job and role as it was an exciting project for the healthcare sector, I was concerned as well. I was looking for stability and was worried that my colleagues, many of whom were permanent staff, would treat me differently.

After a short stint at that job, I worked with other organizations both on a permanent basis as well as on contract roles. True to my concerns, initially people treated me differently. In one of the projects, even after being part of an important deliverable, my project director didn't invite me to meet with the high-profile head of the client who had invited the entire project team. The project director told me that since I was a contractor, I didn't need to meet the client's head.

Gradually, I observed things changing. A permanent role did not guarantee permanency anymore and contract roles started fetching more remuneration. Being a person who finds it difficult to feel excited about routine work and always craves new challenges, the consulting industry provided me with a variety of choices to entertain my inner explorer. But having the option to choose projects, clients and locations provided extra opportunities to fulfil the wanderlust, experiences and lifestyle I valued. It was easy for creatives and consultants to do this in the past.

Today, many people choose to gig—freelancing their expertise, talent and wisdom—to various clients around the world, for short and long terms. Internet makes it easier for gig workers and employers to find each other. And the gig workers love the independence and variety that comes with their work. Though the picture looks rosy, it has the tendency to isolate people due to the lack of long-term association with others and that might affect their mental health, if not handled with care. Nurturing good self-concept, self-awareness, people management and self-care skills would help us handle such circumstances effectively with a positive and healthy mind.

9. The dawn of the Asian age

Today, three out of the four largest economies in the world are in Asia. By the end of 2025, Asia will have two-thirds of the world's population. Industry 4.0 is the era of Asia. With China and India emerging as global economic and political powerhouses with huge innovative potential and with Southeast Asia becoming the focal point of finance, the geopolitical compass is shifting to Asia.

If you take a look at the various countries across Asia, one thing that stands out is civilizational states. Many of these countries come with rich history and many of them like India, China and Southeast Asian nations have an abundance of ancient wisdom, practices and tools to facilitate a thriving society. In the past two centuries, due to colonialization and thereafter western financial and political dominance, Asian cultures were trying to assimilate into western ideologies and thinking.

We are already seeing the spread of Asian soft power such as yoga, mindfulness, martial arts, cuisines and technology, across the world. But, are the people of Asia fully cognizant of our role as individuals here? In order to embrace the Asian age, Asians need to continuously learn how to embrace new skills and talents and polish their people management skills.

In the future, Asia has the potential to become the job hub of the world, attracting talents from in and outside the region, working both physically and remotely. When a region becomes the job hub, it has the potential to become the education hub as well. We have seen that in the case of the US. Today Asian students form a big chunk, fifty-three per cent, of foreign students enrolled globally. In 2019–2020, there were around 800,000 Asian students studying in the US. When these students come back to their native countries, they are bringing not just the subject knowledge, but the cultural and lifestyle aspects such as Thanksgiving. Asian students and immigrants have also increased the awareness of various Asian cultures and at the same time become the catalysts for the dawn of many new industry sectors and businesses. In the future, when Asia becomes a melting pot of people of various cultures and age groups, we will see more people who are different from us. In order to make the age an Asian success within the window of opportunity, it is imperative for Asians to rise to the occasion and cultivate skills, behaviours and thinking styles that are rich in accepting others, assimilating from others, and leading others while proudly presenting the various cultures of Asia, so that all this will direct us to a more inclusive society.

If people, countries and cultures in Asia learn how to respect the cultures and customs of other Asian countries, it is easier to build a more cohesive Asian age in the coming decades. As Asians unearth their hidden potential to embrace and take advantage of their rich culture and knowledge base and, combine it with the mainstream wisdom from the West, they will be well positioned to create a more balanced world.

Why every shock is a stellar opportunity?

As we have seen in the meta-trends above, we live in a highly volatile world rife with various disruptions. However, in spite of possessing talents, skills and resourcefulness to be successful, we see many people succumbing to situations such as career stagnation, lack of clarity in goals, lack of purpose, lack of willpower, lost opportunities, failed relationships and so on. Have you ever wondered why these people are not getting a breakthrough in their life? Due to the lack of proof for the cause of their failure, many people brand themselves as 'unlucky' when they get into such situations. Such situations in life lead to stress, self-doubt, a decline in self-esteem and self-confidence, lack of sleep, health issues, financial instability and general dissatisfaction with life.

It is interesting to note that, there are also people who achieve success and life satisfaction amidst all the changes we experience, even when they don't start as talented or skilled, compared to many others. What makes it possible for them? People like to call them 'lucky'. But do they create their own luck or are they special? The truth is, the 'unluckies' are as lucky as the 'luckies'.

New developments in physics and quantum mechanics tell us that we have enormous potential within us waiting to be unleashed. But, what makes that unlimited expansion possible? If you want to convert every shock into a stellar opportunity, the solution is to unlock your hidden potential. Developing the skills to understand the power of intrinsic resources and availing of these resources systematically, will help you expand and thrive despite the disruption and incessant shocks.

Chapter 2

How will this book prepare you to unlock your hidden potential?

Having established that the world is on the cusp of many shocks and disruptions and that people who are well positioned to succeed in this environment are those who know how to unlock their hidden potential, this book gives you the Three Gates framework, to unlock your hidden potential in a systematic manner. Inside the pages of this book, you will find the Secret Codes and Drivers to unlock the Three Gates so that you can prepare yourself to boldly face the future like a tardigrade and emerge triumphant no matter what challenges and shocks you may face.

As a long-time management consultant, mindset coach and edupreneur, I have spent more than two and a half decades observing and studying the effects of mindset in a wide range of people and organizations from executives to teachers and students. I have had the opportunity to work with various industries from start-ups, technology giants, research organizations and governmental agencies. Problem-solving is a skill that I have been polishing throughout all these chapters of my career. The insights I gained from these experiences were further enriched when I wrote my books *Infinite Possibilities: Unlock your real potential with the secret recipes from superachievers, Great Growth Mindset Challenges* and *30-Day Gratitude System*, and lead-authored the book

Breakthrough: Secrets of growth, happiness and bouncebacks from women around the world. In addition, I have developed many resources on mindset for corporate and education sectors. I have also had the opportunity to interview leaders from various sectors. One thing I feel fortunate about is having got the rare opportunity to work with a vast range of age groups from children to seniors. Such experiences have given me a unique perspective on mindset, intelligence and leadership. I will be sharing the wisdom from these efforts, experiences and interactions, on how you too can unlock your hidden potential to clarify, plan and achieve your dreams, no matter how big it may appear initially.

The Three Gates

I have mentioned the terms 'The Three Gates', 'Secret Codes', and 'Drivers' several times now and you may be wondering, what exactly are these Three Gates? What are the Secret Codes and Drivers that will help you uncover them?

To put it simply, the world is a stage. Our place on that stage depends on how we are playing in each of the Three Gates. Unlocking these Gates will help you play various roles on that stage and find success and contentment from it. There are Secret Codes to open each of these Gates, and each of these Secret Codes is a combination for certain Drivers. The Drivers of the Secret Codes are skills and behaviours, and as you systematically build proficiency in using those Drivers, the corresponding Gate opens up gradually to lead you to find success and contentment in your personal, professional and social circles.

The Personal Gate helps you develop the skills, attitudes and behaviours to build your personality and your purpose. The People Gate helps you develop your skills, attitudes and behaviours to establish your place among others, confidently and resourcefully. The Universal Gate helps you develop skills, attitudes and behaviours to initiate and lead changes and be a changemaker.

There is no rule that says you need to open these Gates one after the other. You can get familiarized with the Drivers belonging to different Gates at the same time. However, the more proficient you are with the Personal Gate, the more competent and confident you will feel to explore the People Gate. Likewise, the more familiar you are with the Personal and People Gates, the more competent and confident you will be to identify yourself with the Universal Gate.

With the Three Gates framework, you will be able to shape and sharpen your intrinsic resources, which will help you approach any challenge with courage and self-confidence. For that, you will of course need to take a closer look at what these Three Gates are.

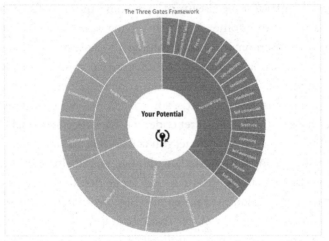

1. PERSONAL Gate

Here you find the intrinsic resources we use to develop an unbeatable 'self'.

Celebrated 19th-century poet and playwright Oscar Wilde said, 'Be yourself; everyone else is already taken'. But do you know who you are and what your powers are? If you do a Google search for 'Who am I?' it returns a whopping ten billion search results. That is way more than the total number of people on the planet, which means, people are searching this more than once and are not finding a convincing answer yet.

This demonstrates the interesting fact that who we truly are is a perennial question, and it has been perplexing the mind of mankind since the dawn of time. Everyone has their own interpretation of it too. During my coaching and mentoring sessions, something I often hear from my clients is, 'I don't know who exactly I am or what exactly my purpose is. If I knew that it would be easy for me to plan my path to growth.'

Most people have definite ideas about how they want to live their lives, many have ideas about what they want to become. Some dream of becoming the next Warren Buffet or Oprah Winfrey, some dream of becoming the next Einstein or Shakespeare and some dream of saving the planet or ending hunger or discrimination or becoming a top executive. However, as we take action to fulfil these dreams, we come across many challenges and roadblocks and many end up quitting their dreams. If you look inside their minds, you will see something interesting. They haven't found the secret code to unlock their Personal Gate.

Inside your Personal Gate, you will find the intrinsic resources you can develop by yourself, with minimum help or influence from others. A strong Personal Gate is the first thing you need in discovering your inherent potential, feeling confident in your own skin, finding your place in this world, and living a purposeful life. It plays an important role in understanding ourselves and thereby relating to others. In Part 2 of this book, you will discover twelve Secret Codes that you can use to unlock your Personal Gate. These Secret Codes will reveal the exact practical skills and behaviours that will help you to understand yourself better, and charter a Development Plan to exercise those skills and behaviours. Once you develop that practice, those skills and behaviours will become your second nature, which will position you well to open the other two Gates.

More importantly, unlocking the Personal Gate will lead you to a state of mind where you will realize that attaining your goals and dreams is a conscious yet enjoyable process even in the face of disruptions and shocks from the meta-trends.

2. PEOPLE Gate

Here you find the intrinsic resources we use to establish our position among others.

One of the quintessential factors that determine success is, how good and effective we are in dealing with other people in our personal, professional and social worlds. Believing in your personal power is important, and unlocking your Personal Gate to prepare for that is also important. But, getting other people to invest their time, energy and resources in your purpose is a leap of growth towards your next levels.

In an interconnected world of rapid changes and disruptions, working with others is unavoidable. Though we all might agree with that, people management is a major headache for many. When we have the skills to connect with people, influence them to understand our views and collaborate with them to fulfil each other's purposes, the journey to success gets faster. When people management is an underdeveloped skill, it becomes difficult to find progress in many of our dreams and hence many people end up achieving less than what they are really capable of. In my coaching and consulting practices, I often come across many exceptionally skilled and talented people, who fail to scale up in their careers just because of their lack of confidence in dealing with other people. Those who don't put their efforts into identifying and growing their people management skills may start feeling unlucky and undervalued, and eventually succumb to mediocrity. What is important to note here is that people management skills are already there inside you and that it is possible to bring them out. If these people knew what exactly they need to do to uncover their people management skills, instead of frustratingly quitting their jobs and dreams due to people issues, they would be able to enthusiastically chase their dreams with the support and help from others. That is where the People Gate comes to your help.

Inside your People Gate, you will find the intrinsic resources you can use to develop long-lasting relationships with other people in your personal, professional and social circles. There are four Secret Codes to unlock your People Gate. By learning to decipher these codes, you will be able to identify where you stand in people management skills and be able to create a Development Plan for yourself to systematically build such relationships to trust, understand and support each other and fly high on the wings of success. These codes are important skills and behaviours, and once you develop the practice of that following the Drivers of People Gate, you will feel more confident in your skin to collaborate and work with others seamlessly.

In today's interconnected world, we can leverage on the help and support from others to expand our ideas and realize our purpose faster and easier, by unlocking our People Gate. You will discover more about the Drivers of People Gate in Part 3 of this book.

3. UNIVERSAL Gate

Here you find the intrinsic resources we use to become part of the bigger picture. The ability to relate your personal goals to bigger issues and causes in the universe increases your self-belief, your commitment and the chances of getting it done leaving long-lasting effects in the lives of people. And as you fulfil your purpose in this manner, you realize that you are indirectly helping others fulfil their purposes as well.

At such a stage in your life, you will realize that many people look up to you as inspiration and many work for you directly and indirectly. This happens when other people start noticing your ideas or products or services and take an interest in those.

This could also happen when your ideas and dreams become so big that you voluntarily reach out for support from the masses or from people who are much more influential than your usual circle. In both cases, you are influencing the masses and hence you need to develop more skills to give justice to the position you are in and act responsibly. This is the stage where many people get disoriented with a lack of knowledge about how to behave. Then, there are many people who take it for granted, act uncivilly and with total disregard for the people who are looking up to them and end up self-sabotaging. In both cases, what they are missing is the skills related to Universal Compass.

Once you have become natives of both Personal and People Gates, and on the way to becoming a native of the Universal Gate, you are not only in charge of your own growth and development, you are influencing the world as a changemaker. And that comes with the responsibility of helping and supporting others to find the Secret Codes to the Three Gates. For that, you need to look at the world you are influencing with a bird's eye view, anticipate and solve issues—and that is what you will find out in Part 4 of this book. The Universal Gate is at a higher plane than the other two Gates for a reason. Being at a higher plane doesn't mean the people operating at the Universal Gate have a higher status, but that they need to position themselves at a place in order to enable themselves to help others identify and unlock their own hidden potential.

So, how do these Gates work? When you develop your Personal Gate and People Gate, you will realize that you have the ability to play a role in benefitting the greater world by expanding your faculties further. You will also be able to see how your own actions, for profit or not for profit, could become the catalysts in effecting a universal cause or your own ideas. Furthermore, you will be able to give a universal purpose to your own actions and initiatives. Universal Gate elevates you to a universal connectedness, where you will be able to bring collective wisdom, knowledge and resources together to fulfil your mission and vision.

Having discussed about the Three Gates and their impact on our success, sceptic minds might still ask, 'Is it going to work? Do we really have such infinite potential?' For that, let's examine what we can find in psychology and neuroscience about this.

Psychology says you have the fire to grow limitlessly

Based on the studies by Stanford psychologist Carol Dweck, there are two types of mindsets: fixed mindset and growth mindset. On one side of the spectrum are individuals with a fixed mindset, who believe that their talent and intelligence are set at birth, and they have no influence in changing that. When a person has a fixed mindset, it is common to find them using phrases such as 'That is the way I am', 'I will never be able to do that', 'Math is not my cup of tea, I am more of a right-brained person'. Their accentuated fear of failure and tendency to guard their self-projected image dampen their growth prospects.

On the other side of the spectrum are individuals with a growth mindset, who believe that their intelligence and talents are malleable. That is, they know how to significantly increase their intelligence and talents by incorporating lifelong learning, effective workstyle, and other mechanisms for continuous improvement. This focus on learning and development accelerates their progress and growth. You would hear them saying things like, 'I have never done it before, but let me give it a try', 'I couldn't make it this time, but let me see where I went wrong and plan for the next time', 'She did it commendably well, let me see what I can learn from her'.

People with a growth mindset are characterized by their willingness to learn new skills, seek feedback, reflect on mistakes, and reach out for help. They see failures as opportunities to learn and take risks to explore the unknown with positive efforts or possible learning. Individuals with a growth mindset focus on the process that leads to desirable outcomes rather than fixate their focus solely on the outcome. They leverage the natural abilities of the brain to unleash their infinite possibilities. They believe that they can make a positive influence on their future with the power to change their intelligence and talents with effort, experience, and exposure, which leads them to the path to success. Whereas individuals with a fixed mindset believe that their intelligence and talents are fixed at the time of their birth and that they have practically no influence in changing it, and often you will see them stuck in their pursuits.

People with a growth mindset are not interested in labels like, 'I am intelligent', 'I am smart', or 'I am lucky'. At the same time, they are also not for, 'I am dumb', 'I am so unlucky', or 'I can never become as good as him/her'. However, they may think, believe, and perform using process-focused identifiers such as, 'I can work hard', 'I can learn from others', or 'I can learn and apply it in my life'. People with a growth mindset learn from the failures and successes of themselves and others. They boost their talent by seeking knowledge from others and sharing their own knowledge. They set their goals, and plan and focus to achieve those goals. They try to identify and follow the skills, behaviours and attitudes that lead to excellence.

It is the growth mindset that leads a demotivated job hunter to suddenly start building himself up and land an excellent job and an underperforming student to start performing well all of a sudden. It is also the growth mindset that enables the best in the field to perform even better and an average performer to become the best.

We are all a combination of a growth mindset and a fixed mindset. But, if we can identify our mindset towards each of our pursuits and beliefs, we will be able to grow our growth mindset in leaps and bounds. If you listen to your conversations to yourself and others, what do they sound like? Do they sound growth-minded or fixed-minded? Many Drivers you come across in this book, especially in Part 2, will equip you with the skills to understand your mindset and take on the path of growth.

It is important to note here that even people with a growth mindset have their own moments of self-doubt and struggle.

However, they are aware that they can learn to overcome such circumstances, and therefore they tend to be more motivated than others. Mindsets are not created equal, but any mindset can be upgraded. A growth mindset leads you to pursue more opportunities and unlock your infinite possibilities.

Neuroscience suggests that a growth mindset is a physical phenomenon

In the past, neuroscientists used to think that our brain is wired permanently to a certain extent at the time of our birth and we don't have much influence in rewiring it. That gave rise to the belief in the scientific world that either you are born with high intelligence, creativity etc., or you are not. Up until the 1970s, they believed that the brain, its structure and functions are changeable only in early childhood. However, the new technologies and scientific advancements after that established that our brain is indeed malleable throughout our lifetime.

The eighty-six billion neurons, the brain cells, in our brain network with other neurons to enable us to function in our daily life. These neurons are capable of creating trillions of connections with other neurons to help us live our lives and, be more intelligent, more skilled, more creative and so on. Our behaviours and responses are also controlled by these neural connections. And, the brain is able to make such connections throughout our lifetime.

With that knowledge, the next question that comes to our mind is, how easy it is to make these connections or wire our brains for increased abilities? For that, we need to know about neuroplasticity. The word neuroplasticity originates from the brain's ability to modify and reorganize itself in response to various experiences throughout our life, just like how plastic takes the shape of its mould. Each of our thoughts and actions is controlled by a corresponding set of neurons. Every time we do something, the neurons make connections by firing chemical signals to other neurons. The more times we do the same action, the more adept these neurons get in signalling each other, and hence the brain can process the action much faster compared to another action with a weaker partnership. This explains why we perform better when we practice piano on a daily basis or give public speeches regularly or wake up early every morning. Our internal resistance in taking that action gets weaker with time that those actions become part of our nature, and that indicates the establishment of a certain level of neuroplasticity for that action.

You have read above that neuroplasticity is the result of repeated action. But, that is only partially true. When you learn a new skill, it is common that we come across some difficulties. Some people tend to leave it at that, and some don't. Here is the trick to achieve neuroplasticity faster. When you come across difficulty in learning or doing something, let the brain experience the challenge by prolonging your sincere efforts to get around the challenge a little while longer. When you do that, the brain releases the neurochemicals responsible to create solid neural pathways, and that initiates the building of neuroplasticity for that task. But how do we prolong the moment when our mind clearly tells us to stop doing it? This is where we take the help of another neurochemical, dopamine. For that, think positively about the task, such as how learning this task will help you progress towards your goal, while you are trying out that difficult part. Such positive thoughts trigger the brain to release dopamine, which is responsible to fill us with motivation and will further motivate us to stay on task for longer and establish neuroplasticity. So, if we stop working on it at the first instance of coming across a challenge and come back the next day to try it again, it will take longer to create neuroplasticity.

Though you can develop neuroplasticity at any age, it slows down with age. The youth brain is a playground for neuroplasticity as they try out many things without prejudice. However, once we cross our mid-twenties and are clouded with prejudices, the rate of neuroplasticity slows down. Adopting a conscious practice of developing neuroplasticity as we discussed above, will help our brain learn new things quicker irrespective of our age.

As per Prof Carol Dweck's studies on growth mindset, the more we know about how we can influence our brain to learn, the more success we find in learning new skills, behaviours and habits. On one hand, it is clear from the meta-trends that we need to up our game to stay relevant, and on the other hand, we know that we can influence our brain to get better at our game to strive and thrive. The growth mindset and neuroscience details above form the necessary understanding for the possibility to unlock our hidden potential and rise, just like how tardigrades wake up from their tun state. Now let us move on to learn about the Three Gates, unlocking which will help us to unleash the potential which is hidden in the tun state inside us.

This book is for everyone such as leaders, executives, artists, innovators, homemakers, students and so on. Irrespective of what phase you are in the journey of your life or of your purpose, you might come across something that could be of help in bringing clarity and robustness to that journey. I hope the practical wisdom from this book will help you develop your mindset, attitude, skills and strategies to face your present and future with renewed passion and energy.

As you learn the Drivers to uncover various Secret Codes to unlock the Three Gates in this book, reflect on which areas of your life you can apply them. Based on that, make your own Development Plan for your personal growth and future breakthroughs as you see fit. You will see me mentioning the Development Plan occasionally in future chapters. As you read the book and discover the Drivers that you need to improve, you may include that in your Development Plan regardless of whether I mention it or not.

Part 2

The Secret Codes to Personal Gate

Chapter 3

Develop an unbeatable self-identify

Who am I?

In late 2017, I came across an eleven-year-old boy, Jerome. He was there to take part in the Public Speaking Camp run by As Many Minds, the organization I founded to support children and teachers in reimagining and experiencing better learning and teaching. The students love to be in the camp and parents are enthused about the transformative effect of it, and it is normal to see both timid and confident children from Singapore and abroad looking forward to being part of this.

It was the first day of the camp, and one by one each child came to the front of the class to introduce themselves. When it was Jerome's turn, he walked to the front of the class, introduced himself and told his classmates they can call him 'Jerome, the President'. Naturally, the other children asked him 'Why?' He said, 'When I grow up, I am going to become the President of this country.' The other children had this quizzical look on their faces that said, 'Here comes another dreamer.'

During the break Jerome told me, 'I saw many students trying to stifle their laughter when I shared my dream earlier. But I am very serious about my dream, and I know how difficult a journey it is to become the president of this country. I know that to become eligible to become the president, I need to have experience in running an organization handling millions of dollars. I am studying my best so that I can get a good job and fulfil that criterion. I know that public speaking is a must to become a capable politician and that is why I am here to learn from the best. I know I need to be a good debater to present and debate on matters related to the country, so that is my next step after becoming a good public speaker.' I was thrilled to learn about the passion and determination in the voice and body language of that eleven-year-old.

The next day, his primary school results, which is called PSLE in Singapore, came out. He had scored among the ninety-nine percentile in the country and had got accepted into his dream secondary school. A few months later, I got an opportunity to attend the National Debate Championship. Guess who we meet there? Jerome was representing his school in the championship, with teammates three to four years older than him.

It was an inspiring experience to watch how Jerome's self-identity was fueling the potential in him to dream big and act big, to achieve those big dreams. Since he believes sincerely and confidently that being the president is his future, he doesn't consider the hard work and time he puts into it, as chores. He does not care about the teasing looks and giggles he sometimes gets from others. He is making his intentions public and uses the responsibility and pressure that comes from that positively to nurture his dream.

We find Jerome's tale inspiring because not all of us dream so big, plan so big and act so big about our aspirations. But our appreciation for Jerome tells us that we would also like to be like Jerome, yet we probably are not as brave as Jerome to take full responsibility to pursue those aspirations. Since many of us are reluctant to admit those dreams to ourselves, let alone to others, we do not find the courage to pursue those dreams.

Is Jerome going to stick to those dreams when he grows up? As he learns more about the world and the possibilities around him, he might keep the dream alive or opt for other pursuits. We can't predict that now. But what we can predict is that even if he does change his dream in the future, he is going to show the same sincerity and passion in achieving 'his new' dream. Sometimes, we are afraid that our dreams might change in the future and hence it is better to not take any action on the current dreams we have. On one hand, there are people like Jerome who seem to be very aware of who they are, what their likes and dislikes are, what they want to become in life and what they need to do to become that. On the other hand, there are people who are unable to conclude what they want to do with their lives.

Most people agree that change is inevitable. It is perhaps easy for us to imagine a change in the physical sense, such as changing appearances or moving to a new home or driving a new car. However, many people find it difficult to believe that their personalities and behaviours could change. Have you listened to people using fixed qualifiers for themselves, such as 'Sales department pays well, but I won't be able to join the team because I am not a great communicator' or 'You see, I am not good at working with others, I like to work alone. So, I am not applying for that job'. There are many studies that outline the fact that people change their personalities over time. If you are not a good communicator now, it does not mean you won't become a great communicator in the future. Similarly, if you are not a good collaborator now, it does not mean you won't become a master collaborator in the future.

So, what if you imagine yourself as a salesperson and see yourself communicating well in front of clients and other people? What if you pick up Jerome's attitude and, identify the skills you need to develop and take ownership of those dreams?

A future-focused self-identity

We change our personalities, our values, our skills, and our outlook. More often these changes happen without our knowledge, but there are circumstances where we actively initiate and effect these changes in ourselves. Today someone might be giving more value to making money and having a secure life, but in ten years, their primary focus might change from making money to leading a minimalistic life or helping underprivileged children. You probably are not able to think about waking up at five in the morning today. But in two years, you might be waking up at 5 a.m. and doing your daily meditation with ease. You might be terrified about high altitude today, but in three years, it is possible that you might be bungee jumping at Macau Tower. If I tell you there is a possibility that you might be able to do the very thing you are most terrified of doing, in four years, will you believe it?

When you are on the path to discover your hidden potential, cultivating a future-focused self-identity is of high priority. However, we find it difficult to envision ourselves as someone different from who we were in the past and who we are in the future. Using his famous the Hierarchy of Needs theory, American psychologist Abraham Maslow described how human motivation changes as we move from one stage of achievement to the next. The needs that line up in the hierarchy are physiological needs, safety needs, love and belonging needs, esteem needs and self-actualization needs. In order to engage our inherent need for change, we should be prepared for changes in our thinking, aspirations, and goals at different stages. So, what we can do is to be committed to our goals at any point in life and develop a self-identity around that, just like Jerome.

My friend Anil Kumar has an amazing personal story of transformation. Anil is currently the vice president of business development for the Asia Pacific region in a leading digital automation and energy management firm. He holds an MBA and an undergraduate degree in Instrumentation Technology. He is a fantastic photographer, a good singer and always handles a significant role in all the events in the community where we live.

Anil said, 'If you had seen me thirty years ago, you wouldn't have guessed that I was to become what I am today. I have been interested in competitive rifle shooting, nature photography and trekking since my teenage days. All these fields were so well complementing that I spent most of my teenage days doing just that, neglecting my studies. Though I passed high school, the marks I scored were so low that I didn't manage to get an offer from any university. In those days, not going to college meant you are doomed for life. I managed to get enrolled on a diploma course. If I finished that course, I would have become part of an engineering team doing what the graduate engineers would ask me to do. When I imagined what I would be doing ten years after I complete the course, I had chills. I realized that that was not the life I wanted.'

The future looked bleak in Anil's eyes, but he had a self-identity of himself living a future better than what the present situation presented—not a life where he would be struggling to make ends meet, not a life where he will always have to follow other people's plans and directions, not a life in which his family will look down on him. He didn't want to become a burden to his well-to-do siblings or his elderly parents. Apart from all this, he didn't want to be the follower of a leader with little prospects of attaining that leadership position. He knew he had leadership potential, but he didn't think the course he enrolled in gave him the opportunity to become a leader in the workplace.

Anil decided to change the future that the present offered. He imagined how he wanted his life to be, what he wanted to do with his life, the sort of job he wanted to land, and the kind of luxuries he wanted to enjoy. He concluded that just dreaming is not enough, he needed to take control of his life trajectory. Consequently, dropped off from the current course and he made up his mind to make himself eligible to join an undergraduate course in engineering from a reputed university. That being the case, Anil opened his high school books once again, this time to genuinely study and he took his high school exam once again. He had to learn how to focus for an extended time in his studies, something that was alien to him, and learn certain concepts from the basics. According to Anil, the struggle was more about keeping the motivation alive and following a pattern of disciplined efforts to make his self-directed learning sustainable. His drive and efforts paid off, he graduated with flying colours and got admitted into his dream engineering course, where he further practiced and polished the newly discovered passion for studying and completed the course with flying colours.

Anil realized that he didn't want to live the future that his past and present had predicted. He created a strong self-identity of what his bright future is and believed that he can reach and achieve that future. Sometimes, the gap between the current and the future may seem too wide and unbridgeable. Many people give up thinking that it is impossible to build any bridge there. But some people make up their minds to believe it is possible. Create your imagery and belief so strong and tell yourself, 'If there is no bridge, I will fly on an airplane or row a boat or dig through the underground to reach the other side because that is where I belong.' Help your brain leverage neuroplasticity to build a strong future-focused self-identity with your thoughts, beliefs, and actions.

Drivers to develop an unbeatable self-identity

In this section, we will explore how you can develop an unbeatable self-identity with the seven Drivers of self-identity.

1. Who was I (Past self)?

When you look back, do you think you have remained the same in the last ten years? If you are an adult, do you still speak like your fourteen-year-old self? Do you still hang out with the same group of friends? Have your aspirations changed? How has your definition of success changed over time? What were your likes, dislikes, values, habits, and beliefs at that time? Do you still have the exact same personality as your ten years younger self? Let me ask you, do you think you could have achieved more if you were not as self-critical as you were and believed more in your potential? What stands out in the case of people like Anil and Jerome is how their future-focused self-identity managed to outpower their self-critical tendencies and the defeatist and disempowering remarks from others.

When we look back, we come across many glimpses of our character. You might see how brave or courageous you were in the past, how idealistic or rash your thoughts were, how rude or polite you were, how punctual or tardy you were, how composed or impulsive you were in critical situations and so on. You will see that your personality has changed over time.

2. Who am I (Present-self)?

We saw how Jerome cultivated a future-focused self-identity. He had a pretty good idea of his strengths and weaknesses in skills that he thought were important to achieve his dream future. He knew that he was a student who put a lot of effort into his studies. He acknowledged the wide skill gaps he had to bridge, such as public speaking and debating. When we look at charismatic politicians, we see them speaking effectively. Jerome didn't consider himself any less because he couldn't speak as eloquently as them, but he devised a plan to develop that skill by learning from the best. Similarly, while acknowledging his areas of improvement, Anil didn't allow himself to be chained down by his past or present.

Doesn't the reflection on your past and present life provide you with irrefutable proof of your ability to change? If the skills once hidden are in plain sight today, it is possible that there are more things hidden today which are waiting to be revealed in the future.

Ten years ago, if somebody had told you your personality would be what it is today, would you have believed that? Which areas of your personality have changed? Let's create the transformation trend for the areas you identified. How do you feel about what you are now compared to what you were in the past? How do you feel about what you are now compared to what you were in the past? What sort of transformations you have gone through? Have you picked up new skills? Did you drop some old habits and behaviours? Establishing your past transformation trend is a powerful tool you can use to convince yourself you will be able to transform exponentially in the future as well. And that conviction will help you design your future-focused self-identity.

Establishing the transformation trend from the past to the present in various aspects of life comes in handy when you guide and mentor children to uncover their potential too. There are many children who feel inferior because of the world around them, and use the realization of their transformation as a great boon to blossom. Once a fifteen-year-old boy told me how his self-identity of being shorter than his peers, restricted him from dreaming of anything big in his life. Delving into his transformation story made him realize there are other areas of life where he has thrived and that he can find the motivation to dream big, act big and achieve big by creating a future-focused self-identity which doesn't have anything to do with his height.

3. Who will I be (Future-self)?

In his TED Talk, Harvard psychologist Dr Daniel Gilbert talks about the 'End of History' illusion. Through his studies, he found that the rate at which people change decreases as we age.

For example, the rate at which a young adult changes is slower compared to the rate at which a baby changes. Babies change in weeks, but teenagers may take months. Likewise, the rate changes as we age older. However, what he also found is that the rate of change that we estimate for ourselves is much lower compared to how much we actually could change. As we age, many among us tend to think 'It's the end' and that we are unable to change any further or make any influence on our 'fate'. Dr Gilbert calls it the 'End of History' illusion. What it means is, that once we cultivate that thought, we stop to visualize a grand future, or we stop believing in our ability to transform ourselves into that grand future. But our chance of transformation is way bigger than what we actually think we are capable of. We severely underestimate our potential to change. As Dr Gilbert said, 'Human beings are works in progress that mistakenly think they are finished'. A future-focused self-identity is one where you throw away your End of History mindset and carefully cultivate a 'beginning of the self-revolution' mindset.

Twenty years ago, if someone had told me I would become an author, I would have brushed it off as a joke. I loved reading, and I respected authors, but I didn't even dare to dream about becoming an author. I was insecure about my language skills, I didn't believe that my opinions and knowledge made any sense, and I didn't even think I liked to write. It wasn't until people started asking me about my books and inviting me to be part of writing books that I realized my self-identity, which was fixated on the past, was playing a huge role in limiting my potential, that my beliefs about myself were not allowing me to dream big and act big. Why don't we dare to visualize ourselves as someone much different from who we are today and who we were in the past?

If you think it from the perspective of neuroplasticity, we can arrive at a logic around this reluctance. We find things easy if the neural connections are already established, and that is the case with our life until today. However, the neural connections from tomorrow are not yet established, at least not as elaborate as in the past. So, we find it difficult to imagine and trust our future. But we don't face the difficulty with the same intensity in every aspect of our future. Take the case of a promotion at work you have been very keen on landing. As you dream more about that position, it is easy for you to imagine yourself performing the tasks relevant to that position and interacting with others in that capacity. Initially, it probably started as an aspiration, but with your belief and effort you have made a future-focused self-identity around that position. You don't find it wrong to have that identity. If you can visualize and develop a future-focused self-identity without guilt about this position, why do you sometimes feel guilty about creating a future-focused identity around bigger things?

There are four major components that contribute to the making of an effective visualization routine for your future self. The first component is formulating your objective for becoming that future self. A clearly defined purpose as we will discuss in the next chapter is of essence here. However, there are times we visualize our short-term objectives. For instance, if Adi has identified visiting all countries in the world as his purpose, he might be visualizing a future-focused identity of how he will be after visiting all those countries. But when he strategizes his purpose, along with the visualization of the grand outcome of visiting all countries, he might also be visualizing a short-term future self of himself visiting the first country, getting immersed in the culture and landscape of that country, meeting new people, and gaining new experiences. Based on where you are in the pursuit of your purpose, make your objective clear to yourself.

The second component is to attach emotions to your objective. The more feeling you put towards your objective, its importance and connection to you increases in your mind. Think about situations such as what difference it will make in your life as well as in the lives of people who are associated with you and how will you feel when you achieve your objective, and the dopamine release that comes with these positive feelings about your future would provide you with the right motivation to stay in course to achieve your goals and purposes.

The third component that contributes to effective visualizing is forming vivid images of the future self in your mind. Imagine the way you behave, speak, dress and look, coupled with the right emotions when you fulfil your objective. Imagine more details such as how will other people treat you and what kind of life you will be living after that.

The fourth component is the additional techniques you can use to enhance the strength of your future self. One of the techniques many people find effective is creating vision boards. A vision board is a visual representation of your future self. In it, you can include all kinds of images and short texts that contribute to your future self. Going with the idiom 'a picture says a thousand words', placing the vision board in your line of vision will act as a reminder of your future and it helps in triggering the right emotions within you. Creating a vision board is especially of use if you find it difficult to see vivid images in your mind. Another powerful technique you can use is journaling. Journaling helps to clarify and elaborate our thoughts and ideas. You will learn more about the staggering benefits of journaling and its Drivers in Chapter 6 of this part of the book.

Once you develop a vivid image of your future self, the next step is to develop the belief in the possibility for you to become that future self.

4. Develop the belief in your future self through optimism

In an interview with Tom Bilyeu of Impact Theory, Trevor Moawad, a sports psychologist who was named 'Sports world's best brain trainer' by Sports Illustrated, narrated a powerful anecdote of how beliefs and behavioural changes result in personality transformation. In that interview, Moawad talked about a boy who was raised by a single mom. He was struggling at school, and his mom was worried about the future of her son. She made him promise that he will take the SAT test, which is the college admission test in the US. He didn't prepare for the test though, but when the result came, he had scored 1480, a very high score, that placed him in the top one per cent, which even his mom suspected he got by cheating. A score as high as that guaranteed him an Ivy League education.

After he got this high score, his entire personality changed. He felt that he was a person capable of getting that score, he was a person capable of studying in an Ivy League college and that he was a person who was born to do bigger things in life. Once that outlook changed and he created a brighter self-identity of himself and his future, his habits also started changing. He started attending classes, he started hanging out with people with high ambition. When he started transforming his behaviour, habits and personality, people around him started treating him differently, and eventually, he got into an Ivy League college, had a great education, and became a successful magazine entrepreneur.

Years later he got a letter from Princeton university, which administers the SAT test. In that letter, they said the SAT board had done a periodic review of the results from the year in which he took the test and found that he was wrongly sent the wrong score and that his actual score was 740, which was half of what they had communicated initially. But it didn't matter anymore. That wrong score had transformed his personality and life for the better. He was the same guy with the same IQ, but a change in his self-identity resulted in a change in his mindset and behaviours. The new mindset and the behaviours he cultivated, created new neural connections in his brain and since he persevered on those habits, those connections became very solid. A true example of a growth mindset at play.

Not all of us get such a great letter with such power to boost our confidence, the belief in ourselves and transform our personality. But what we can do is to visualize an optimistic future and develop and boost a self-identity as powerful as if we got that letter. That said, the real challenge many people face is not in visualizing that future, but in believing it. Let us examine what happens when we visualize a glorious future—the inner critique starts asking questions, prompting you to doubt what you are visualizing. Many people are familiar with catastrophizing or thinking about the worst outcome of a situation.

Michael, one of my friends, shared his catastrophizing thoughts with me recently. He is young and is working at a mid-management level, and his goal is to become the CEO of an organization that he has identified, in fifteen years. He said, 'Whenever I try to visualize my future self, there is a bombardment of defeating thoughts and questions that hold me back from believing what I am trying to visualize.' Some of the catastrophizing thoughts that stop him from believing in that future self are 'But I am not good in strategy', 'Oh, I was such a disappointment last time when I became the leader of a small team, and it's funny that I am now daydreaming about becoming the CEO', 'I am not good at networking, how can anyone choose me to be a CEO when people wouldn't even notice my existence?'. Many studies in positive psychology have found that optimism is a powerful tool for boosting our resilience to work towards something. Similarly, there are many studies that point out the detrimental effect of catastrophizing on our resilience.

While people like Michael doubt their ability to achieve their objectives, there are others who get frightened about success. There are many causes for the fear of success such as the negative experiences from past success, worry about how others are going to respond to a success, self-doubting the ability to perform up to the expectations from the success and so on. As we can notice, there are many things that could stand in the way of an effective visualization exercise. What is worthwhile to remember is, that visualization is daydreaming with optimism. It is about believing in your glorious future and keeping your doubts and fears at bay. The following growth mindset-based thinking is a great way to remain realistic and optimistic while daydreaming your glorious future. As in the sentence above, 'yet' is a powerful word you can incorporate into your vocabulary to remind yourself that you are on the way to your glorious future self. When you couple 'not yet' with your plan on developing yourself, you will realize that achieving your dream is not magic, but the result of carefully curated processes that you will be able to follow through.

Interestingly, having the belief in our future self provides us with many other benefits as well. Practicing optimism has been found crucial to our overall well-being. Studies have shown that it increases social support, the chances of succeeding in tests, the chances of successfully selling as a salesman, and satisfaction in relationships. It has also been proven to reduce stress, depression and the chances of cardiovascular diseases. So, practicing optimism not only helps you with developing a strong future-focused self-identity but also increases your overall mental, physical, emotional and financial wellbeing. Optimism in any situation is a thought. And it is our thoughts that take the lead to set our feelings, beliefs, perceptions, and action. No wonder optimism showers all these wonderful benefits to our overall wellbeing.

With the help of that unbeatable self-identity, you will be in a position to plan for your development to realize the future you envisioned.

5. Bring clarity on how you are planning to continuously develop your self-identity

Developing a healthy future-focused self-identity is an ongoing process. And the closer you reach the set identity; you will see it evolving further. Research has shown that a person who builds an effective future-focused self-identity identifies what holds them back from trusting their future self and makes use of that information constructively. People with catastrophizing tendencies find those situations as threats, expect the worst outcome out of it, convince themselves it is not possible to negotiate through those threats to a successful outcome and succumb to the belief that their future self is something that is unapproachable for them. However, a person who consciously practices optimism to develop their future-focused self-identity sees the barriers as challenges and looks for more clarity.

The clarity of your self-identity is an important factor that determines how effectively you are going to enact the chosen self-identity. Lack of clarity results in a lack of success. If you do not know what exactly your personal barriers are and the reason behind them, it is easy to spiral into the vortex of despair. The people who uncover that information take the effort to clarify what they can do about bridging these barriers. Many people find tools such as self-reflection, feedback, mindfulness, meditation and journaling useful in clarifying the challenges. They identify opportunities for learning, unlearning, and relearning to work out those challenges. They go deeper into identifying their exact development goals, such as attitudes, skills, and behaviours they can incorporate into their life to see through the challenges to their future self.

Once they have their development goals, they create a pact with themselves with a plan to learn those development goals as well as to apply those learnings. Nowadays there are so many ways to learn and develop. The personal development market size was valued at USD thirty-five billion in 2020, and it is expected to rise by forty-nine per cent to USD fifty-two billion by 2028. This means that there are many existing avenues to develop and unlock our hidden potential and new avenues are opening regularly.

You may sign up for a course online or face-to-face based on your learning preference. Or you may look for a mentor or a coach to fast-track your development. The right mentor or coach can help you customize your development based on your unique strengths and needs. Of course, you may come up with your own strategies to change habits, such as listening skills, empathy and so on. You might have reached the current stage in your life with a certain set of skills and behaviours, developing which was essential for you to reach here. But that set might not be enough for the next leap in your career and life.

Another major factor that can help you bring more clarity to your self-identity is identifying your core values and character strengths. We will discuss that in the next chapter.

When you design a future-focused self-identity, it can bring clarity to a lot of ambiguous thoughts in your head. When there is clarity and a Development Plan, you know what your identity is, what kind of attitude, behaviours and skill goals you are going to achieve and how you are going to achieve those.

6. Do it (Start it today)

Nishi, a successful and ambitious human resources professional was a client of mine. She told me, 'Early on in my career, it was easy for people to notice me because I have developed good communication skills since my school days. I used to speak up in meetings, so it was easy for people to notice what I was doing and capable of doing. However, as I climbed up the career ladder, I am at a loss now.' Nishi felt that people started considering her communication in meetings as oversharing and attention-seeking. The communication skill that was held up by her superiors in the past started showing up as a disadvantage in her performance reviews too. Together we developed a Development Plan for her to help her focus on improving her listening skills. Once we formulated a development strategy for her, she stuck to developing this new skill. She reminded herself of her plan before every meeting and important phone calls and made it a point to provide her viewpoints only where it was needed. However, she made sure that when she spoke, she showed her authenticity with enough clarity and content. Furthermore, she spent time learning how to speak effectively and concisely. It was a gradual process that demanded a lot of planning, self-reflection, seeking feedback, and patience. Nevertheless, now after spending two years developing and practising this skill, listening comes naturally to Nishi and she is receiving much more respect because of that. She shared with me, 'I have noticed that people value my inputs now as they know when I speak up, it is something important.'

Once you have made a Development Plan, put it into practice. There are some attitudes, behaviours, and skills you can straight away start to demonstrate while there are some that you learn and apply. Then there are developmental plans that you learn and apply. Following through your developmental plan is important to ensure yourself more of your future self and to create the necessary neuroplasticity in your new behaviours, skills, and attitudes.

One of the major hurdles that many come across at this step is when they face disappointments. When facing unfavourable test scores, personality tests, interviews, and personal rejections, sometimes we may tend to say, 'I am still a loser, what is the point of having a made-up self-identity when I can't even do this well?'

Whether you are facing disappointments or not standing up to your own expectation is part of the journey, that does not make you a loser and that doesn't mean you are fake. The more you succumb to the feeling of inadequacy, the more you are going to build your self-identity around that, which could be detrimental to your goal. Upon facing disappointments, these people take the disappointment at a core personal level and attribute it to their bad luck, and conclude that they don't amount to anything.

Martin Seligman, the director of the Positive Psychology Centre at the University of Pennsylvania, who is known as the founding father of positive psychology, explains this tendency as 'learned helplessness' in his book by the same name. People who nurture learned helplessness, learn to look at every bad situation as something not under their control and accept that as their fate. Since they don't believe that they have control, they don't try to develop themselves or improve the situation. You will hear those people saying or thinking, 'Hey loser, you lost it again', 'I knew this was going to happen', 'I am so unlucky, nothing I do can change my fate'.

On the other hand, people who think that they have control over the situation acknowledge the situation but do not attribute their disappointments to their personality at a global level. They identify the specific circumstances that led to the disappointment and empower themselves to develop further. Their thoughts and talk do not create detrimental effects on their self-identity. They do not waver from the belief in their future self and their inner dialogue would be in the effect of, 'Hey future-self, I am still on the way to you. Let me figure out what happened here and plan my development from this experience.' Martin Seligman calls this learned optimism, which is about cultivating your optimistic beliefs in every situation, even in the face of disappointments. Those disappointments are temporary derailments since you are still figuring things out and your brain hasn't yet made the right neural connections with enough practice. We will learn more about handling disappointments and setbacks when we discuss willpower later in this part of the book.

Every time you apply what you have planned in your Development Plan to realize your self-identity, ensure that you acknowledge your efforts, your progress and how it is adding up to your future self. You may practice future-self-identity-focused communication to motivate your children and team as well.

For example, if you tell a child or teenager, 'You were very kind there. That is a great attitude, and if you continue to practice it, it will help you when you become the vet that you are planning to be', you are helping that child to associate what behaviours of theirs are helping them to reach their desired future self. Similarly, when you tell your colleague, 'You didn't lose your patience though the client was very aggressive regarding the issue they encountered today. That is a great attitude you can keep cultivating since you are interested in applying for the position of a client account manager', you are reaffirming that their actions are bridging the skill gap to reach the future self.

7. Evaluate how your current self is transitioning towards your future-self

When you consciously design and develop a future-focused self-identity, it is not a one-time activity. As self-identity itself is constantly evolving, you need to know where you stand. Reflecting on the steps you take and evaluating how you are doing is an essential step to strengthening your self-identity and uncovering your real potential. If you are working on your development goal of speaking up more in meetings or to lead better or save better, how will you know whether your strategies are working? How do you know how your communication is helping the meeting? How do you know you are communicating effectively? Personal reflection and feedback help in identifying the pluses, trends, and areas of improvement in your plan and action. I have mentioned self-reflection and feedback a few times in this chapter. Later in Chapter 10, you will learn more about the Drivers for self-reflection and feedback.

As they work on a future focused self-identity, some people may feel that they are cheating themselves and others by assuming a fake personality. Here is the difference between a fake personality and a future-focused self-identity. A person with a fake personality tries to make other people believe what they are not, whereas as a person with a future-focused self-identity, you are on the pursuit to sharpen and uncover your own potential to become that person you genuinely wish to become. Self-awareness is a major trait that aids in creating your self-identity, we will discuss about that later in this part of the book.

Developing a healthy future-focused self-identity can help us in establishing the right neural networks to support that future even before the future becomes a reality. And those networks will strengthen and expand over time and will make our transformation to our future self more efficient and faster. As you unlock your hidden potential, you will realize that having a healthy self-identity and nurturing it with tender care is as important as having a well-defined purpose. You will learn about the Drivers for a well defined purpose in the next chapter. As the 19th century American naturalist and writer Henry David Thoreau said, 'The secret of achievement is to hold a picture of a successful outcome in mind.'

Chapter 4

How to find your purpose?
The Perplexing Question of Purpose

Niravu is a tiny hamlet of one hundred and one households in the state of Kerala, India. In 2006, a voluntary group of students from the neighbouring women's college did a free lifestyle survey for all residents of Niravu. The survey found that many people were suffering from various diseases. What alarmed the villagers was that seven people among them were cancer patients and five of them were women. Niravu was an inner village, away from the pollution of the city. Seven was a large number for the villagers to come to terms with, that too with a high percentage of women. The villagers turned to find the real reason behind it and see how they can save people, especially women from the disease. They formed an action council to apprehend the cause and work out a solution. Traditionally women in the village didn't smoke or drink, so that could not be the reason for the high percentage of cancer among women.

They looked at the lifestyle of the women in the hamlet, but they didn't know what to look for. So, they reached out to experts. Kerala is a state that has achieved great strides in social development on par with developed countries in many categories. However, the development came with its own pitfalls as well.

Though a tropical paradise with fertile soil, it is a consumer state, largely owing to the high labour costs and labour strikes. As a result, the backyards and farmlands were left unattended without farming and the vegetables and pulses were purchased from the market where it came from other states. This buying habit introduced plastic into the society and environment. To dispose of the excess plastic, women in Niravu, who mainly did the household work, burnt the plastic. The toxins from the smoke were identified as one possible issue affecting women's health. Women were handling the produce bought from the market, which was not locally produced and was laden with pesticides. This was identified as another factor that affected the villagers.

The action council decided to reduce the pesticides in their food by cultivating their own produce. They turned to the elders in the hamlet for the ancient wisdom of farming and cultivation. With guidance from them and from experts, Niravu started producing organic food, vegetables, and dairy products. The backyards and farmlands once dominated by wild weeds were replaced with bananas, yams, and rice. The sight of free-ranging chickens and cows enjoying the open fields and backyards of Niravu became a norm. The hamlet became self-sufficient for fruits, pulses and vegetables. They built their own biogas plant, produced their own organic compost from waste and developed a sustainable waste management method targeting zero-waste. With the focus on a collective purpose, Niravu turned into sixty-one acres of land where, nature, animals and humans thrive in harmony looking out for each other.

What is a purpose and how do we know what our purpose is?

Merriam-Webster defines purpose as 'something set up as an object or end to be attained.' A purpose is an intent in which you are invested with your mind, emotions, and efforts. Though a purpose sounds like an end from its definition, it is not a destination, it is the process of achieving various goals. You find a certain sense of satisfaction when you achieve the various goals associated with it, and the satisfaction you feel is much better and bigger than the satisfaction and contentment you get from your other pursuits. That is exactly what you find in Niravu and in their purpose to live a healthy life.

When we talk about purpose, one of the questions that arise is how to differentiate between a purpose and a goal. We have seen that purpose is something that we believe will provide us with contentment. When we consciously align our actions with our purpose, the milestones, and the successes we chase become goals that lead us to that purpose. However, you may use the Drivers for clarifying your purpose to clarify your goals as well.

When I conduct mindset development programs for educators, I begin by letting them connect with their beginning— why did they choose to become an educator? A large percentage of teachers choose their profession because they believe in the transformational power of that profession, and they want to play their part in transforming lives. But many teachers have shared with me their reality too. In the face of the aggressive demands of their profession, they do not get the time to think much about the reason behind their choice of profession. However, when they get a chance to remind themselves of the real purpose behind their pursuits, like when I ask them explicitly about their purpose, it is impossible to miss the renewed drive to persist and persevere to make a difference in their teaching journey and in their students' learning journey.

What we see at Niravu is a community that discovered a problem, found its purpose in solving that problem and with their commitment towards fulfilling it, expanded their purpose to a bigger level. Likewise, is it possible for individuals also to be equally focused and resourceful to formulate and achieve their own purposes?

A few years ago, I got an opportunity to interview Jack Horner, the great paleontologist who helped modern civilization understand dinosaurs the way we know them today. From the time coming across the fossil of a dinosaur at the age of six, Horner was extremely fascinated with the world of those giants that ruled our world millions of years ago and wanted to know more about them. Despite his passion for dinosaurs and paleontology, he did poorly in school and didn't achieve any substantial academic merits. He didn't graduate from university, and nobody thought he would amount to anything substantial. But his self-identity was different from the identity other people had cultivated about him. At a young age itself, he identified that his purpose was to learn more about dinosaurs, and he developed a future-focused self-identity around that purpose. His childhood passion for unearthing the secrets of dinosaurs didn't frizzle out as it happens with many children, it stayed with him, and he continued his own personal research on dinosaurs despite all the academic setbacks he faced.

Even after Jack failed to graduate from the university, he continued his personal research on dinosaurs, while working as a truck driver. Along with that, he applied to natural history museums all over the English-speaking world, to gain a doorway to paleontology and dinosaurs, but his lack of educational qualifications remained a barrier to that. In the end, he got an invite from Princeton University to work in their natural history museum and it was there, in his thirties that he got diagnosed with dyslexia. That diagnosis came as a relief to him because he now had proof that he was not lazy as others liked to call him during his school and college days. While he was working at Princeton, he got an offer from a museum in Montana, where he continued with his research. Although Horner got the job, he still faced a lot of hurdles in his research career as he didn't have a PhD. Many of his colleagues didn't consider him qualified enough to pursue his work or to do certain administrative tasks related to his research field.

Horner had a well-developed purpose, had developed a self-concept around that, was committed to that purpose and was ready to work towards that purpose. While the discovery of your purpose gives you the passion to achieve it, a clear sense of the purpose gives you the drive and clarity to relentlessly pursue and achieve it. It bestows you with the power to charter your path, face off roadblocks on the path and compels you to take risks.

Drivers of purpose

Having a well-defined purpose is the result of clarifying various factors that are part and parcel of the purpose. Let's discuss how you can find and clarify those factors. One important factor to consider here is, purpose and self-identity work hand in hand, and the Drivers you use to strengthen each of these help to strengthen the other too. You may use the Drivers discussed below to identify and clarify your purpose.

1. Identify the dreams that pull you towards it

Jack Horner knew what he wanted to do with his life—he wanted to study about the giants of the past. He faced many roadblocks in that pursuit, including poor performance at school, ridicules he was subjected to by his peers and teachers at school, the humiliation he faced in the scientific world because of his lack of qualifications and his learning difficulty, yet he didn't let any of that come in the way of his pursuit. His passion and belief in his purpose was so well developed that he didn't consider any of these roadblocks powerful enough to deviate him from this purpose.

However, many people encounter the reality of not being clear about their purpose. If you are facing this confusion, a little inward observation, and a few questions to yourself might steer you towards your purpose. Asking yourself questions such as the ones listed below would be of help to identify how serious you are about a certain dream you have and whether you would want to wholeheartedly pursue that.

- 'What pulls me towards it?'
- 'What makes me feel it is meaningful to contribute towards it?'
- 'Does it make me feel happy beyond monetary and power benefits?'

There are some misconceptions about purpose being all about pursuing something for charitable causes. However, it doesn't have to be. Your purpose doesn't need to be altruistic for you to make a difference. The foremost important criterion is that you find it meaningful to pursue even if you separate the monetary benefits from it.

For example, billionaire investment guru Warren Buffet is one of the wealthiest persons alive today. Despite having the means to afford anything that most people are unable to own, Buffett is known for his modest lifestyle. In 1998, at a lecture he delivered at the University of Florida School of Business, Buffett talked about his ideas of a happy life. He said we can't reboot and restart our life from day one, but what we can do is make positive changes in various aspects of our life such as our goals, career, finance, health, and relationships and derive our happiness from that. When you look at the investment methodologies and principles he has adopted, we arrive at the realization that it is not money that is driving him, it is the passion to perfect the art of investing that fuels him, and that money is a result of his relentless pursuit of that purpose.

There are many things we strongly feel about—it could be anything such as landing a certain position in your career or building a business empire or uplifting society or sharing your knowledge with others. And many a time we are pulled towards multiple things and that might put us in a confused state—should I work on climbing the career ladder or become part of the activism against climate change? At this point, what is important to acknowledge is that it is normal to feel that confusion and that you have a multi-faceted personality.

You may even find that many of these dreams are eventually pointing you towards a single purpose that is a common factor of all these various dreams. For example, you might be able to combine your aspiration to become a corporate leader and your penchant for climate change activism by setting a goal to lead an organization working on products and services designed to curb climate change. If there is no common element for all those things you identified, it may be as simple as that you have multiple purposes that you strongly feel about. However, you may find that the priority you give to each of these purposes is not the same. You may even pursue different purposes simultaneously or decide to pursue one after the other.

Once you have identified a purpose that you feel the strongest about, you identify yourself with that purpose as we saw previously when we discussed self-identity.

For Horner, recognition and accolades were not part of his purpose or self-identity, and hence the lack of those didn't bother him. Through his work, a lot of unknown dinosaur species were discovered, and many species of dinosaurs are even named after him. He also played a huge role in bringing into light what we know today about the social behaviours of dinosaurs. He wrote many books on dinosaurs, including children's books, that paved way for the popularity of dinosaurs in our society today.

While Horner was busy studying dinosaurs, the bestselling author Michael Crichton was busy writing a fiction book on dinosaurs. The book was published in 1990. Unbeknownst to Horner, the central character of the book, Dr Alan Grant, a palaeontologist, was loosely based on him. When the famous film director Steven Spielberg came across the book, he made a deal with Crichton to make the book a movie. In the movie, Spielberg modelled Dr Grant's character after Horner. Spielberg also offered him the position of scientific advisor for the movie. Jurassic Park, the blockbuster franchise, was born in 1993. The rest, as they say, is history. Jack Horner has served as the scientific advisor for all films thus far in the Jurassic Park franchise.

So extensive was Horner's research on dinosaurs that it became impossible for the scientific community not to acknowledge his contribution to palaeontology. While the universities were apprehensive of his qualification or lack of that in the first part of his career, they were queuing to give him honorary degrees in the latter part of his career. He received honorary doctorate degrees from the University of Montana and Pennsylvania State University. The Society of Vertebrate Paleontology awarded him the Romer-Simpson Prize, the highest honour a paleontologist can receive from the society at that time. In his speech at Science Centre Singapore in 2013, he said 'Stop reading, start doing', which was very apt in his situation. He had decided not to let dyslexia stop him from pursuing his dreams. He designed his own methods to pursue his dream—that was to find it by doing.

2. Strengthen your optimism and belief in your purpose

Going back to our original example of the villagers of Niravu, their biggest secret was their optimism and their passion fueled efforts in staying true to their purpose. Their purpose was bigger than their individual goals, and with a collective belief in that purpose and the willingness to collaborate, they became the inspiration for many. Niravu's waste management process was adopted by various schools, colleges, and many residential councils within and outside the state of Kerala. It didn't end there, they were approached for providing waste management consultancy services to the nearby Kozhikode International Airport, and which led to them providing consultancy services to other airports and railway systems in the country.

Likewise on a more personal level, if someone has a purpose to lead a healthy lifestyle, but if they absentmindedly stress eat consistently, it doesn't help their purpose. Similarly, if you blame others for your smoking or stress eating, it means you are not building the habits to help your purpose, instead you are entrusting the agency with others to change their habits to fulfil your purpose. In such a case, it is not a surprise if the person slowly disconnects from the purpose in due time and laments that they are not able to pursue their purpose because everyone else was putting hurdles in their path.

I believe you don't feel a pull towards something if you are not capable of doing it because that pull demonstrates how passionate you are to fulfil that purpose. It is not the impossibility of the purpose that pulls us back, but the doubt in our abilities, to pursue and fulfil that purpose. Let's hypothetically think you already have all the skills and talents to fulfil your biggest dream. Would you still take a step back from those dreams? The answer is obvious here. A 'dream' is never a 'dream' if there is no challenge associated with it. As we discussed in the previous chapter, a fear, or doubt about success in the future is a call for a Development Plan and its implementation of it. Whenever you doubt yourself, remind yourself consciously that you can build yourself neuroplasticity in any field, along with the right efforts, if you let your brain release the right chemicals with optimism and positive thoughts to entertain the neural pathways to fulfil that purpose.

We explored the importance of optimism and the ways to cultivate it when we discussed self-identity in the previous chapter, and those techniques are relevant in building your optimism in your purpose as well. One obstacle that holds us back from being optimistic is self-doubt and fear of failure. When something bothers us in the form of self-doubt or fear, the first step to removing those obstacles is to admit those feelings to ourselves. Being optimistic means that you believe in a bright future, and that you can build yourself to overcome all those doubts and fears. There are many ways to clarify your feelings such as self-reflection, mindfulness, meditation, journaling, visualizing and affirmations. We will explore the Drivers behind these Secret Codes in later chapters in this part of the book.

The villagers of Niravu were not experts in waste management strategies or organic farming or management consulting. They didn't start off to get famous for their movement or methodologies. What they instead did was not give up on their purpose, thinking they are not capable to carry that load. In fact, their willingness to remain optimistic, learn, unlearn, and relearn helped them not only achieve what they set forth for their community but also to become the flagbearers of establishing healthy lifestyles in other communities as well. Similarly, Horner didn't have the perfect conditions to realize his dreams, and people around him had written him off as a lazy boy. But he didn't give up his dreams, he believed in his purpose, took ownership for achieving that, remained optimistic amidst the chaos, of a bright future, and reinforced his optimism with consistent habits and action, which paved the way to fulfilling his purpose.

3. Your past holds the thread to your purpose

Take some time to walk through memory lane and identify the defining moments in your life. Why did those moments become defining for you? Defining moments played a big part in shaping the person you are today. These events might have given you happiness or sadness, such as beginning a new partnership or realizing that you got cheated in a partnership. It could also be a disappointment about something that you did or did not do. If something has left a strong feeling in you, that time could not erase, that incident somehow connects to you beyond the superficial. Irrespective of whether it was positive or negative, those events helped you realize something about yourself or the way this world works and possibly provided you with more information about what is truly meaningful for you and that helped you to define your identity.

For me, one of the earliest defining moments in my life was in middle school, when a teacher told me, 'Sindu has potential.' She was talking about my math skills. I struggled with word problems, did poorly in exams and dreaded math class. The teacher picked me for solving math questions in front of the class on a daily basis, scolded me in front of the class for not doing it and didn't stop picking me even after realizing that I couldn't solve a single problem. I used to get frustrated because I felt she was picking me to humiliate me on purpose. On one such occasion when I was called in front of the classroom, she scolded me for not following a simple instruction, got extremely frustrated and sat down on her chair and said, 'Sindu has the potential to do very well in math. I don't know why she is not trying enough.' As I listened to her words, I realized that she didn't want to humiliate me, but was trying to bring out the potential hidden inside me. This was a defining moment in my life that prompted me to find out what potential she saw in me that I didn't see myself. That exploration took me to the realization that I could in fact understand math, learn math, and score well in math if I put in the right effort. The aftermath of this incident was that I formed a self-identity around the fact that I am a person who can put sustained efforts patiently to achieve something which I perceived as too big to even dream about. This experience early in life guided me in taking up challenging tasks and responsibilities in the future and working hard towards its success.

While each of the defining moments may seem like silos, in hindsight, you might be able to find the common thread that binds all or many of them together. As I became an adult, in my professional life in consulting, I could recognize various factors that helped or hindered people's and organizations' success and I could relate those factors to mindset in one way or another. Along the way, there were many moments where I realized that I did find pleasure and fulfilment in helping and guiding people. I did also realize how I could help others find their potential and these realizations helped me see that the connecting thread, my purpose, was 'mindset'. Further introspections helped me see that everything I happily did or aspired to do pointed to the fact that my purpose is unlocking the hidden potential in me and in others by focusing on our mindset. And that my various pursuits, such as books, courses, coaching, consulting, magazine, and events like International Youth Leadership and Innovation Forum, are all mediums I used for achieving that purpose in various ways. Searching and finding the common thread not only helped me to clarify my purpose, but also to believe in it.

The frontal lobe of our brain helps us with decision making and executive functioning, such as thinking, planning, decision making, problem solving and behaviour among other things. Basically, this part of the brain helps us plan and organize our efforts towards long-term and short-term goals. When you actively think about the past experiences that directly or indirectly are associated with the purpose you are clarifying, your brain accesses the behavioural strategies associated with those past experiences and that helps to form new strategies and improve confidence in your purpose.

While you firm up the purposes that you care about, it is likely that you feel that you don't amount to achieving that and this is something you have never put much effort into. These imposter thoughts can make you conclude that it is indeed not your purpose and that you are fooling yourself with some fancy dreams. This is where you need to build the thread of defining moments from your past. This thread will act as proof for you to believe in your purpose and unlock your potential to fulfil that purpose.

4. Align your core values and strengths with your purpose

When I conduct return to workforce programs for women, I come across many women who left their work for various reasons. At first, when they introduce themselves, they talk about their past career with great pride, and then they share what they are doing in the present—homemakers, caretakers and so on. What I have noticed with many of them is that with the loss of their jobs, they have also lost part of their self-worth. They let that affect their self-identity. Many of them feel that they are wasting their life. One of the many reasons behind their getting back to work is their desire to take back the self-identity and self-worth they lost. At the same time, they do not feel confident that they will be able to return to work.

When you attach your self-worth to your profession, your self-worth undergoes a huge decline with the loss of that job. But when you attach your self-worth to your values, character strengths, skills, and your ability to upskill yourself, you are building an unbeatable self-identity. And that puts you in the right place to pursue any goal optimistically. As we take these women through the process of identifying their values, character strengths and abilities, they peek into their life journey and realize that they have their own individual powers even in the absence of a job. Some realize that it is their logical skills that helped them in the past to be good programmers, some realize that they are good at bringing people together to work towards a common goal, some realize that their affinity to keep a clean and organized home stems from their organization skills, some realize that their emotional intelligence is what makes them form friendships, and some realize that it is their productivity and humanity that helped them in getting involved in various activities in the community.

As they come to terms with their powers, they realize that their past jobs didn't define them and that it was just a result of who they were. And that they have the skills and strengths they built before, during and after their career in the past, to present to a new employer. And above all, they recognize that they are people with certain sets of core values and that they exhibit their own character strengths in order to lead a life based on their values. I have witnessed this new realization becoming a catalyst in boosting their self-identity and injecting the drive and confidence to define their goals and dreams, and in some cases to change their goals. Identifying your core values and character strengths helps you in two ways—on one hand, it tells you if and why your purpose is important to you, and on the other hand, you can make use of your values and strengths as the foundation for achieving that purpose.

A logical question that arises in this context is, 'What is the difference between values and character strengths?' Core values are the personal principles that guide you in every aspect of your life, such as building relationships, making decisions, way of working, way of living and so on. These are the virtues that are important to us, and we strive to exhibit them. Courage, justice, humanity, wisdom, etc. are examples of core values. Whereas character strengths are the personality strengths we exhibit confidently in our lives. Traits such as perseverance, fairness, love, curiosity, etc. are examples of character strengths. So, you could consider character strengths as a subset of core values. And, because of that reason, character strengths are sometimes referred to as values in action (VIA). For instance, you might value financial independence as your core value, but that doesn't mean that you have already achieved financial independence, you might be in the pursuit of achieving your financial independence.

Do your purpose and goals align with your values? The best way to understand that is to look within to find whether you feel guilty about your purpose. Sometimes you feel that you can't agree with what you are trying to achieve with a purpose or a goal. For instance, someone who gives a lot of importance to personal freedom and independence might not feel it right to work for someone else, although it is not ethically or morally wrong to work for someone else. Generally, if you are pursuing a purpose or a goal aligning with your values, you would not feel that you are doing something wrong to yourself. While ethics is a system of belief based on moral values which are generally practiced by a group, values, as we have discussed, are different for each person. We can see values at play everywhere, in interpersonal relationships, professional partnerships, marriages, and relationships between countries.

This reminds me of an incident my former colleague Clarissa shared with me. She and another colleague Martin were at the client site, which was a large consumer electronics company, for the final presentation of the project they did together. Clarissa admired Martin's expertise in bringing in new accounts for their firm, and she wanted to improve her sales skills. She had previously asked Martin if he could mentor her on that. During the presentation they got the impression that the executives of the client had another project in their mind which they might want to start soon. After the presentation when the executives were having a discussion among themselves outside, Martin asked Clarissa to follow them and listen to their conversation. He said, 'Clarissa, there are many tricks in this field. We need to use all tricks up our sleeve to get a new account.'

Clarissa felt like she was hit by a hard rock on her face. She thought, 'How dare he ask me to do something so nasty? I can't even imagine I sought to be mentored by a person who eavesdrops on other people to get ahead in his work?' We can observe the different value systems that Clarissa and Martin practiced, in this scenario. Martin gave importance to building his career at any cost. Since that was his main value, he did not find it morally wrong to eavesdrop on people. Career progression was important for Clarissa too. However, she valued honesty and integrity too. Though she was also ambitious, she did not want to carve a career based on the actions that she considered against her values. This points to how our values and character strengths encourage or discourage us from pursuing our purpose.

If you observe, you will notice that values and character strengths play a significant role in our daily life and relationships too. An example we commonly come across is in parenting. Parents want the best for their children, but the parenting style adopted by each family may differ. One family's style, based on the values they believe in, might not seem ideal for another family which values a different set of core values. And hence, this gives rise to the judgements we see in society. Social media comments are rife with examples of such judgements.

In every interaction, if we know the values that are important for the other party, it is easy to engage in that relationship. If you know that your friend is very particular about punctuality, you might try to be on time for your lunch with them. If you know your manager promotes collaboration in the workplace, you might not try to take sole credit for the results of teamwork. If you know family is important for your wife, you might not criticize her choice to have weekly dinner with her parents and siblings.

One of the main advantages of identifying your own values is that you will be able to live a guilt-free life by making decisions and choices based on your core values. For example, Clarissa would not feel guilty for not eavesdropping on the client's conversation if she does not get the next project as she knows that honesty and integrity are part of her core values. And if she cultivates her sales skills around honesty and integrity, she will feel proud that she is pursuing her goals with values in action. Don't you think the phrase 'accept the other person as they are' stems from the reality that different people from their opinions based on different values?

I know a socially responsible teenager, who felt more at ease when she moved to a school that gives high importance to service and she was happy that being in that environment would give her opportunities to develop and polish many of her character strengths. An executive who gives high importance to socio-emotional socio-emotional work culture, felt motivated to work for the new organization he joined, as it considers mindfulness as its core value. Walmart's founder Sam Walton had created a culture of listening to everyone in the company. By instilling a culture based on this value, he figured out ways to get the employees to talk and act on their ideas and frustrations. Studies have shown that employees feel empowered to work for companies that share values that are similar to their own.

Our values are determined by our environment, exposure, and the people around us and they get updated from time to time. Children learn a lot about values when they are young, from their home, school and society. However, when they get older, step into the outside world, and gain more experiences, they may hold onto some of those values, add more values and release some. Our value system evolves continuously, and hence if you observe that your value system has altered from before, it doesn't mean you have forgotten your roots, it means you had some powerful experiences and realizations that resulted in re-examining and re-defining part of your value system. Furthermore, these updates in your value system play a role every time you revisit your self-identity.

Once you identify your core values and character strengths, aligning that with your purpose helps you understand whether you will be able to sustain the passion for the purpose for a long period. Asian American students have been consistently found to do better in standardized tests and score better at school compared to other children. They are also more likely to finish high school and attend elite colleges. A growing body of evidence suggests that one of the main reasons for this is some important values Asian parents instil in their children from a young age. These values include collectivism within the family, where each person in the family considers they are responsible for the overall advancement of the family and hence they are there for each other. Another set of values is related to motivation and self-control. Asian parents give high value to education and teach their children to respect educators. They emphasize the importance of being a good student and attribute success to hard work rather than intelligence.

There are times we find admirable values in others and wish we had exhibited the same values. If you want to cultivate yourself a new value, first thing you need to check is whether it aligns with your existing value system. After that, check whether it is rational enough to adapt in your situation.

Values and character strengths are your personal powers. The more similarities you find between your purpose and your values, and the more you utilize your character strengths in pursuing your purpose, the more connected you will feel towards your purpose.

5. Take ownership of your purpose

The people of Niravu didn't start off with a clearcut purpose, they didn't know they were going to change the way their community experienced life, they didn't know they were going to be part of a cultural change, they didn't know they were going to become the agents of change in other communities. It all started off with a survey by an external organization which threw out some information about themselves. They started off with a simple goal for their community—the right to live and let others live healthily. However, as they stuck to their purpose, their purpose got bigger, and their influence got deeper and wider. But their journey was never smooth. It required expanding many skills for the action council members as well as for the villagers. The villagers had to change their way of living, eating habits, purchasing habits, disposal habits and thinking habits. They had to change their routines to adapt to farming and living harmoniously with nature. The action council members had to develop and improve their influencing skills, patience, technical skills, and negotiation skills to move things within and outside Niravu. They had to rise from ashes many times when someone from the community wanted to give up and go back to their previous way of living.

What made the villagers of Niravu remain optimistic and stay on their purpose although others didn't consider them as likely candidates to achieve their dreams? Likewise, what made it possible for Jack Horner to stay on his purpose though he had all the odds against him in becoming a paleontologist? It is their ownership of their purpose that made it possible for them to rise against all odds. We see many people blame others for the failure of their purposes. We come across people who blame their friends for their addiction, blame spouses for their poor eating habits and blame parents for their destructive behaviours. It is quite possible that other people played a role in deciding who we are today. But, if we continue to make them accountable for our future too, we are passing the control of our life to them. Accepting what happened and planning what is good for the future and taking accountability for following those plans is ownership. If we can cultivate that habit, we will see our inner potential unlocking the gates of success and accomplishments that we have been dreaming of.

In the rest of this book, we will uncover how we can unlock our hidden potential to achieve our purpose and goals. At this point, if you find and clarify your purpose and goals based on what we discussed in the book so far, you will be able to take tremendous leaps with the lessons from the upcoming chapters of this book, in making those goals and purpose a reality. The Drivers shared in this book to unlock the hidden potential behind each of your Gates are not standalones. As you get familiar with a Driver, introduce a new Driver that complements the Driver that you are working on. Observe and review your progress and adjust wherever necessary.

Chapter 5

Self-awareness and limitless expansion
Lay the foundation for your limitless expansion

Shortly after taking charge as the CEO of Microsoft, Satya Nadella said in an interview to New York Times, 'I fundamentally believe that if you are not self-aware, you're not learning. And if you're not learning, you're not going to do useful things in the future.' It is self-aware leaders with confidence and vision that make effective organizational cultural changes. Nadella, whom Microsoft founder Bill Gates described as 'humble, forward-looking and pragmatic', re-designed the culture of Microsoft from a company obsessed with its financial statements to an organization that is built around empathy, self-awareness, respect and a growth mindset. Self-awareness has been found to help people and organizations grow leaps and bounds with improved decision-making, improved relationships and improved confidence.

Have you ever attended an interview where the interviewer asked you about your strengths and weaknesses? Most of us might come across this question at one point or the other, and it is likely that you might have already practiced the answer to that question. But we have also learnt the formula to answer that question. Pick up a weakness and present it in a way to demonstrate the strengths you are utilizing to tackle that weakness. Pick up a strength and present it in a way to show how that will help you in the job you are interviewing for. But you ask yourself, would you fully agree with the answer you are giving in your interviews? Do you remember the first time you wondered how to answer that question? Many people find it extremely difficult to answer. In the initial years of my career that was the question I dreaded the most in interviews. Those days when the business world distanced itself from emotions and introversion, I wondered whether it was self-sabotaging to say I am kind or that I would rather listen than talk in meetings.

Though self-awareness is an often-discussed topic, many people tend to perceive it as something deeper than it is and associate it with consciousness, which is quite complex. Self-awareness is not consciousness, but being conscious of our thoughts, feelings, and our behaviours, and how these are affecting ourselves, others and the environment around us. Many people go through life unconsciously without realizing what they do, why they are doing it and what response they receive. This is where self-awareness helps us.

Self-awareness is our ability to read our thoughts, emotions, actions and how others reciprocate them. In addition, it helps us to understand whether our actions align with our purpose, values and character strengths. Self-awareness is crucial to forming a self-identity close to reality.

People who are on the path of unlocking their potential are also seekers who are trying to innovate themselves to rise to the next level. Self-awareness is the basis from where we start this. The benefits of cultivating self-awareness are far-reaching. It helps us with improved decision-making skills and critical thinking skills, understanding right from wrong, and improved self-confidence among other benefits. In the workplace, it helps us with leadership effectiveness, career progression and job success, in addition to the other benefits listed above. No wonder so many organizations give importance to hiring self-aware people for leadership positions.

Self-awareness helps positively to the overall effectiveness of teams also. As part of a study by Eric Dierdorff and Robert S. Rubin, two associate professors of management in the Driehaus College of Business at DePaul University and co-directors of BusinessEducationInsider.com, fifty-eight teams and three hundred leaders from a Fortune 10 company were put in a competitive business simulation activity. The self-awareness of the team members was assessed as part of this study. What they discovered was that teams with fewer self-aware team members made wrong decisions, they collaborated less, and they were less effective in conflict management. They found that when there were more self-aware people in the team, the probability of better decision-making and conflict management increased more than double and that of coordination increased more than three times. Furthermore, the study found that the level of high self-awareness in an organization is also positively linked to business matrices such as customer awareness, market share, productivity and many other important KPIs.

If self-awareness is an important trait, how common is it for people to be self-aware? Based on a five-year research by executive development firm The Eurich Group, ninety-five per cent of people rate themselves as self-aware. However, only ten to fifteen per cent are self-aware. That means, though we may feel that we know ourselves fairly well, there is still a lot more left for us to learn about ourselves.

As per the research by Tasha Eurich, organizational psychologist and the founder of The Eurich Group, there are two types of self-awareness—internal self-awareness and external self-awareness. The difference between these two is like our social media profiles. If you go to your social media profile pages, you will get to see yourself in two ways—how it looks for you and how it appears for others. Internal self-awareness is how you perceive yourself—that includes your self-identity, strengths, weaknesses, passions, values, aspirations, actions and how all these fit within the environment where you function. A good internal self-awareness can help us be happier, content with ourselves and manage stress and anxiety better.

External self-awareness helps us perceive how others see us. That includes what we know about how others see our strengths, weaknesses, passions, values, aspirations and actions. External self-awareness helps us to improve the environment where we function. Having a well-developed external self-awareness helps us strengthen our relationships and hence leadership skills.

Drivers of self-awareness

Self-awareness is a learnable skill and there are some simple, but effective ways to develop your neuroplasticity in self-awareness. In fact, self-awareness is the main premise of all the other Drivers we are discussing in the subsequent pages of this book as that will help you with sufficient knowledge and tools to practice the other skills to unlock and expand your true potential. In this section, we will explore some of the Drivers you can use to assess your self-awareness and get better at knowing yourself.

1. Proactive self-reflection and feedback

Self-reflection and feedback are the tools that help to develop your internal and external self-awareness. These tools help you delve deeper into identifying your thoughts, emotions and actions and the reasons behind them. With the help of these two tools, you will be able to understand yourself better through two different lenses—your own and the people whom you seek feedback from. You will learn more about the effective practicing of self-reflection and feedback later in this part of the book.

2. Meditation and mindfulness

Meditation and mindfulness help us to be conscious of our thoughts, feelings and behaviours. In fact, you will see these techniques useful in uncovering many of the Secret Codes we are exploring in this book. You will read more about the Drivers of meditation and mindfulness in Chapter 9 in this part of the book.

3. Psychometric tests

Psychometric tests provide general information on your personality to gain some insight into who you are. Your personality profile you receive from such tests is based on the answers you provide on the test. But keep in mind that your personality is not permanent, it is constantly evolving, so a test from a year ago might not be a true indicator of who you are today. At the same time, it is very generic and might not reflect your circumstances and individual situation. Furthermore, many people know how to manipulate the answers in such tests. So, if you do that, the personality profile you get might not reflect your actual personality.

Apart from the tools we discussed in this chapter, there are other powerful practices such as journaling, self-compassion, and gratitude, that will help you to learn more about yourself. We will explore more about these practices in the upcoming chapters of this part of the book.

Ultimately, the people who choose to develop their self-awareness are the ones who become successful in building their lives in a way that complements their own purpose and expectations from it. They are the ones who gain more insights into human behaviour by observing and modifying their own behaviour, and gain profit from interacting, collaborating and leading others. Exercising self-awareness will bestow you with a shortcut to unlock your Three Gates to unearth your hidden potential.

Chapter 6

Journeying the joy of journaling
Confide and connect the dots for clarity

Perhaps the most famous journal we have today is of Anne Frank. In it, she wrote, *'I hope I will be able to confide everything to you [her diary], as I have never been able to confide in anyone, and I hope you will be a great source of comfort and support.'* In Nazi-occupied Netherlands, as a Jewish teenager, Frank used her diary to understand herself, her relationships, and the political turmoil around her, hiding behind a bookshelf from Nazis. For Frank, her journal which she named Kitty was the go-to 'person' to confide in and clear her thoughts.

People have been journaling since the time writing was invented. Its therapeutic benefits have been sworn by people in various adverse situations. I have heard and read about burn survivors, domestic abuse survivors and trauma survivors who spoke about the healing and motivating effects of journaling. I have heard from people about how journaling helps them in dealing with guilt, failures and mistakes.

Initially, I was not planning to talk about journaling in an entire chapter. However, I changed my mind realizing that this is an easy-to-do activity with far-reaching benefits. Numerous studies have shown that effective journaling can positively transform several areas of our life and help us improve the overall quality of our life. It has been found to help in almost every aspect of life that we are talking about in this book.

As you unlock each Gate of your potential, you are introducing new behaviours, skills and knowledge into your life. Journaling is a remarkably beneficial activity to reflect on your efforts, review your progress, manage your mental health, and keep up your drive. Consistent and effective journaling has been linked to improved working memory, improved symptoms of depression, reduced absenteeism at work, higher grades on tests for students and improved mood. It has also been shown to improve physical health by reducing blood pressure and improving immune system functioning, lung functioning, liver functioning, and overall wellbeing.

Journaling takes our mind into a reflective mode and catches hold of a lot of information we otherwise would miss out in the plethora of thoughts we have day to day. Also, journaling is a great medium to pour out our dreams, agony, and doubts. Not surprisingly, journaling provides clarity to our thoughts and is a great tool for improving self-awareness. I use journaling to make peace with my failures, disappointments, sorrows, and other negative and demotivating feelings. I use it also to share my big and small accomplishments, daily experiences, conflicting thoughts, and happiness. In my journal, I catch a lot of my insecurities, and that helps me to use the right tools to handle those insecurities and lift my self-confidence. For me, my journal is a part of me to whom I can share my feelings as they are and bring out the answers. Writing in my journal is an extremely intimate and peaceful activity for me.

If simple journaling can provide us with self-assurance, self-confidence and overall psychological and physiological well-being, without spending huge money or enormous effort, there is nothing that should hold us back from this simple yet so rewarding daily habit.

Drivers to cultivate your personal journaling habit

Upon seeing all the benefits journaling can bestow us with, the natural question that comes up is, what can we do to start a journaling habit? The answer is 'just do it'. But the following information may help you on the way.

1. Find your preferred medium

Some people find using a physical diary, and some people find digital journals convenient and more secure. Find the medium most suitable for you so that you don't give yourself an option to complain and back out from this habit. The way we express ourselves differs from person to person. If you like writing or would like to improve your writing, journaling gives you the opportunity to practice your writing. However, if you are not writing because you feel that your writing style or language is not good, that is not an excuse. Your grammar and language do not matter when you write. What matters is whether you are expressing your thoughts and emotions in their purest form. Furthermore, there is a hidden advantage here. By writing regularly, you will also be able to improve your writing skills and language proficiency.

I started with a physical diary, and I used to carry it around in my purse. One day, I found out that someone took it out and read it, hiding it from me. Though it didn't have any confidential information in it, I was hurt that they did it behind my back. So, I shifted to digital journaling, and that is my preferred medium now. Some people find it easy to express themselves better with art. Some people record their daily journals verbally. There are people who draw, paint or doodle or write poems or use some other medium of art to express themselves. Some people use a combination of different mediums, like the way renowned Mexican painter, Frida Kahlo poured her heart out through prose, poems, and watercolour illustrations. Then there are those who want to limit time for writing, and they go for a bullet point journaling approach. Your journal, your rules.

2. Be true to yourself and to your emotions

In a journal, you are having an intimate conversation with yourself. This is a place where you can share even those things you were not ready to admit to yourself. This is a place you don't need to be diplomatic. Try to pour out the true incidents, facts and emotions. Studies have shown that journaling helps to reduce the intensity of negative emotions. A journal is also a place where you can share your dreams without fearing whether it is too big to achieve. As you have that conversation with your own mind in your journal, you might come across interesting situations where you are asking a question to yourself and answering it yourself. Having that back-and-forth conversation is a fertile ground for problem-solving and ideation.

Journaling has given me the confidence to acknowledge aspirations that I otherwise wouldn't have identified. It has also helped me with understanding my own nature as well as of others. It is a valuable Driver that helps me to organize my thoughts about various situations and observe situations from various viewpoints. I use journaling as a tool for self-compassion, which we will explore in detail in Chapter 8 in this part of the book. Journaling truly is a tool that could help you to boost your self-awareness and to plan and assess your progress in the pursuit of your purpose.

3. Multi-purpose journals

How many types of journals can you write? Basically, you can write as many types of journals as you like. Some people focus more on reflective journaling. Here they write about their day-to-day life experiences, special incidents, dreams, goals, and emotional journeys in a reflective mood. This helps to bring clarity into the situation, your actions and other people's actions. At the same time, it acts as a learning tool for how to deal with circumstances and people and to plan better for the future.

Then there is gratitude journaling, which I am very fond of. In gratitude journals, people usually tend to write about how grateful they are for the big and small things in life. Like, how grateful you are that you called your mom today or that you could see the sunrise or that someone helped you during the meeting at the office today. A gratitude journal reminds us of the small steps that we take towards our purpose and goals. It has helped me tremendously to connect the dots between my purpose, goals, actions, and emotions. When you are in a reflective mood, you think about your aspirations and your actions, and it helps you to remind yourself about how each day of your life is contributing to your aspirations, and this itself can help your brain to release the chemicals required for making your neural connections stronger on the topic you journaled about. People who do it vouch that their overall quality of life has improved after making gratitude journaling a habit.

Other than these regular journals, there are people who do travel journaling, hobby journaling, nature journaling, food journaling and so on. Mark Twain, who is known as the 'Father of American Literature', used to journal about his travels, and the ideas for new stories, in his pocket notebooks.

4. You can develop the habit of journaling at any age, but consistency is of important essence

You can start journaling at any age if you are able to share your thoughts and you write consistently. Parents can start asking young children about their day with leading questions such as, 'How did you feel then?' or 'What are you grateful for?' and make them feel comfortable to answer their thoughts and emotions. Provide them a safe environment where they feel comfortable sharing about the mistakes they made and the failures they experienced. You could share with your child about your day incorporating feelings, ideas, events, and thoughts, to encourage them to think and share about their own day. Write at least once a day. You may even plan a daily Family Journaling Time where the family comes together, but each person writes their own journal.

At last, use a journal for what it is, it's not a cure-all, though it has many benefits. If you write with the objective that it is soon going to solve all your problems and frequently assess its efficacy, it is going to backfire on you because of the stress you put yourself into.

So, enjoy your journaling, use it as a companion who is always there to listen to you. It doesn't take much effort and it bestows us with numerous benefits. And in return, you will learn more about yourself and the purpose of your aspirations, and you will pick up the courage to unlock the Three Gates to fulfil your purpose and aspirations. Doesn't that provide you with enough reasons to start your journaling routine today?

Chapter 7

Nurture a resilient mind through gratitude

Discover how small things are connected to the big picture

The ancient Greek philosopher Heraclitus said, 'Change is the only constant in our lives!' How apt was that when all of a sudden our lives changed when Covid-19 lockdowns kicked off in 2020! Who said wishes don't come true!

Many people wished to be at home doing nothing.

Many students wished they didn't have to go through the pressure of exams.

Many people wished they could eat homemade food every day.

Many wished they could watch Netflix all day.

All of them were sure that their wish will bring happiness in their lives if granted, but none of them thought their wishes were going to be fulfilled. Lo and behold! A magic wand appeared from somewhere in the form of Covid-19 and all those wishes were granted.

But are we happy? Two years after that, and still struggling to come to terms with the post-Covid world, some of the words that we got more familiarized with are 'anxiety', 'resilience' and 'mental health'. If you scroll through social media pages or if you are a coach like me who hears from others, you know that more people are seeking help for their mental health issues. Ironically, though people got many things they wished for, they are still anxious. And, rightfully there are many reasons to be anxious.

So here is a lesson from human psychology. We chase what we don't have, thinking that is where our happiness is. While happiness resides right in front of us every day, we fail to lock our eyes with it. How different our life would be if we are able to 'see' all those things that make us happy and appreciate those? As per studies, consistent practice of gratitude has the power to bring us face to face with the efforts that contribute to our happiness. An attitude of gratitude is the habit of reflecting on the good experiences and efforts that you were able to give or receive or experience. In the section below, we will take a glance at the various ways in which the attitude of gratitude enriches the quality of our life.

Benefits of practicing gratitude

Gratitude is a social emotion that plays a major role in unlocking all the Three Gates to our hidden potential. The fundamental driving force behind that is the fact that gratitude helps us to be more in touch with our thoughts, emotions, perspectives, actions and responses, and that in turn boosts our self-awareness. This self-awareness leads to acknowledging and understanding our abilities, priorities and aspirations. Throughout this book, you will come across many Secret Codes which list gratitude as one of the Drivers. And as you read the rest of this chapter, you will learn how gratitude truly deserves that spot.

According to studies, a habit of consistent practice of gratitude showers us many benefits in our personal and professional life. This is because gratitude triggers the release of dopamine in our system. As you have read earlier in this book, dopamine is a neurotransmitter responsible for happiness, pleasure and motivation among many other things. No wonder dopamine is counted among the happy hormones. The happy hormones help us with mental and emotional well-being, focus, energy and overall satisfaction with life.

Regular practice of gratitude provides us with great mental clarity as well since it puts us in introspective and self-reflective behaviour. As a result of that, we notice our daily efforts towards our purpose and goals. These self-reflections are instrumental in unlocking our hidden potential, which we will in discuss in Chapter 10. Furthermore, the daily practice of gratitude brings us face-to-face with how we give and receive in relationships.

Another important benefit of the consistent and effective practice of gratitude is that it boosts our ability to think from other people's perspectives. When we deliberately look positively at how someone else helped or supported us or how we got the opportunity to help and support someone else, we learn our own lessons on the working of the human mind. This is a great lesson that helps us to grow behaviours and traits such as empathy, likeability, influencing skills, interpersonal skills and collaboration skills. In the next two parts of the book you will learn that these skills play an important part in unlocking your People and Universal Gates as well.

Gratitude plays a huge role in getting rid of toxic emotions. This is because the feeling of gratitude has been found to activate parts of brain that are associated with regulating emotions. This helps in managing toxic emotions by releasing neurochemicals, including dopamine, that elevate our mood. Furthermore, dopamine in the system balances the stress hormones in the system and leave us in a positive mental and physical state.

Listed below are the Drivers that you can practice to cultivate this habit yourself.

Drivers to cultivate gratitude

1. Ensure a steady and natural supply of dopamine

Having already established the connection between gratitude and dopamine, it helps to know whether and how we can use it more efficiently. The answer for that lies in the little tweak we can do in the way we take account of our achievements.

When we chase specific goals, such as money and position, which definitely are important, we tie the reward to whether we are achieving those goals and the magnitude of that achievement. And when we achieve that goal, the brain releases dopamine and we get a dopamine spike. But neurologists have found something interesting regarding that feeling.

The dopamine spike you hit after achieving a goal, doesn't stay for long, there is always a dip after a spike. However, a dopamine dip doesn't mean that the dopamine level goes back to the baseline and stays there. When dopamine drops, it oscillates an equal amount to the other side. It has a wave pattern, every spike is associated with an equal dip. So after we celebrate a win, when dopamine drops and oscillates to the other side, we feel tired, moody, unmotivated and sometimes even depressed depending on how high the dopamine level was during the spike. This is one of the reasons we find it difficult to sustain our motivation, drive and excitement after a great win or a big celebration. But, if we have a steady supply of dopamine that motivates us, but doesn't push us too low, we can sustain our motivation and excitement.

This is where we can tweak our perception of the win. For that we need to look for motivation in something other than the goal itself. Neurologists have found that we can create a habit of dopamine spikes and resulting pleasure and motivation even when there is no big win. A great way to accomplish that is to train ourselves to observe and celebrate the pursuit of the goal, rather than waiting for the final goal to celebrate. If we acknowledge and celebrate small wins such as the completion of various steps towards the big win, our brain gets accustomed to dopamine spikes.

This is where an attitude of gratitude comes in handy. Regular practice of gratitude helps us take notice of the small wins on a day-to-day basis, and the resulting dopamine spike provides us with enough motivation to sustain our effort a little more. Since these dopamine spikes are not massive, the ensuing dopamine dips are also not as low as to drive us to a demotivated state. So gratitude plays a major role in elevating our motivation and drive, and living a happy and contented life. If we do not acknowledge these small wins, we don't get to make use of the dopamine spikes and the motivation associated with them.

At this point, some people may ask, 'Isn't just acknowledging the small efforts and wins enough? Why do we need to be grateful about it?' Acknowledging small wins and efforts provides great benefits. In fact, this is where the basis for the phrase 'focus on the process rather than the result' stems from. The answer to that is that social emotions such as gratitude have been found to have a role in elevating our dopamine levels. Now that we are undoubtedly clear about the fact that gratitude plays a major role in elevating our motivation, mood and overall satisfaction in life, let's examine some everyday situations and see how you can find the reason to be grateful for those.

- You got the chance to tell a story to your child: That is the small step you took today towards your goal of building a lifelong bond with your child.
- You got the chance to cook a meal with your better half: That is the small step you took today towards your goal of forming sustainable relationships.
- You got the chance to read a book: That is the small step you took today to discover your long-term plans.

- You were able to hold a critical business meeting with a client on zoom: That is the small step you took today towards boosting your influencing skills even when you were physically not there.
- You were able to apply the negotiation skills you learned in a business discussion today: That is the small step you took today towards your self-development to achieve your next promotion.
- You kept away your phone when your partner came to talk to you: That is the small step you took today towards your goal to pay full attention to people when you are with them.
- You held yourself from telling your child to stop talking because you are in the middle of your work: This is the small step you took today to create a happy and lively home.

These are simple things, but they go a long way in ensuring that you are indeed on the right track and that will further provide you with additional motivation to pursue the underlying goals.

2. Be your own cheerleader

Appreciate yourself. The unbeatable self-identity you developed as we discussed in Chapter 3 will be of great help in appreciating yourself for being the wonderful person that you are. Use positive and process-focused describers such as hardworking, patient, kind, learner etc. to compliment yourself, as we saw in the previous Driver, and be your own cheerleader.

Find out ways to develop a habit of saying gratitude for each of the simple things that happened in your life. Trust me, that won't go astray. I have experienced the calming and strengthening powers of a gratitude practice in my own life and that is what led me to write my book *30-Day Gratitude System* in 2020.

3. Use a gratitude journal

We have discussed the therapeutic and psychological benefits of practicing effective journaling in the previous chapter. Doing gratitude journaling is just an extension of that. Incorporate every small thing you are grateful for in that journal.

You can also go creative by using mediums such as gratitude jars, online gratitude sites and so on to express your gratitude.

4. Use the three-step gratitude process

When you write or express your gratitude, there are three things you need to consider.

1. Gratitude towards other people for what they have done for you: Your gratitude for people who used their time, money, possessions, efforts, gestures or words to help or support you.
2. Gratitude for what you could do for others: The opportunities you received for helping and supporting others through your time, money, possessions, efforts, gestures or words.
3. Gratitude for the steps you took to fulfil your goals and purpose: Each day comes with a promise of great things. However, there are some days we are able to do more, then there are those days we do not manage to achieve much. This is where you look for every step you took, regardless of whether they were small or big, and connect those to your purpose or goals.

5. Use your own mediums and methods to express gratitude

As we practice gratitude, we sometimes suddenly realize how certain people were instrumental in helping us reach wherever we are today. You might have or have not realized their roles in your successes until now. Whether it is long-lost or prevailing connections, the gratitude activity would be much more beneficial and joyful if you try to express your gratitude to them personally, in addition to writing it in your journal. You may use telephones, emails, messages, cards etc. to convey your gratitude to those people and create an environment of positive and uplifting emotions.

6. Attach good emotions with your gratitude and pursue a goal right after

By now we know that unlocking the Three Gates is all about creating the right environment for beneficial neurochemicals to establish lasting neural connections. Attaching good emotions to your gratitude practice is a great way to influence the release of those neurochemicals. For example, instead of writing 'I am grateful that Martha helped me today', if you write 'I am grateful that Martha took the time to brief me about my new work and answered all my questions patiently. I am grateful that she encouraged, motivated, and helped me to be at ease on my first day'. When you include relevant details of the incident in your gratitude practice along these lines, you are reminding yourself of the material and emotional benefits you experienced from that situation, and that would trigger positive emotions and hence motivation in the present moment too. And, you can make use of the motivation to pursue something you care about right after your gratitude practice in order to maximize the dopamine spike and the motivation from it.

7. Recruit a gratitude buddy

If you want to enjoy expressing gratitude, it is essential to make it a habit through consistent practice. Try to do it at least once a day for reaping all the benefits of this. One of the ways to achieve consistency is by involving like-minded people in this practice.

Having an accountability partner is a great way to do that as both of you can encourage and push each other in practicing gratitude on a daily basis. As we have seen earlier, you may also consider family Gratitude Time where your family members can come together to express or write gratitude separately at a given time. This is especially useful if you would like to impart the practice of gratitude to youngsters in the family.

In conclusion, practicing gratitude is not limited to a feel-good effect, it also helps keep our motivation up to pursue our dreams and goals. The mental, social and emotional benefits from this simple practice showers us with the resolve and resilience to persevere and persist. A daily gratitude routine can greatly accelerate your efforts to unlock your hidden potential many folds.

Chapter 8

Use self-compassion to build yourself up
Develop a passion for caring for yourself

A few years ago, Chelsea joined our growth mindset and learning skills program for teenagers. Chelsea was a happy thirteen-year-old student with big dreams about becoming a dietician. However, academic reports showed that she scored C and D in her exams, and she was worried that she might not get a chance to study her favourite course at the university. She attended the Growth Mindset program during her holidays with the intention of improving her scores. When she came back for the catch-up session after a month, she excitedly shared that she scored A and A* in all her subjects except Mandarin, for which she scored a B. She said, 'I am seeing such good results in my tests first time after four years.' As she was proudly and cheerfully recounting the efforts that led to her progress, she said, 'I used many techniques you taught me during the program. I practiced memory techniques to study effectively, and I used mind maps to organize information. I prioritized my tasks and planned my time as you taught me. I am consciously practicing stress management skills to stay relaxed, and I am improving my organizational skills now. However, the most important thing that helped me to achieve all these was deciding to be kind to myself.' She further explained,

'I used to beat myself up for not using my time effectively. I used to feel guilty after playing computer games with my brother for wasting my time. I used to be angry at myself for not being able to control gaming and blamed my brain for forgetting the concepts I learned. And I used to beat myself up for not scoring as well as my friends at school. But now I am looking at myself with more empathy and more understanding.' When Chelsea sat down to study, the self-blaming and the guilt took over her valuable time. That didn't let her enjoy the fun moments fully and utilize her study time productively. This not only affected her focus and academic performance, but also her mental well-being.

That was the first time we had introduced self-compassion in our program and several other students echoed Chelsea's feelings and shared how self-compassion helped them to focus better on their studies as well as improve their overall satisfaction with their efforts. Over the course of time, we have heard several stories from students such as how self-compassion helped them to deal with their anger, how it helped them to adjust their learning style to suit themselves, how it helped them to improve their self-identity and self-confidence and so on. When the outside world mainly focuses on advising teenagers about what they should and should not do, they are missing the whole point of what kind of internal blaming is going on within these children.

It is not just students who blame themselves for what happens in their life. In the workplace also it is common. When your colleague got the promotion that you had been meticulously working towards, when you couldn't achieve your performance targets, when you had a conflict with your colleague—you will be surprised to notice how easy it is for us to find reasons to blame ourselves in any situation.

Like Chelsea, many leaders and entrepreneurs I coach also recount how practicing self-compassion has helped them to achieve breakthroughs in their professional and social life and how it has helped them to increase their overall satisfaction with their life and relationships.

Why do we need to practice self-compassion?

Nowadays we hear about compassion and empathy very often and the importance of these behaviours have long been understood. But that paradigm was one-sided and unbalanced. What we often learn is how we should be abundant in showing our compassion to others, but at the same time how we should be tough towards ourselves. It gives the impression that there is no room for self-compassion during hard work. Mainstream literature on concepts such as hard work, perseverance and persistence have inadvertently created the belief among the masses that we should be tough towards ourselves as we work towards success. Some people shared that they count showing compassion and empathy towards self as an act bordering on narcissism. That brings up the question, how can you dare to think about yourself without self-labelling yourself a narcissist? Let me create the case for the need for self-compassion.

1. Self-judgement is paralyzing the growth of people

I have observed among people of all ages that everybody feels the need to boost their self-confidence. I have even seen successful people whom others admire for their leadership and people-centric nature quietly wish, 'If only I were more confident'. Many years ago, when we were doing an event for our children's edutainment magazine, The Kidz Parade, at an elementary school, an eight-year-old boy approached us and said, 'I would like to subscribe to the magazine.' He continued, 'I heard that you have a section that gives tips on how to handle bullies. I want to learn how to build my self-confidence to stand up to bullies.' You see a need in people to feel confident at every age and every stage in every walk of life. I have had teachers telling me how they wish to develop their own self-esteem and self-confidence to mentor high school students effectively. The biggest hurdle that stands between you and your greater self-confidence is your self-judgement.

We have read about many stories of personal success through resilience. But what drives people's resilience and perseverance when they see only roadblocks everywhere? We have heard about how Colonel Sanders of KFC, at the age of sixty-five, failed 1,009 times before he succeeded in selling the fried chicken recipe of his by then closed roadside restaurant to the first franchisee and how it became the brand KFC. What if Col Sanders had beaten himself up after the 10th, 500th or 1000th rejection? What gave him the confidence to knock on the 1010th door after the 1009th rejection? If he was hard on himself and blamed himself, 'You are useless to even think that you will make anything out of your own recipe?' he wouldn't have gathered the perseverance to drive around the United States for two years, living in his car, to search for potential customers. He would have probably believed that he was incapable to expand his horizons and remained desperate, cynical, and miserable in his life. Yet for all that, he had the self-compassion to accept his situation and to look at his disappointments kindly and hence he found the self-command to trust in his future expansion, learn from disappointments and motivate himself genuinely to stay on in his pursuit.

Have you felt not at ease when you are not happy with your performance or progress? Studies have shown that self-judgement causes stress in humans and stress leads to mess. Self-judgement induces the secretion of cortisol, the stress hormone in our system, which in turn triggers the mammalian fight or flight response in our system. It builds up the energy to act and suppresses the energy to think and respond. The sustained stressful situation could affect our heart, cause fatigue, and interfere with the efficient performance of our memory system. Our brain builds neural networks based on our thoughts, beliefs, actions and behaviours. And it strengthens those electrical circuitries based on how often we do it. So, if you have a habit of judging or blaming yourself, your brain builds those circuitries so strong that self-blaming roots itself unconscious influence on you. Like Chelsea, you will always be finding something to blame yourself for in every situation. Self-judgement is detrimental to your imperishability. When you break free from such an established neural network, you will open the doors to better physical health, mental health, memory skills and overall performance.

2. Seeking self-esteem could crush your growth

It is well understood from the studies of many researchers that Asian cultures are predominantly collectivistic and Western cultures predominantly individualistic. Living at a time when the world is predominantly being led by western philosophies, standards and societal norms, people around the world generally feel the pressure to demonstrate their personal accomplishments. In the pursuit of achieving personal success, many suffer huge setbacks in their self-confidence. A lot of them do not know how to handle that and consequently their self-esteem suffers. When the world is focused on victorious stories of individualistic pursuits, it is easy to guess why people are giving so much importance to self-esteem.

If we look at why we need better self-esteem, we know that it is because we like to project our individuality and self-worth in front of the world. Yet studies have shown that self-compassion is a better way to accomplish all the benefits that self-esteem offers. Moreover, self-compassion also gives some additional benefits and helps to not practice some unwanted character traits that are associated with self-esteem. It has also been found that a person's self-esteem shifts based on what they have achieved, whether they were successful in something or not.

Jean Twenge PhD, an American psychologist and a researcher on generational differences, studied the narcissistic levels of US college students over twenty years and depicted how self-esteem is linked to narcissism. Her study found that self-esteem rose with narcissism. You will see people's self-esteem suffering when they come across disappointment or failure in life. However, with self-compassion, success and failure aren't an end game. Self-compassion has the power to instil belief in yourself and cultivate a healthy self-identity that provides you with all benefits of self-esteem. Would you choose self-compassion over self-esteem now?

3. Perfectionism hinders contentment

The feeling of achievement is associated with contentment. But, when perfectionistic tendencies are followed by self-blaming, it could plummet your self-confidence and stall your progress. Let's take the example of Gavin. He is a bright business development manager in a trail-blazing advertisement firm and was just back from a client presentation. He came back to his seat and said, 'I blew it.' Gavin had been working on this pharmaceutical client account for a few weeks now. He was excited about this new client. He had spent weeks researching the details, meeting with the client, discussing with his own team and optimizing his slides for this account. When he presented the proposal, the right words didn't come out of his mouth, nervousness overtook his confidence, and he didn't remember to say many things that he had meticulously prepared to speak about. He felt his presentation didn't have the impact he had carefully worked for.

Gavin kept on chiding himself after he went back straight to his seat. 'I am useless', 'Why do I always do this?', 'When will I learn not to dream high and live in a fool's paradise?', 'It is high time for me to accept the fact that I am not as great as I think I am'. The rants changed their course from frustration about the current situation to generalizing that he is ineffective and incapable of anything in life. Many people unknowingly fall into the trap of negativity and low self-confidence just by ranting. In fact, if we could listen to our negative thoughts, we would be ashamed to realize that we are so crude that we talk the worst to ourselves and expect the worst from ourselves. Though it comes out from our frustrations and disappointments, this behaviour does not help us in getting better in any manner, and it is in fact detrimental to our progress.

If Gavin had waited to listen to his clients and colleagues after the presentation, he would have heard how much they appreciated his presentation. More importantly, he would have got an opportunity to address some of the points he had missed in his presentation during that extra time with the client. But his penchant for perfectionism clouded his thoughts with self-judgement and self-blaming instead of taking the opportunity to improve the situation.

Gavin's self-criticism gradually made its appearance in the way he treated others as well. Even when his son brought home a great result, his feedback focused mainly on why the child didn't push for something grander. Gavin was never happy about anything he did or anything others had done for him. Moreover, this attitude of his was hampering his progression to better roles he looked forward to. Whenever he sat for a performance review meeting with his manager or a job interview with another organization, he was unable to show excitement and enthusiasm for the past work he had done, and that made the other party doubtful of his abilities and contributions. Gavin kept wondering why he was not getting any good opportunities despite having a great resume and participating honestly during the discussions. His colleagues tend to make him the scapegoat when things went wrong and stole the credit when things were on the right track. The colleagues who worked with him on the same projects climbed up the career ladder, but Gavin hasn't, although he has contributed much better than others in those projects. He had been known as an energetic high potential person among his friend circle in his younger days but has reduced to a mere shadow of that.

You might have come across one or several Gavins in your personal or professional life. There are many ways people create the perfect situation for self-blaming. People in their pursuit of perfectionism often feel guilty that they are incompetent compared to someone else at work. Feeling guilty about not finding enough time to have dinner with family, feeling guilty about not being the perfect parent or child portrayed in self-help blogs, feeling guilty about not managing time while you were burning the midnight oil to finish your work commitment, feeling guilty about ignoring social life and personal fitness, the list goes on. There are studies that suggest that perfectionism is linked to depression, social anxiety and eating disorders.

In a world where there is no dearth of tips and advice, it is not difficult to find imperfections in yourself and the ensuing negative bias. Neuroscientists have found evidence that there is more neural processing in the brain in response to negative stimuli compared to positive stimuli. Due to this we have a much stronger emotional response to negative stimuli that, in turn, affects our decisions and actions and it could also stimulate another set of negative thought waves and perhaps actions. Evolutionary psychologists think that negativity is built into our survival mechanism to look out for dangers and act.

Unrealistic portrayals of life in movies and social media have induced unrealistic expectations of personal effectiveness. Bosses are expected to be perfect bosses, subordinates are expected to be perfect workers and spouses are expected to be perfectly companionable. There is always something you need to get better at; to level up. Mothers are expected to be the perfect mothers, they get condemnation by keyboard fighters on social media for things such as being forgetful, introducing some discipline to their children's life or letting their children enjoy their life. Many teenagers experience the pressure to look like Instagram models and entrepreneurs feel the pressure to find success within a short period. People feel the pressure to create a fairytale life, present intricately decorated food, design enchanting homes and go for fun-filled holidays. Many people are becoming victims of perfectionism in this make-believe world of social media moments.

In moments of despair and despondence, have you ever felt 'If only there was someone out there to understand me?' or 'If I had someone there to comfort me without asking me any questions?' You are that person. You are a person who can feel one thing and at the same time think about something else. As you feel the despair, you are the sufferer, and you are the observer of the suffering too. When you give that observer the hands to comfort you with words of empathy, you are creating an environment for self-compassion. The good news is self-compassion can effectively lead you to reduce your self-judgement and guide you to form a better self-identity. Moreover it helps you to build a better relationship with yourself.

So, we know that there are many reasons for us to cultivate a habit of self-compassion in several areas of our lives. When we talked about the journey of thought earlier, we have also seen how thoughts impact our lives.

Later in this chapter, we will explore the Drivers you can use to cultivate a habit of self-compassion and capitalize on that to develop a strong Personal Gate.

4. Retrospective thinking ruling your life and thoughts

My friend Viji got transferred to another department in her research institute last year. This was a transfer she had requested for, but a few months into her new role, I noticed that she didn't look as happy as she used to. During a recent catch-up, she opened her heart and told me, 'My new boss Christina has a short fuse, and she is looking for opportunities to find fault in everything I do. Because of her sharp tongue, I often don't respond to her taunts. But I can't stop myself from thinking about how I should have responded in each of those situations. I feel that she is ruling my thoughts too.'

It is well proven that looking back at our past experiences and gaining insights from them is something that will help us to thrive in life. However, when these retrospective scenes become the reason for increased frustration and inadequacy in your life and when it destroys your mental equilibrium, it is high time to say 'No' to self-critical thoughts that lead to self-sabotaging.

Adopting a timid nature was something I resorted to as a child when I felt that my thinking style was different from others around me. Timidity was good as it would also help me to avoid a lot of personal questions people would ask in my little town where everybody felt it was their business to know everybody else's business. Timidity was a good facade that people didn't expect me to share my views when I didn't want to. As I practiced timidity consciously, it started coming naturally to me, timidity started becoming me. And it came with its own disadvantages too. When you don't speak for yourself, many people would find it convenient to blame you right on your face, right in front of others. Many people would find it easy to share the ideas you shared with them privately as their own.

In the middle of all these pros and cons, what I suffered the most from was, the constant self-reminder of what I could have done in many situations, such as claiming my ideas as mine, defending myself when people found it convenient to blame me, sharing my viewpoints that would give away my true personality and beliefs. It took a while for me to accept myself as who I was, to find my own voice and to stand up for myself. Even then the retrospective thoughts kept asking me what I could have become if I had stood up for myself earlier. Self-compassion is something that helped me to rediscover myself and to prepare myself for future possibilities.

Feeling guilty or shameful about bad decisions, embarrassing situations or wrong actions is not something new to many of us. When that happens, those thoughts may come back and haunt you numerous times, especially if it is something severe. But what happens if keeps regurgitating for long term?

I have listened to people saying how some negative decisions or actions from their childhood or adolescence come back into their thoughts regularly, curtailing their enthusiasm and self-confidence, making them doubt their own potential. It reappears in the thought stream whenever they feel they made a stupid decision or took a wrong step. Obviously, these retrospective thoughts are not putting you in a confident zone related to your past and it surely is not giving you much confidence to tackle your present challenges or future situations. Now the question is, is there a need to nurture these retrospective thoughts? The answer is obvious.

We have seen that negative retrospective thinking itself is detrimental. Then there are people who inflate their mistakes and treat that as something unique to themselves. This makes it even more detrimental as such thoughts are accompanied by the belief that it is rare and unsolvable.

In the example we read about earlier, when Gavin felt that he had made some mistakes in his presentation, some of the thoughts that went through his mind was, 'Why am I the only person who makes such mistakes again and again?' What if Gavin looks at the situation and tells himself, 'This time a couple of things went amiss. This is something that could have happened to anybody.' When we look at Gavin's situation as a third party, we can relate to it and understand that this is a mistake that anybody could make. Furthermore, we can also relate to how Gavin would be feeling about it. But when we face it ourself, we do not feel it as a human error. We feel it as 'my mistake' or 'I am the only one who would make such a horrendous error'.

When you inflate your mistakes and give them an identity of 'nobody else makes such mistakes', it ceases to become the product of a situation, but it becomes you. And that further triggers and enforces limiting beliefs and fears.

Drivers to build self-compassion

Let's face it. It is impossible to be your best at all times and it is impossible to live in the memory of unpleasant situations forever. Sometimes, the soil you remove when you dig up the past could bury your future. That is where practicing self-compassion can help you. You might probably have identified some areas and situations in your life that you could make brighter through self-compassion. Discussed below are the Drivers you can adopt to practice self-compassion.

1. Catch your thoughts and emotions

Thoughts are cultivated habits. Over the years, we unconsciously cultivate the habit of thinking the same thoughts with the same mood frequently. These thought patterns and mood take over our minds and it becomes part of our nature. Self-blaming and self-judgements are also habits of our thought pattern. The more we judge and blame ourselves we find more opportunities to do the same.

The first step in getting rid of any habit is to become aware of when you exhibit that habit. Taking a check on ourselves such as 'What was I thinking now?' is a great way to catch our thoughts. I have a friend who asks herself that question whenever she sees a number with repeated digits. There are people who practice the habit of catching their thoughts at repeated intervals, such as when the clock strikes every hour or by keeping an hourly alarm. There are people who ask this question whenever they sense a mood change in themselves. A thought is heavy. It originates from another thought and becomes the originator of another thought. And it comes with its own feelings and emotional response. If you develop a practice to catch your thoughts with all these companions, you will be able to understand your thought process better. Mindfulness, meditation and self-reflection are ways where you can tune your mind to be more alert and catch your thoughts.

Catch your thoughts when it moves into a self-sabotaging path. Does the thought introduce stress or demotivating feelings in you? Are they retrospectively judgemental or perfectionism fueled or catastrophic or are they really superior problems in nature? Identify those thoughts as your self-judgemental thoughts.

2. Correct your story

When we discussed our thought patterns, we saw how our thoughts might not portray the right perspective. Our thoughts fuel the shaping and reshaping of our personal stories. If you have been looking at a certain situation from a self-critical perspective, it is quite likely that thinking about your perspective on that situation is influenced by your self-judgements, perfectionistic tendencies or the need for self-esteem or retrospective thinking.

Like in a movie shooting, say 'Cut' to those scenes and ask yourself, 'Is that the real story? If an independent observer was there at the time, what would their perspective be?' Replace the self-judgemental story that you have in your mind with the version of the independent observer. This corrected version of your story is less likely to threaten your future growth and expansion as the previous version.

3. Practice the best friend talk

Next time when you frustratingly ask yourself 'Why did you do that?' change your condescending tone to an empathetic tone. When you talk to yourself, assume that instead of you it is your best friend or the person whom you love the most who got into that situation. Will you tell them, 'You are the most incompetent person I have ever come across' or 'You are useless'? It is very unlikely that you would do that. You wouldn't even be their best friend if you did that. Instead, you would console them with words such as, 'You wouldn't have done that if you knew better' or 'This is just one incident where you lost your cool. This doesn't define who you are' or 'I don't consider you irresponsible at all. It is just that there were other angles to this situation which you didn't know before'.

In a healthy relationship, constant criticism has no room. Be that ideal best friend for yourself. Make yourself feel that you are there for yourself. Give that best friend talk to yourself so that you can feel valued and valuable .

4. Choose your mode of communication with yourself

Some people find it difficult to sustain a soothing conversation with themselves, even if they are doing it in their minds. They don't really feel it, especially when they initially start to practice self-compassion or self-talking. Also, some people are more expressive when they write things down compared to talking. If you prefer writing, consider writing a letter to yourself. How would a well-meaning and motivating mentor write to you? Use that style when writing to yourself.

Use self-compassion as your mature and empathetic personal coach and mentor who is anytime at your disposal. Let that mentor help you to quieten your inner demons and to steer you towards focused thoughts for future advancements. There is no point in punishing yourself and sabotaging your present and future for your mistakes and failures from the past.

5. Accept other people's admiration for you

There is often a gap between how people perceive you and how you perceive yourself. A self-judgemental person usually has a much lower self-identity of themselves compared to how other people perceive them. They take other people's admiration for them with a pinch of salt. They may feel that others admire them either because they don't know who they really are or doubt their intelligence or feel that they are doing it for gaining some favours. The more you put your effort into bridging that gap to understand the perspective of people who admire you, the more you will come to terms with the real person you are.

6. Watch how you treat others

The root of many of our self-judgement is based on how we were treated by others and what we heard from others. For example, if a parent punishes a child for their mistakes, irrespective of how well-meaning the parent is, the child grows up with the opinion that treating yourself hard for your wrongdoings is the right thing to do. When emotions are not addressed in relationships, self-criticism and personal suffering become the norm. While it affects the sufferer, this reinforces self-judgement and self-blaming in the other person too.

It is important to create a culture of self-care around you by acknowledging the emotions and feelings of the people around you, such as your family, friends, colleagues as well as yourself. If you are a parent or a youth developer, be a role model and guide the younger generation towards self-compassion so that they will get a jumpstart in acknowledging and processing their emotions with empathy. Let them learn from you how to compassionately look at themselves and extend it to others.

7. Accept yourself as a part of the collective human experience

Research shows that when you identify failures and personal ineffectiveness as shared human experiences instead of suffering in isolation, it helps you to treat yourself with more kindness.

Each human being is a beautiful medley of two facets; the yin and yang of 'our strengths and weaknesses'. When there are two facets, it is possible for a certain facet to appear more prominent in certain situations. Observing others is a great way to feel compassionate to ourselves without any weirdness. As you observe weakness and strength in others you accept that you are as strong and as weak as others. This helps you to reduce your self-judgement and look at yourself in a more humane light. Transform your self-identity from an incompetent person to a person who can make good and bad choices. So, a misstep or a missed deadline or a miscommunication is a human error. Give yourself that permission. Tell yourself, 'I forgive you. It just shows that you are human.'

Empathy and compassion start literally with you. The more you know about your own emotions, the more you will be able to empathize with yourself, the more you will be able to be compassionate with yourself, and the more you will be able to show all these traits and social emotions to others. Self-compassion is not just the way to your self-wellbeing, it is the way to establish your empathetic and compassionate self with others and at the same time achieve your goals and mental wellbeing.

As the world comes to accept the importance of mental wellbeing, empathy and emotional intelligence in the workplace, it is essential to establish an organizational culture that encourages and promotes self-compassion at work. Spread that culture by elevating yourself to be the promoter and flagbearer of self-compassion at your workplace and in your team.

Chapter 9

Discover the real 'you' with mindfulness and meditation

Find yourself in the backdrop of a tranquil mind

When the Covid-19 pandemic and the lockdown started, like many people, I felt extremely constrained. I love nature and large space, the vastness of space around me has a therapeutic and calming effect on my mood and it sets my mind free for exploring new ideas and concepts. And I considered these as the backbone of my creativity.

My typical creative idea generation process looks something like this—go to a cafe with outside seating having an unconstrained view. Though it is difficult in urban Singapore, I did manage to find such places easily accessible from my office and home. I would do my research, read and contemplate sitting there devouring my shot of caffeine. This also gives me an opportunity to watch people as they conduct their everyday business. It is in those cafés that I arrived at business ideas, course ideas, speeches, the detailed conceptualization of my books and other creative pursuits. Singapore's weather of sun and rain, the space, the smell of coffee, and the conversations with myself about new ideas—it was not just the environment that stimulated my creativity, I considered these rituals as part and parcel of my creativity. Once

I had a solid concept for a section of the book, I did the writing at home or office.

When Covid-19 lockdowns happened unexpectedly, initially the cafes were closed. But, when they reopened, my favourite places didn't reopen the outside seating area. Forced to stay at home, I felt that my creativity got constrained and often got this mental image of my hands and legs tied down with chains. Gradually I stopped conceptualizing and writing my book.

Without even realizing that I had given away the control to the environment, and that I was sabotaging my own progress with this book, I took several extensions from my publisher. The immense guilt of keeping her waiting and the shame of not being able to keep my own word hit me hard. I tried my willpower to will myself to write, but the change in the scenery of my creative exploration was affecting my psyche. It led me to question my own ethos to write a book on this subject.

I moseyed around the land of uncertainty and fixed mindset, hoping that the world was going to go back to the past normalcy. But as the guilt was taking over me, I realized that I was not practicing what I wanted to share in this book. After a lot of self-reflection, I got convinced that I had to recharge myself and keep my motivation level up. And I told myself, 'That's easy. How many times have I taken myself out from a demotivated state of mind!'

Soon I realized that I was not reaching anywhere with the motivation part. The worst part was that I was not letting go of my beliefs about the source of my creativity, reframing my thoughts, recouping myself or stepping up to the changing and challenging times. I felt worse than before when I realized that my willpower failed me. And I got a firsthand experience of how the failure of willpower negatively affects our confidence in our abilities and skills.

The baggage of writing the book was putting additional pressure on me; even feeling that as baggage surprised me.

This was not a feeling I had experienced ever before in the past; I enjoyed writing, the topic was so close to my heart, and I was excited when my publisher approached me for a book. That made me think—perhaps I need to give a massive lift to my mindset and motivation, which I thought I had enough in the past, to sail through unprecedented times of challenges. I needed to discover more about myself and figure out what else I could apply to myself from what I wanted to write in this book.

The first step I did was to separate my willpower from the book. I split my goal into two. The first goal was to build up my willpower and the second was to write the book. In general, my willpower certainly needed a shakeup. When we feel that we are beaten by life, our willpower gets pulled down by our negative thoughts, environment, and company or the lack of it. To give an overhaul to my willpower, the gratitude practice, which I did once a day even before now progressed to three-four times a day. This is because I started writing my gratitude journal whenever I felt low. However, I was looking for something even more sustainable, something that can fill me with a shot of positive energy for the whole day. And that is when I set foot in the land of meditation.

The meditative mind

Meditation is not new to those of us who were brought up with some Asian roots. From the Indian Vedic era thousands of years ago to Buddhism, to Taoism to the modern mindfulness revolution by Zen master and bestselling author Thích Nhất Hạnh, meditation in various ways has been in continuous practice in our collective culture for centuries. Meditation was the go-to practice for mental clarity and mental well-being in the past. Whereas mental tranquility and looking inside for answers were considered a norm in the past, with colonialism in several parts of Asia and later with globalization, as we got more and more introduced to other cultures and started adopting those, we have also neglected the various meditative practices.

Over the years before the pandemic, I had attended many yoga and meditation programs, but the practice of it had weaned off, mainly because I didn't feel any pressing need to do it at that time. A year before the pandemic I had attended a yoga program in a reputed institution which included meditation too, and that gave me answers to many questions and I started regular practice from then onwards. However, due to two ankle injuries, one after the other, unrelated to the yoga practice, over the span of six months, forced me to stop the daily practice. I was still tending to an injured ankle in the initial few months of the pandemic.

When my ankles recovered, I restarted my yoga and meditation practice. I took up yoga and meditation in the pursuit of self-awareness, and that took me on a journey to discover more about why I became so demotivated. As I got deeply invested in finding myself and my self-development, I gradually realized that my mind was getting clearer and to my surprise, I got answers to even some long-forgotten questions from the past. My life journey till then was getting clearer to me and I realized more strengths and areas for improvement. It also helped me to be more vulnerable and to own myself with all my strengths and weaknesses.

Being an analytical person, I needed logical answers to these experiences, and this is something that I found. A study from UCLA found that the brains of long-term meditators are preserved well compared to others. The long-term meditators have also been found to have more grey matter volume, the information processing centers, than non-meditators. In another study conducted by the University of Pittsburgh and Carnegie Mellon University, the researchers used MRI brain scans to analyze the effect of an eight-week practice of mindfulness in 155 healthy adults. They compared the brain images before and after the six-weeks meditation practice and made some interesting observations. They found the amygdala, the region of the brain that is associated with fear and stress, shrinking. Along with that the researchers also observed the pre-frontal cortex, the part of the brain that is associated with executive functioning, got thicker. Furthermore, the study also found the connection of the amygdala with other parts of the brain weakening. These structural changes suggest that consistent practice of mindfulness results in a reduction in stress and, improvement in higher order brain functions such as focus and decision making.

Daily practices such as meditation, yoga, deep breathing and even walking in nature has been found to help clear toxins in our brain and keep our memory healthy, reduce our stress and keep other mental processes healthy.

I discovered how my heart fluttered or my stomach got butterflies or legs started dancing or my head started swaying, or sometimes even felt miserable when I listened to a vast array of classical and traditional music from India, the middle east, and eastern Europe. I always loved to get lost in pure music but realized that the hectic life had put that in that mental basket that we all pile up for our retirement life. It was not just music that I focused on. I chanted and listened to chants from different religions and cultures and listened to guided meditation. I let myself enjoy the process of listening to my body's response to various sounds, something I rarely did in the past. Since I had considered finding my willpower as an important goal, spending time on all this didn't make me feel guilty about wasting time, which I would have otherwise felt.

What ensued was a lot of direct and indirect benefits. I became more self-aware. I started knowing more about my likes and dislikes and the reasons behind those. I started understanding the reason behind my emotions. As I was learning more about myself and my emotions, I started understanding and relating to others better. I got better at sharing about myself with others without fearing how they will treat me after listening to some of my views. And I stopped being the person who would let others treat me badly. The better I knew about myself, the better I was able to accept myself, be happy with myself and be more open to setting goals and dreaming about a brighter future. I became braver because with the self-awareness I was developing, I knew that I was not the person some people chose to make me believe I was, to fulfil their own egos. If you have a habit of believing every negative comment people make about you, and spiral into a negative self-identity, what you need is to develop more self-awareness. For me, it was the practices of meditation and mindfulness that helped me to get clarity about myself.

Waking up for my early morning meditation, helped me with a boost of positivity in yet another way. When I was a high schooler, I used to wake up early in the morning and study, voluntarily. There was no pressure because I was conscious of what I wanted to achieve. But after I enrolled in my undergraduate engineering course, I lost my interest in studies as I realized I was not passionate about the subjects I was studying and with that the habit of early morning waking weaned off. Occasionally when I did, it was the day before the exam or later when I had to finish up some presentation for work. And oh boy! I hated waking up early. I wondered whether I would ever be able to re-establish my early waking routine.

But to my disbelief, I enthusiastically woke up in the mornings to do meditation, because I was doing something that I enjoyed. It felt like I was getting my high school years back. Waking up early became a habit, I didn't need to force myself. There was no drop in willpower, the entire pot of willpower I needed for the day was available and it was brimming with excitement because I started the day on a positive note. Now I was getting my dopamine spikes from the morning itself—from the happiness of waking up early, the pleasure of achieving my daily goal of meditation, and from the neurological benefits from the act of meditation itself. Hence my motivation and self-awareness were at an all-time high, and without any provocation, one day I felt that I was ready to start working on my book again. And here it comes in your hand, the result of the hardest willpower challenge I faced in my life, which I would never barter for anything else.

Meditation is about practicing focus—that is focusing on what you are meditating on. In some forms of meditation, you try to detach as many thoughts from your mind as possible, whereas in some other forms of meditation you try to take in as many things around you as possible. In either case it is about bringing your focus on to something.

While meditation is a dedicated practice, mindfulness is meditation in action. Being mindful is about bringing your complete focus into everything that you are doing—that includes what you think, what you feel, what you hear, what you say and what you do.

If you think about it, it is interesting to note that focusing is all about meditation—meditating on the task at hand. Practicing meditation helps you with the necessary motivation and preparation to remain mindful throughout the day, and mindfulness trains you with a sustained focus on various short activities to prepare you to be focused for your longer meditation practices. Both complement each other. In a mindful state, you make honest conversations with yourself. During those conversations you ask yourself what you are thinking, feeling, and doing, and why you are thinking, feeling, and doing so. This may sound too mundane. But this is what paves the way to conscious response to emotions, thought-out decisions and informed actions.

Drivers for developing your own meditation routine

As you will be seeing throughout this book, meditation and mindfulness play a critical role in unlocking the Three Gates discussed in this book. Hence learning and practicing it the right way is very important. Experts have very strict rules about teaching yoga and meditation. I am a practitioner of both meditation and mindfulness, but I am not an expert to teach either. So, I choose to refrain from giving any advice on how to practice it. My recommendation for you to practice meditation is to find a good teacher who will be able to answer your questions and guide you step by step. What I want to do here is to give a few pointers that will help you to get around your meditation practice.

1. Choose a meditation practice that you can relate to

Select a meditation practice which you trust will help you to create the right internal environment before you start the practice. There are various methods in practice.

Meditating focusing on a sound: In Yogic practices, meditating on the primordial word 'Aum' is recommended. However, there are mantras and chants in different cultures that you can meditate on. Then there are various apps that come with soothing instructions that take you through the various phases of meditation. You will come across chakra meditation music available online, you may explore these and see whether any of those suit you.

My late uncle Rajasekharan Pillai had the left side of his body fully and the right side partially paralyzed at the age of eighteen when he was a freshman in university. That changed the life of that tall, handsome and intelligent person forever. He had to drop out of college to focus on his medical treatments. I have never seen him walking, but I have never seen him sulking either. My father being the only sibling he had, he lived with us and having him around when I was growing up, positively shaped me in several ways. Every morning I woke up listening to the Sanskrit mantras he chanted, every evening he had a new story to tell me and my brothers. He taught me Math and he had a clear perspective on everything that happened in the world. He was a business owner, an author, a Sanskrit scholar and a lifelong learner. It was when I reached my teens, that I started thinking about what kind of mental and emotional impact he might have had with the unfortunate turn of his life trajectory at an age when we seriously start thinking, dreaming and planning our future. When I asked him about this, he said the mantra meditations every morning gave him the mental strength to accept the truth, create new dreams and most importantly find happiness and satisfaction in leading his life. He continued with the practice of that meditation till the time he passed at the age of seventy-two.

In every culture, you can find a meditative practice. If you are religious, you will be able to find a meditative practice that your religion teaches. It could be a simple prayer that you could practice easily or a series of steps that you can pick up and practice. And if you are not religious, there are numerous meditative practices that are devoid of any religious affiliation.

There are focusing meditations where you focus on the mental image of a flame or a spot on your body. Additionally, there are breath meditation techniques in which you meditate by observing your breath. Then there are various courses, trainers, and masters you can go and get trained.

As per a study by Dr Dave DeSteno, professor of Psychology at Northeastern University, it doesn't matter whether you are attending meditation training with a guru or following an app. What matters is whether you are doing it the proper way and are consistent with it.

Not all meditation practices are for all of us. By trying a few techniques, you will be able to find a practice or a combination of practices that suit your personality and circumstances. Getting trained in the beginning by an established organization and gathering more knowledge with my own practice and research helped me to trust the process for my own benefit. You will be able to find your favorite method with practice and observation.

2. Do not fall prey to unrealistic expectations

A popular myth about meditation is that we need to be completely free of our thoughts when we meditate. Of course, it is good if you can do that. However, most of us are not Himalayan yogis or monks to attain that perfection, at least in the beginning. In fact, I consider it a first breakthrough when you are able to catch the fact that your thoughts have diverted to something else and may be experiencing some emotions related to it because sometimes we wouldn't even realize that our thoughts have diverted. Once you catch yourself losing your focus, don't serve tea to that thought and entertain it further but acknowledge it and say goodbye to it. Meditation is a habit that you develop with practice. It is natural that initially, you may feel that your thoughts are taking over your meditation. Accept that fact and trust that with practice, you will be able to gradually boost your focus. When you trust a process, you are minimizing the resistance to it, and you are doing it with positive emotions and that triggers your brain to provide you with more motivation by releasing dopamine.

3. Do not feel bad if you feel like not doing it sometimes

Consistency is what our brain looks for in terms of setting habits and beliefs. But we are not creatures of instinct, we are creatures of our mind. And sometimes, we feel like not following the habit. Do I still feel like taking a cheat day? Of course, sometimes. Do I take that cheat day? I try my best to sustain my practice. However, if I can't resist and have a good reason, I take a cheat day. For example, if I feel too tired to wake up in the morning after a long night, I say no to it as I have learned to listen to my body. After all, whatever we do to help us relax our mind and bring more clarity should not be a forceful practice, right?

But the difference here is, I don't beat myself up for taking a cheat day. And I consider that as part of the process. That thought itself stems from the deep self-compassion that originated from my meditation practice. Even after taking a cheat day, I feel that I am still part of it, or meditation is still part of me. I don't feel guilty or think that I derailed. Meditation has become part of my self-identity, which we explored in Chapter 3.

Meditation and mindfulness are the roots that determine how tall and strong you can grow withstanding strong winds, heavy floods and severe droughts of life. This is the reason you will come across these two concepts as the Secret Codes to unlock the Three Gates from time to time throughout this book. Use these Secret Codes to derive your mental clarity and self-awareness, and channel that to accelerate your journey to fulfill your goals and purposes.

Chapter 10

The complementary voices of self-reflection and feedback

The voices that step up your growth

A 2020 study at Queen's University Canada reveals that an average human mind processes six thousand two hundred and forty thoughts a day, which is exactly 4.3 thoughts every minute. It is impossible for us to keep up with that speed and register each of those thoughts consciously. Self-reflection is the process of consciously enquiring about one or more parts of our life, with ourselves. It is an introspection of our own thoughts, feelings, actions, reasonings and solutions. If we practice this introspection about things that matter to us, the findings from it can be used to create revolutionary improvements in several areas of our lives.

For example, nursing is a profession that demands a lot of social emotions along with professional expertise. While helping patients with their health issues, nurses become privy to a lot of complex emotional and personal issues the patients and their families are facing. As part of a 2015 study in Taiwan, 260 nursing students were trained in developing a self-reflection practice. Six months after that, it was found that the performance these nurses had improved and that the improvement in performance was related to their practice of self-reflection.

Practicing self-reflection regularly can provide many benefits in our personal and professional life. This is a practice that will help you gain deeper insights into who you are, what you are capable of and what your real potential is. And as you will see throughout this book, this is also a quintessential Secret Code in unlocking the Three Gates to your hidden potential and soaring to greater heights.

The systematic process of self-reflection

Do you know what kind of unconscious emotions and behaviours you embark on a day-to-day basis? Let us look at the following examples:

1. Jaden hates others overtaking him on the road. In the mornings he comes to the office in a bad mood after yelling and honking at other Drivers on the road. He tells his colleagues that the city is full of road bullies and that that spoils his day. If Jaden was patient enough to observe his actions on the road, it would be easy for him to understand that he needs to control his reactions to others and focus on safe driving and polite road manners.

2. Vincent is an entrepreneur. Most of the time he works from home engrossed in his work and thoughts, and many of his reactions are absent-minded. He doesn't respond to questions from his wife and children, gets frustrated with slight noise in the house and his responses are absent-minded reactions. His wife is drifting apart from him, and the children are behaving distant. But he feels that he is not getting the love he deserves from his family. If Vincent consciously observes his thoughts and behaviour, he would be able to see the gap between his thoughts and actions, and still would be able to take some conscious steps to align his feelings for his family and his actions.

Majority of the thoughts that pass through our mind are unconscious. Though we don't recognize these thoughts, they affect our behaviour, responses and psyche. Self-reflection helps us to capture at least some of those thoughts, and evaluate our actions, behaviours, thoughts, aspirations and responses. Some people might ask, 'Isn't that what we usually do?' The answer to that is, yes we think about ourselves a lot. But there is a huge difference between self-reflection and thinking about ourselves. When you self-reflect, you consciously perform it in a systematic way compared to having passive thoughts that come and go without any structure or plan.

Drivers of systematic self-reflection

The following Drivers are a series of questions that could be of help to approach self-reflection in a systematic manner.

1. The story: What did actually happen?
   Be very objective and non-judgemental when you answer this question. Try to bring out the true story at this stage—no what ifs and why nots at this stage of reflection.
2. The analysis: Why and how?
   At this stage you analyze the incident or the situation. You will analyze things such as,
   'Why did it happen?'
   'Why did I behave like that?'
   'How did my behaviour impact the situation?'
   'What thoughts or ideas led me to behave so?'
   'What was my emotions when it happened?'
   'Why did the other person behave like that?'
   Try to keep this stage as objectively as you can without any biases or judgements about you, others or the situation.
3. The lesson: What if?
   At this stage you consider things such as,

'What could have I done differently?'

'What could have been the outcome if I hadn't approached it that way?'

'What behaviour could have resulted in a better outcome than this?'

4. The next step: Now what?

Here you will think about

'What behaviours and habits do I need to develop?'

'What skills do I need to learn or strengthen?'

'What can I do to control my impulsive responses and reactions?'

With this four-step approach to self-reflection, you will be able to get a better grasp of your behaviours, feelings and thoughts. Keep in mind to stick to the objective and not to ruminate when you self-reflect. We will learn more about the perils of rumination when we discuss about feedback.

Various studies have shown how the practice of self-reflection can help us in all realms of our life. Self-reflection has found to be instrumental in catching the big picture of things, boosting our self-identity and clarifying our purpose. It helps to reduce anxiety, burn out and stress, develop better relationships and enjoy better sleep. It helps to bring perspective into your feelings and actions and to identify the fears and doubts that are causing inner blocks and demotivation. In conclusion, this is a practice that will be instrumental in unlocking your Personal Gate and, as you will find out later, it will help you unlock your People and Universal Gates too.

Solicit feedback

Garry is a magnet for people who seek advice. He carries the secrets of many people, and he doesn't fail the trust of his friends. Garry feels that people confide in him because he is very secretive. Although that is true, the points he misses is that he is non-judgemental and is always ready with a listening ear and empathetic advice for his friends. If he knew all the traits that make him likeable to his friends, he would be able to use those traits in other areas as well.

One of the top qualities that set self-aware people apart from others is their conscious choice to seek feedback and take appropriate action. Feedback is the mirror that shows your blind spots. This is a great way to improve both our internal and external self-awareness. You give a great presentation; some people come and tell you that you did a fantastic job. Some of us feel good, some of us feel very conscious, but we get a good feeling as it is an affirmation of the efforts we put into it. Do you get the same good feeling, if someone tells you, 'I didn't understand many points you shared towards the end? I wish you were a bit slower.' Feedback is a gift, but it may not always be easy to listen to.

Drivers for handling feedback favourably

All feedback irrespective of whether they are good or bad give us an opportunity to inspect whether we need to explore some hidden potential of ours. Here's a quick look at the Drivers that will help you make the best out of a piece of feedback.

1. Be rational, not emotional

Prepare yourself for the feedback. Tell yourself, 'This feedback could be the shortcut to my next level.' So, accept the fact that everything is not going to be rosy in a feedback, keep your emotions in check and prepare yourself to listen with an open mind.

In the earlier example we saw, if Jaden takes some time to have an open conversation with some of his colleagues, he would be able to get an alternate perspective about how his behaviour is affecting the spirit and culture of the team. Furthermore, Jaden will also be able to understand how others deal with incidents like the ones he faces on the road. However, Jaden needs to prepare his mind to keep his emotions and reactions in check before that.

2. Be vulnerable. Keep your self-defensive shields away

In the example we discussed earlier about someone giving you negative feedback about your presentation, what would happen if you decided to wear your self-defensive shield and told that person, 'Many people said they liked the pace of my presentation', that person might decide not to share such feedback anymore. However, if you choose to be vulnerable, listen to the criticism and ask for more details, it will encourage the person to share their views more freely.

Let's consider this example: Li Peng is in her thirties and hangs out with a group of friends she has had since high school. A few months ago, there was a huge argument between her, and her friend Dennis, and they are not in talking terms since then. Her friends think that the argument happened because Li Peng made some unnecessary comments about Dennis' relationships which made him feel insulted. But Li Peng doesn't want to listen to her friends or take their feedback seriously. She feels that Dennis does not trust her even after all these years of friendship and that he should apologize to her. However, if she listens to her friends, she will know that it was not her intention, but the way she communicated it that gave way to the tension between the two. Her friend circle is a safe place for Li Peng to come to know about her out-of-line speaking tendencies. She could solve this issue by apologizing to Dennis. But, if she does not want to be vulnerable enough to listen to her friends' feedback this time, she is losing an opportunity to learn about herself and modify her future behaviours accordingly.

3. Be curious

Seeking clarity on the feedback will give you an opportunity to see the situation from a different perspective. Getting quality feedback is not that easy. So, if you find that that person's feedback makes sense, try to dig out more information from them. What if you ask 'I am sorry that you couldn't catch certain points. What could have I done in your opinion?' to the person who gave you negative feedback about your presentation in the example we saw earlier? Tasha Eurich, who has done tremendous research in the field of self-awareness, says that 'What' questions help to bring more clarity to the situation.

Asking the right questions will also give you an opportunity to check whether you overanalyze or ruminate over your actions and speeches. For example, Simran went to her colleague Tina's desk to ask about a project they were working on. Her colleague politely answered her questions and went back to work. Simran felt bad that Tina didn't engage in further talks. This made Simran think, 'Was I rude when I asked her for help? Maybe she felt offended by what I said in the meeting yesterday?' Simran couldn't shake off that nagging feeling and she blamed herself for Tina's behaviour. Overthinking and overanalyzing can affect our performance and mental peace. A person with sound self-awareness would have a better idea of how they behaved or why the other person behaved in that manner and if needed, take appropriate action instead of overthinking. Asking for feedback from the right people and comparing their feedback with your own self-reflections is a great way to improve your self-awareness. Furthermore, it helps to reduce your ruminating tendencies, which will help you improve your self-reflection as well.

4. Analyze the feedback

All feedbacks are not created equal and all feedbackers are not created equal. You don't need to implement all the feedback.

Some people come and give feedback just to make their presence or power felt. Some people might not have enough background information or knowledge about the situation. Analyze whether the feedback is valid and whether it makes sense to implement now or in the future. If you are confused about a particular feedback, ask someone else who was in the situation or discuss it with someone who can give you non-judgemental views on it.

5. Reframe the feedback

Many people dread receiving feedback. And it doesn't mean that they have an aversion to feedback or improvement. The real reason is that many feedback sound accusatory.

We can't expect that everyone has learned the Three Gates to handle their dealing with themselves and others, like you. They might not have developed self-awareness or effective communication and influencing skills. As a result, some of the feedback you receive may sound negative and demotivating. However, if you consider feedback as an opportunity for growth, reframing negative feedback could provide you with peace of mind and a path to progress.

What is the reframing of feedback? Reframing feedback is the process of rephrasing negative feedback to make it not accusatory but positive so that you can use the reframed feedback to spur your growth.

For example, if your boss tells you, 'Your mistake cost us the project', it may crack open a lot of wounds. However, no negativity is strong enough to abandon a piece of feedback before evaluating whether it carries any room for your growth.

Firstly, keep your cool and follow all the Drivers listed above for handling feedback. After that, with the details you gathered, you summarize the feedback and rationally check by yourself or with someone you trust and admire, whether it carries any message for you to develop any of your skills or behaviours. If your answer is 'No', it would be a good idea to find out why the other person is unnecessarily blaming you.

But, if your answer is 'Yes', it is time to reframe the original negative feedback to motivating feedback, so that you can update your Development Plan with new skills and behaviour and learn those. You may reframe the example above as, 'We had a great proposal. But we lost the project because we didn't have a backup for the main technical guy who happened to fall sick on the day of the presentation and take leave. This is a great lesson and from now on, I am going ensure that we have a backup for every crucial member of the proposal team so that they can cover each other if similar situations arise.'

The positive aspects you incorporate in the feedback by reframing it has a great effect on the effort you put in to develop those skills and behaviours. This is because motivating thoughts help your brain release more dopamine and that in turn will help you work more focused and effectively towards your growth.

6. Work on the feedback

Once you have decided to implement the lesson from a piece of feedback, include it in the Development Plan and assess whether you want to implement it now or sometime in the future. Check whether you need to educate yourself with new skills or behaviours and create a plan for that. Put your plan into practice and review its effectiveness periodically.

Self-reflection and feedback help us to be more self-aware and that helps in developing a realistic self-identity. Moreover, it helps in understanding how we impact the people and environment around us. In a nutshell, upskilling ourselves using the Drivers of these two Secret Codes helps us heaps and bounds in unlocking all the Three Gates and unearthing our hidden potential.

Chapter 11

Bring time at your disposal
Prioritize and manage your activities

'I don't have time', a very familiar expression. Yet it is loaded with many meanings. Depending on the context, people may interpret its meaning as, 'I am not important for you', 'You are avoiding new tasks', 'You are so not organized', 'You are doing something else', or 'You really have no time'. Lack of time could destroy relationships, reduce productivity, decrease contentment, trigger unhappiness and low mood. And all these factors can affect our mental, physical and emotional well-being. But are we really these busy people who are struggling to find time for important things or are we wasting our time on frivolous matters?

So, are we talking about time management? Not really, we are not yet capable of managing time, time just passes, but we can manage our activities. And that is the core of productivity—managing our activities within the time we have before it passes. Now, let us look at productivity. With all the work that we are busy putting in, we should be very productive, right? Yet, we have a gloomy picture there too. How often have you felt satisfied with the completion of your tasks at the end of a busy day? How often do you feel that you have been fair to completing your professional and personal responsibilities for the day? Studies show that an employee is engaged in their work only two-three hours a day.

In economics, the term productivity is defined as the rate at which the output is produced per unit of input. The input is labour, capital, and other resources. That sounds very formal, so let's make it more personal. Productivity is all about maximizing our returns from our effort, time and investment spent on a task at hand. In this chapter, we are, however, focusing more on the first two resources—effort and time.

So, in simple terms, productivity is about managing our current efforts in such a way that we can make use of the rest of our active hours doing things that matter to us. I have heard from many people about what they want to do in their life so that they could feel that they are living fulfilled lives. Some dream about starting a side hustle while they are working on their current job but fail to find the time or energy to do it. Some dream about finding time to spend more time with their family or start a daily workout regime but fail to do so. Some feel the pull towards learning a new course but fail to find time out from their work schedule or family time. Some feel that they are more or less living their dream life, but just want more time to relax or engage in a hobby. Productivity is about utilizing the time we have, to feel contented about how and where we spend our time and efforts and what we accomplish from it. Usually, we don't see words such as 'contented' or 'accomplish', in any definition of productivity. Let's get it right. If we don't feel contented and accomplished, we don't feel that we are using our time, efforts, and resources productively. This is something I sometimes feel when I spend too much time on research without accomplishing much from it. With careful observation I have found that this doesn't happen all the time, but only when I spend time reading research papers with the full knowledge that this research doesn't contribute to what I am researching about. Though I gain knowledge from it, this was not the time I allocated for that purpose and hence it is going to impact the schedule of the task I had allocated this time for. So, contentment comes from the focused use of time for the task at hand.

Drivers of Time

There are a few areas that we need to take care of when driving productivity, that includes prioritizing of the tasks, scheduling of the tasks, and focus management. In this chapter, we will explore how we can practice prioritizing and planning to make use of the definite amount of time we have and increase our productivity and improve our wellbeing. We will discuss focus management in the next chapter. Let's take a look at the Drivers that help us manage our tasks within the time we have.

1. Catch and clarify it: Know what you need to know

My friend Pascal Bornet is an author, a C-level executive in a cognitive automation software house and a leading social media influencer on AI and technology. In between managing the challenges of his job, writing articles and books, delivering keynote speeches, book tours, and sharing the latest advancements in AI and technology multiple times a day through his social media feeds and newsletters, he enjoys a good social life as well. 'You seem to have a lot on your plate. But, when I look at you, you seem to be in control of everything. How do you manage this?' is the first question I asked when I talked to him recently. Pascal uses a few techniques. He has delegated his social media content research to a team that makes use of technological tools and manual research to shortlist the best content for his followers. His social media team helps him in sharing the content he approves. Pascal has done a wonderful job with what seems to be a mammoth effort by breaking it into various chunks. When you prioritize your activities and split that into chunks of smaller tasks, you will be able to independently manage those chunks without getting overwhelmed.

Identifying your actual work is important in assessing the workload so that you can plan your tasks efficiently. Though it may sound very easy, it is not so. If we look around, in many workplaces and homes, it is easy to find people who are doing somebody else's work. There are many reasons people take up other people's work. Some of the common reasons that give rise to such behaviours are lack of confidence and communication skills in rejecting unnecessary work, lack of judgement of our own schedule and commitments and the overwhelming need to please someone. There are many homes where a working woman takes up the entire household chore after work because the household follows the conventional set-up of a woman working in the kitchen. Then there are times when people dump their work on you without realizing they are really doing that. Amber, an eleven-year-old girl once told me about the predicament she was facing at home. Amber was preparing for her big PSLE exam that year. She prioritizes, plans and tries to follow the plan. But it backfires, when her mother asks her to babysit her five-year-old brother who distracts her from her studies. The mother doesn't realize how much it affects her studies although Amber has mentioned it to her before.

This leads to the fact that just identifying the work is not sufficient. We need to identify whether the work truly belongs to us. An effective way to do that is using the 4Ds of productivity. As the name suggests, there are four components in it.

1. Delete: Assess whether the task under consideration is something that truly influences any of the goals or your larger purpose. In the example I mentioned earlier about me getting diverted into other areas of research that are not relevant to my

task at that point in time, I ask myself, 'Is this something that is going to help me with my current goal?'

2. Delegate: Is this a task you can delegate to someone else? You could delegate your task to someone else or give back the tasks someone else is delegating to you if that is not your responsibility. If there are people whom you are mentoring or there are junior officers shadowing your work, you may consider passing some of the work you are doing to help them learn on the job. If you are working in a team environment, you may consider how you can reach out to others for help. Depending on your position and the tasks on hand, you may delegate, just like how Bornet delegates his social media tasks, or seek help. Developing the mental strength and skills for effective delegation is a key trait of leaders.

Delegation is a technique Amber can use in order to solve the predicament she has been facing in the example we saw earlier.

3. Defer: There are certain tasks that do not need your attention at present. For example, if you think a colleague is passing their work unnecessarily to you, you might need to give them the signal that you are not a pushover. For that you will engage in a silent questioning session with yourself, such as:
   - Do you need to do this task now?
   - Would doing this now help you towards your goal?

If your answer is 'No', this is clearly a candidate for 'Delete' as we saw earlier. However, if you think this is something you need to do, but not critical or important compared to your other commitments, tell your colleague when you will be able to do that and why you won't be able to do it now. This will also help to send a signal to your colleagues that you work based on your priorities.

4. Do: If none of the above three components works in the case of your task, that means that the task truly demands your

attention and action. You may follow the next two Drivers to plan and execute those tasks productively.

2. Use the art of prioritizing to prioritize your progress

Have you seen people who are busy all the time, but are always behind on their tasks? If this is a trend, then there is some aspect of inefficiency in the way those people are handling their tasks—personal and professional.

In a post-covid business world where boundaries between home and office are becoming seamless, flexibility has become a major value proposition for employers. Gone are the days when productivity was measured in terms of the number of hours you spend in the office. One of my bosses from the initial years of my career used to remind me that 'Here we give more importance to work-life than family life.' It is only after a few of these reminders that I realized she didn't really approve of the fact that I used to leave the office on time. It didn't matter to her that I was focused and was delivering good results within the schedule. However, with the increasing focus on mental health at the workplace, soon there will be employers that would limit the number of hours people spend at work. In fact, countries such as France and Portugal already have policies in place that prohibit employers from contacting workers outside of work. With many companies turning to goal-based productivity measurements instead of time-based, there is a lot of advantage for all of us to choose to do what is useful. But the fact is we get burned out not just from our employment, but the tasks in our personal life also contribute to how burned out, discontent and unproductive we feel.

Consciously prioritizing tasks on hand helps to bring clarity to what is important and what is not. Eisenhower matrix is a prioritizing method that is attributed to former American President Dwight D. Eisenhower. We can use the four quadrants of the Eisenhower matrix to categorize our tasks into varying priorities to bring clarity to our workload. The four quadrants are:

• Important and Urgent Quadrant

The tasks in the Important and Urgent are the ones we must do as there is no more time left to do them. These are the ones we usually fight against time to finish. Hence it belongs to the 'Do' component in the 4Ds of productivity we discussed earlier in this chapter. And these are the ones that stress us out too. In many situations, unless you have been working consistently and diligently on your tasks, tasks get piled up in this quadrant and that would result in delivering less than optimum results if you don't have enough time for these tasks. Piling up tasks in this quadrant also means that you don't get time to complete your important tasks if something of higher priority comes up, such as taking the child to the doctor as in the example given in the table below.

• Important and Not Urgent Quadrant

This quadrant plays a major role in determining how productive you are within the time you have. A child who starts their revision studies two months before the exam or self-directed training as per your Development Plan are examples of this quadrant. These are the tasks that you have a choice to postpone. But the more you hold yourself back from exercising that choice, you will see the items in your first quadrant gradually becoming lesser and lesser.

When we leave things till the last minute, the items that were in the second quadrant, one day will end up in the first quadrant. The more the number of items in the first quadrant, the more stressed we feel. Moreover, this may also lead to abandoning certain items or delivering those items with inferior quality, due to the lack of time. Paying attention and acting on the items in the second quadrant holds the secret to achieving your goals without comprising on the quality and improving the quality of your life.

Some people might feel that there is a contradiction here since we are talking about not postponing tasks here when we spoke about deferring tasks earlier in this chapter. However, there is no contradiction here. You can defer tasks but try not to defer 'Important and Not Urgent' tasks, unless you have no other option. The items in this second quadrant also fall under the Do category in the 4Ds of productivity. However, here you need to apply a little more motivation compared to items in quadrant one as it may create the illusion that you have the luxury of deferring it.

- Not Important and Urgent Quadrant

In this quadrant you can include urgent, but not important tasks. If we relate it to the 4Ds of productivity, this is where you will find opportunities to delegate or defer, such as asking someone from the team to attend a non-critical meeting if you have tasks to finish from quadrants one and two.

- Not Important and Not Urgent Quadrant

This is the quadrant where we park all the unnecessary pursuits, we waste a big chunk of our time in. These tasks do not contribute to our purposes or goals. On the contrary, these tasks tend to take away time from tasks related to our purpose and goals, and hence the quality of the tasks in all other quadrants suffer. You will usually see items such as mindless scrolling of social media pages and doing somebody else's work because you are unable to say 'No', in this quadrant. These are the items that are suitable of the Delete as we saw in 4Ds of productivity. Here is a sample Eisenhower matrix that will give you an idea about how you can use it to prioritize your tasks.

	Urgent	Not Urgent
Important	• Take child to the doctor • Make slide deck for tomorrow • Order food	• Family time • Prepare for the performance review next month • Train the skill identified in the Development Plan • Meditate
Not Important	• Unimportant calls and messages • Unwanted interruptions • Non-critical meetings • Administrative tasks	• Social media browsing • Online games

3. Plan your time for the prioritized tasks

When we jump straight into planning, it is possible that we wrongly prioritize our tasks. The result of that is, we fail to complete tasks of higher priority and will always be in a frantic mood to complete our tasks with an overflowing quadrant one. When you plan your to-do list after cleansing it with 4Ds of productivity and Eisenhower's priority matrix, you are in for productive planning. And when you follow the plan you created this way, you would be able to give sufficient attention to all tasks that are crucial for your purpose and goals and cut the time from chasing the wild goose.

Prioritizing and planning your tasks provide you with enough time to do things that are truly important for your purpose and goals. And at the same time, it helps to reduce your stress as you have better visibility of your action and progress, and hence find contentment from that. Many Drivers we discussed in this chapter require interaction with others, and that demands the aid of additional Drivers such as communication and influencing, which we will explore in the next part of the book when we discuss the Secret Codes to People Gate.

Chapter 12

Build productivity with focus
A strong foundation for success

You are working on a presentation and stuck on a point since you need more information on something, you decided to research more on that topic, and after fifteen minutes you realize that you are browsing your social media feed or reading some irrelevant news and that your research is still pending. This is a common theme we come across in modern life. Losing focus is a phenomenon that accompanied our technological triumphs. Though distractions were there as long as our species was out there, today's technology makes it easy to get distracted. So, managing distractions and managing focus go hand in hand. Research shows focus is a major driver of success. It is not the focus; it is the sustained focus that works towards success.

There are two types of focus. The first type is the focus you build around achieving a future reality, your purpose. You have envisioned and planned your life and activities trusting that future. The sustained focus you need in achieving this is for a very long period, sometimes spanning years and decades. This sustained focus could in many ways even change the course of your life around it. Then there are smaller goals that you build as milestones on the way towards that purpose you envisioned. These smaller goals would need mental, as well as physical efforts, and sustained focus over shorter periods of time. The lack of focus, in this case, will result in delaying or not achieving the goals that may directly or indirectly affect our bigger goals and purposes.

Have you noticed the times when you are completely immersed in your work, losing the sense of time, environment and the happenings around you? In 1975, in his seminal work *Flow: The Psychology of Optimal Experience*, psychologist Mihaly Csikszentmihalyi outlined that 'Flow' is the most focused state of mind. When you are in the flow state, you feel that the time is moving slowly because you are able to do much more in the same period of time in this state compared to when you are not in it. It is a total involvement with life in a time slice. Imagine how fast and efficient we would be in every task we do if we manage to reach the flow state effortlessly.

There are certain conditions that trigger flow state, which we can try to emulate. One of the main conditions is that there must be a balance between the level of skill and the level of the challenge. But it is not enough to balance it at any level, in order to achieve the flow, both the level of skill and the level of challenge should be high. For instance, this is the case when a highly skilled Sudoku player suddenly gets engrossed in their game upon coming across a highly challenging game or when a painter gets into a meditative world when mixing colours to create the perfect hue they have in their mind.

Drivers of Focus

Focus management is about identifying what distracts us and, finding ways to eliminate that distraction and get into the flow state as fast as possible. There are many underlying distractions that affect our focus. The most common of that is the digital distractions around. However, many people would find it difficult to distance themselves from digital distractions. Since our lifestyle is much dependent on online transactions and digital devices, we can't eliminate the distraction by eliminating the devices. Eliminating root causes like devices is not a sustainable option. In fact, focus management is like finding the balance between the needs and wants by using our own mindset and internal resources. In the section below, we will explore the Drivers that you will find useful to maintain your focus on tasks on hand and rise to the flow state.

1. Work towards a goal

Goal setting is a major component of focus management. When you convert your purpose into goals, you get the wings to fly towards your purpose. It is the goals that provide you with the path towards your bigger dreams. Goals are the milestones on your way to your purpose. When you achieve a goal, it provides you with a mental picture of where you are currently on that journey and what further steps you need to take to reach the next milestone.

People usually associate goals with outcomes that take a certain amount of time to achieve. However, goals are valid in every task we are undertaking. If we ourselves are not sure about the outcome that we are working towards in every task session, the brain would not know what it is targeting and when it needs to finish it. For each task session, create a goal and work towards achieving that goal.

To train yourself to be goal-focused, for each task session, create a goal and work towards achieving that goal. You may have possibly come across SMART goals, where you set specific, measurable, achievable, relatable and time-bound goals. Your mind will be in a different space when you have a SMART goal, compared to when you don't have a goal. SMART goals help you to commit to a plan in your brain and then for the brain to take that up as its responsibility. There is another reason why the brain will work towards its completion. When the goal is SMART, it is a clear, unambiguous goal that provides us with the confidence that it can be attained. Make goal setting and pursuing an integral part of every activity you are undertaking. When you pursue your goals with the assistance of metacognition, you will remain more objective about the goal, stay consciously away from distractions and use the best strategy to achieve your goals. You will learn about metacognition strategies later in this chapter.

2. Find meaning in what you are doing

Have you observed when do you reach for your phone in the middle of a task? Most probably this happens when you are bored with what you are doing. Our boredom demands immediate attention to something that is engaging and enjoyable. The interesting thing here is our engagement is affected by our distractions, but our distractions crave something engaging. What you can do to get out of this situation is to like what you are doing. Attach something of higher significance to your activity. When you feel bored, think about how doing this activity a little longer is going to be meaningful for the purpose or the goal you attached it to. This is like doing five more pushups when you are feeling very tired, visualizing your healthy and fit body in your mind. As we have seen before, these positive thoughts and emotions you put into the task will trigger the release of dopamine and that will provide you with the motivation to stay focused for some more time. Finding meaning in anything can be achieved by tricking our minds in this way.

What positive thoughts and emotions can we invoke? This is where we revisit our purpose, the big purpose of which your activity is a small part. It is these drops of focused activities that take you to the big ocean of your purpose. Each drop that joins that ocean it joins that ocean is not identical, just the way the activities contributing to the big purpose aren't equal. Some drops come from the glaciers of skills, some from the relentless rains of your focused effort, and some others with the energy from the hurdles of waterfalls it had to navigate through. But in the journey from each of these sources, what helps to stay in the journey is the image of the destination, which is the ocean that your purpose is.

3. Avoid multitasking

Multitasking is detrimental to cognitive functions such as thinking, learning and other intellectual skills. Even when we feel that we are focusing on a single task, a lot of us are multitasking when we divert our attention to smartphones and other digital distractions from time to time. Multitasking might also be affecting our EQ. Research suggests that multitasking might be affecting the anterior cingulate cortex, which is part of the brain responsible for EQ. This explains why we lose our temper when someone approaches us in the middle of multitasking.

When we focus on multiple commitments, including digital and other distractions, the brain doesn't get enough time to commit the priority task to memory and hence when you return to the same task later, you work less efficiently. So, although we might get the pseudo satisfaction of progressing in multiple tasks at the same time, the overall time it takes to complete all of that would take more time compared to focusing on doing one at a time.

4. Get enough sleep

A well-rested body comes with an active mind, and sharp thinking skills, with the previous day's experiences and learnings well committed into the memory. This enhances our ability to gain more from less time and effort compared to doing the same task with a sleepy head. Lack of enough sleep practiced over extended periods of time may contribute to physical health issues, which may further deteriorate the ability to focus. So, practicing good sleep hygiene can help you focus better.

5. Keep the neurochemicals in your body in slightly alerted state to better focus

We have discussed earlier the role of happy and stress hormones in our system. Neurologists suggest that keeping ourselves in a slightly alert state, which means a slightly higher amount of stress hormone compared to happy hormones, will help us perform better at the task at hand. These hormones are released based on our mental state, our diet and any stressful situation we are facing now. Knowing your emotional and motivational state and watching your diet, emotions and physical activities to keep these hormones at the optimum state will be beneficial in improving your focus. This points to the importance of developing your self-awareness as we discussed in Part 2 of the book.

6. Use metacognition for self-monitoring and self-control

Metacognition is commonly known as thinking about thinking. It is about being aware of our own thoughts and the pattern behind those thoughts. This is a term we commonly come across in pedagogy, though it is valid for everyone. We are bombarded with various distractions—external influences such as digital devices, and internal influences such as our feelings. Though the influences come from various sources, there is one thing in common in all of them—our thoughts. The ability to capture our thoughts and their influence on our feelings and actions is the basis of our success in self-monitoring and self-control.

Using metacognition techniques is an effective way to train our brain to keep track of what it is thinking and doing. But the essence of that is to ask questions to yourself. And it starts even before you start doing the actual task.

The first step in practicing metacognition is Reviewing. At this step, you try to review things such as what you already know, what you have already done, what you have done similar to it, when you have done something similar, what you are expected to know about the task etc. In essence, you are trying to assess your familiarity with the task you are about to do. The best way to do that is to ask questions yourself and find the answer. With that, you are creating a zone inside your mind for the upcoming task.

The second step is Planning. In this step, you are developing a plan for the task. If you already have a plan for it, this is the time to check and incorporate any missing detail in it and to get accustomed to it. You might want to ask questions to yourself such as the exact goal you are planning to achieve during this focus capsule, the strategies and tools you are planning to use to accomplish that goal, the lessons you are planning to incorporate from prior experiences—your own or others, and so on. As you can see, at this step, you are consciously preparing your mind to do what you are going to do.

The third step is to Self-monitor. During this step, you consciously ask questions to yourself to know whether you are following the schedule, plan and strategy, whether there is any need to change your plan or strategy and whether things are working as you expected. You will also ask questions to understand the challenges you are facing, the right steps you are taking, the mistakes you are making, the skills that are useful, the skills to develop further, the skills and processes you have got better at doing. Your questions will also address whether you need any help, the kind of help you need and so on. With the help of these questions, you are doing a real-time check on your strategy, execution, and further steps. By having a conversation with yourself, you are getting a chance to understand your working style, distractive thoughts, your strengths and areas for improvement at this stage. This is the time your self-expectation and reality come face to face with each other.

The last step is Reflection. During this step you self-assess and evaluate the efforts you undertook. Ask reflective questions to yourself to know about your experience and how well did you align your actions with your strategy and plan. If you feel that you have deviated from your plan or strategy, assess how did the new plan or strategy perform. You will also reflect on the successes, learnings, failures and mistakes you made. You may also leverage on the Drivers for self-reflection we discussed in Chapter 10 at this step.

If you make a set of standard questions for each of these steps and customize it as per the situation, it will help the process of building your metacognition skills easier. As you can see, metacognition is helpful not only for building deep focusing skills, but it can also throw more light into your self-awareness, which we explored earlier in Chapter 5. In addition, you can use metacognition skills to boost the efficacy of your mindfulness practice, which we discussed in Chapter 9, too.

7. Use practical tools to consciously detach from distractions

As we get familiarized with various ways to focus, one thing is getting clearer—distractions are a reality. Now, the question is, how do we consciously detach ourselves from distractions while remaining optimistic about the reward that comes later?

We engage with our distractions physically, such as reaching for a smartphone, and mentally, such as getting lost in distractive thoughts. Keeping the physical distractions beyond your reach while you are at a task, will help in controlling your tendency to reach for it. An important fact to remember here is, not all distractive thoughts are destructive. For instance, when you are doing research about a prospective customer, you suddenly remember the email you need to send out to a colleague. Though you might still be doing the research, your mind may get occasionally distracted by the thoughts about the email.

Identify physical distractions such as your phone or an object placed on your table or certain apps on your device if your work involves working on a device. After that, seek out ways to keep these things away or block the sites and notifications.

The interesting thing about distractions is that when we try to mentally shut down the distractions, they keep coming back to our mind, regardless of whether it is a material distraction or a mental distraction. That is, though we might not be responding to the distraction, we may keep thinking about it, such as the result of a particular soccer game or that email that we wanted to send to that colleague. If you let your mind engage with the topic of those thoughts immediately or entertain those thoughts, your brain loses the efficiency with which it was handling the task on hand due to the shuffling of multiple tasks as we have seen earlier.

Nevertheless, you can solve this issue creatively by creating a Distraction To-Do list. This list helps in mentally detaching yourself from the distraction and the thoughts about the distraction. The first step for that is to catch hold of the distractive thoughts. Mindfulness helps in catching our thoughts and emotions as we discussed in Chapter 9. As soon as you catch your thought, instead of acting on the distraction, write down that distraction, such as the one which reminded you to send out an email to your colleague, in the Distraction To-Do list.

A Distraction To-Do list helps you capture your distraction somewhere outside your mind and free up your mind from the recurring thought of it. Once you have finished the task at hand, you can revisit the Distraction To-Do list, catch relevant items from there and plan when you want to focus on or work on those items. Sometimes, you may realize that many of the things you captured in the list do not sound important anymore. So, by delaying the action, in some cases, you will be able to make use of the time you otherwise would have spent on irrelevant pursuits.

8. Leverage on your most productive hours

There is a daily limit for willpower, about which we will discuss more in Chapter 14, that we can use and it drains our energy. Hence, if you are trying to do focused work or learning at a time your willpower is the lowest or your energy is the lowest, it will deplete more of your willpower. Throughout the day, our energy fluctuates based on several factors, from what we eat and don't eat to whom we spend our time with. If you plan your activities carefully around that time of the day when you feel the most motivated and energetic, your mind will be in a better state to commit to a focused effort. For this, leverage your biological peak time or biological prime time. It is the time when you are the most energetic, or you feel that you are the most productive. It may differ from person to person. There are early birds who schedule their day based on their personal peak time. It is easy for them to get up early in the morning and perform their tasks energetically. There are many famous early birds who schedule their important tasks from early in the morning through the first half of the day as they have found out that that is their peak focus time. Then there are night owls who feel the most energized and productive from late afternoon through late night. You can find your personal peak time by monitoring how energetic and motivated you feel in performing various tasks throughout the day. The metacognition steps and mindfulness Drivers we discussed earlier will be of your help in this monitoring activity.

However, it is true that not everybody has control over their work time, especially if you work on shifts or work a nine-to-five job. In such situations, find out your peak time during your working hours and manage your activities around that time as much as you can. There are people who schedule their meetings or email communications based on peak times. You may consider scheduling your most difficult or least interesting tasks during your peak time, to leverage the productivity spike.

These Drivers are universal for all ages; hence parents and teachers may also make use of these to support their children develop focus management skills. As you can infer, more than keeping distractions at bay, focus management is about developing the right mental and physiological environment to find meaning in what we do and adopting the Drivers outlined in this chapter to achieve that. When you consistently create and maintain that environment, your path to unlock your hidden potential gets smoother and faster.

Chapter 13

Fail perfectly to succeed

The art of transforming failures, mistakes and rejections into success

Most people do not pursue a goal wishing it to fail. Yet a lot of us fail at least in some of our pursuits. All of us have experienced failing at something and from that we know that failures and mistakes seldom take us automatically to a highly excited and positive state of mind. In addition, we may commit many mistakes before we succeed or fail in a pursuit.

You might have heard many people using the example of how Thomas Edison failed a thousand times before he perfected the invention of the lightbulb or, as we have previously discussed, about Colonel Sanders of KFC facing 1009 rejections before his fried chicken recipe was accepted by a restaurant.

We listen to motivational speeches in which people say failure is the stepping stone to success. But is it guaranteed that all failures and mistakes lead to success? Consider the scenario in which a person works hard towards something, putting their heart and soul into it, only to arrive at the hard reality of failure. Most people at this stage feel terribly disappointed, some people blame God, some people blame the people who rejected or failed them, and some people blame themselves. Then there are people who get emotional and overreact. Failures, mistakes and rejections make many people conclude that they are not good enough to achieve their goal or that their goal is not good enough for them and quit their pursuit.

Would quitting lead to success in the future? The popular answer is it doesn't. However, there are times when quitting becomes the right decision to make. Now the question most people would ask is, 'How do you determine whether to stay or quit after encountering a failure or committing a terrible mistake?' In order to determine that, we need to know what happens to our minds when we fail.

Understand how your mind works after a failure

Think about a time you had a glorious win or a disastrous disappointment. Did you notice what influence that win or loses have on your other pursuits at that time?

Social hierarchies are formed based on winning and losing patterns. In a well-repeated study by various research teams, lab mice were tested for the effect of winning and losing in their behaviour. The team of researchers had let the mice enter through a tube chamber two at a time, one from each side. The tube had just enough space for one mouse to pass, so once they meet, they had to either push the other mouse or move back. The one who pushed was considered the winner in this experiment and the other the loser. The winner and the loser were subsequently paired with other mice to repeat the experiment. The previous winners were found to push their opponents more vigorously and previous losers were found to be more submissive. Since the losers were submissive, the aggressive nature of the winners kept reducing as the experiment proceeded, but still the losers kept losing. As a result, most mice with more winning experiences kept winning and all mice with more losing experience, kept losing.

This phenomenon of how winners get driven and go on to win repeatedly is known as the 'Winner effect'.

In a follow-up study conducted at Zhejiang University, a group of scientists did the same test. But this time they identified the group of neurons that are responsible for persistent behaviour and using brain intervention, turned those neurons 'on' and 'off' while the mice were doing the experiment. Irrespective of whether they won or lost in the previous rounds, eighty to ninety per cent of the mice that got the neurons 'on' pushed out the opponents that had defeated them before the brain intervention. The winner effect of the newly dominant mice didn't just stop at the tube experiment, the newly formed social hierarchy was visible in other areas of their social behaviours as well. Similar experiments have been performed on other animals and were found consistent with the phenomenon of the winner effect. Many scientists have come up with anecdotal evidence of winner effect in humans as well.

If the motivation for winning and losing is determined by how active certain neurons are, doesn't it make sense to turn on those neurons to increase our chance of winning in the future? One of the most important conclusions we can probably arrive at, from these experiments, take us back to a Secret Code we discussed earlier in this book—self-identity. Our future successes depend on how we perceive ourselves. If you cultivate a future-focused self-identity of a successful person, that belief itself can direct you to be not affected by failures and disappointments. And as we have discussed before, a strong and well-defined purpose can help us consider failures as temporary phases and remain motivated irrespective of that.

The route from failure to success

The reason for failures differs from situation to situation and from person to person. Also, different people define success in different ways. For some people success is about reaching the top position in their work, for some, it is about becoming rich, for some, it is about building a successful entreprise, for some it is eradicating poverty, for some it is about living a happy life, yet for some it is about travelling the world, the list goes on. Then we have situational failures, such as losing a well-anticipated promotion or failing a test or financial struggles or setbacks in our business or personal life.

In the common literature, we are constantly being preached to not quit. Is giving up on a pursuit bad? Does it make you less suited for success? The secret of successful people is not that they never give up, but they make conscious decisions about what to follow and what to flee from. Our pursuits are the results of such decisions we make at different points in life. Now that we learnt about the winner effect, we know how it influences our minds and decision-making. That points to the fact that in order to ignite the flames of motivation and future success, we need to deal with our minds first, which we will discuss more in the subsequent pages of this chapter.

Let us explore the Drivers we can use to organize ourselves and set us up for success after failure.

Drivers to rise from failures

After a failure, while we are still nursing the disappointment and the resulting emotional turmoil, many of us might not even want to think constructively about the failure.

In this section we will discuss in detail about the Drivers you can adopt to effectively manage yourself after a rejection, mistake, or failure.

1. Take ownership

The former president of India, Dr APJ Abdul Kalam, is also known as the 'Missile Man of India' for his tremendous contributions to India's triumph in space and military missile technologies. He narrated a powerful anecdote of personal ownership amidst a massive failure, at an event in Sriharikota in 2003. Indian Space Research Organization (ISRO) is the national space agency of India. On 10 August 1979, the entire world's eyes were on Prof Satish Dhawan, the chairman of ISRO. The country was about to launch its first rocket as part of its SLV project, the culmination of the efforts of thousands of people in the previous ten years. Prof Dhawan had appointed Dr Kalam as the director of this gigantic mission, known as SLV-3.

On the day of the launch, the countdown started at 7 a.m. Just forty seconds before the launch, the computer detected an issue and put the launch on hold. Six experts in the control center looked at the pictures on the computer and they identified that the problem was caused by some control components. As the program director, it was time for Dr Kalam to make a Go/No-go decision. He decided to bypass the computer and launched the rocket.

As they stood in the control center with bated breath, the rocket took off towards the skies, carrying Rohini satellite as the payload, in the set course to a height of twenty-three kilometres in sixty-eight seconds and completed the first of the four phases as expected. But troubles surfaced in the second phase, instead of rising further, the rocket twisted and rotated, and it didn't reach the expected height. After that, though it completed the third stage, it went into a spin and in the fourth stage, SLV-3 could not put Rohini satellite into orbit, and it plummeted into the depths of the Bay of Bengal. Dr Kalam wished he hadn't made that mistake of overruling the computer warning. But it was too late.

Immediately after the disaster, there was a press conference in which Prof Dhawan took the blame for the failure and said he would support his team so that they can succeed in the future. Prof Dhawan could have put the responsibility on Dr Kalam for the go-decision he had made. But, as the leader of the organization, he took the blame. The ownership Prof Dhawan demonstrated, taking the blame just forty-five minutes after SLV-3 plunged into the ocean is an excellent example of immense character strength and vulnerability in leadership. One of the best services you can do to yourself as you try to grow from a failure is, to be vulnerable— to accept your feelings, your situation, your flaws, and your shortcomings.

Dr Kalam and his team were given another chance and, a year later, in 1980, ISRO launched SLV-3 again. SLV-3 placed the Rohini rocket successfully in its Low Earth Orbit. This was followed by a press conference, but this time the mood was entirely reversed. Instead of the gloomy atmosphere a year before, the room was full of cheer. But this time Prof Dhawan asked Dr Kalam to conduct the press conference. He took the blame for the failure, but he let Dr Kalam take the credit for the success.

Taking ownership of a failure is not about being diplomatic in the eyes of the world. It is about taking responsibility for the next course of action to right it. Every failure comes with added responsibility—to review the failure, identify the causes behind it, dig out the lessons, and plan the next course of action. That is what a 'successful failure' is. A successful failure comes from ownership; without ownership, a failure is a doomed failure.

Taking ownership of a failure is as excruciating as experiencing that failure. Hence, it is not surprising if we feel that we would rather have someone else take the responsibility for the failure than we ourselves. Therefore, we come across many people who blame others for their own failures. In some cases, it is done consciously to protect their job, position, or reputation. Then there are situations where the blaming is done unconsciously when the person responsible harbours a fixed mindset that they can never go wrong. We come across such attitudes in domestic situations too, such as a person blaming their partner when their child makes a mistake or does not live up to their expectation.

Failures and mistakes are treated as taboo subjects which people tend to avoid talking about or acknowledging. In my consulting career, I have come across many such incidents. In one such organization, since I have spent a considerable amount of time there, I was aware of some of the issues they were facing. Those issues were not there in the list of issues they came up with for their innovation targets. When I asked the executives involved in it about it, their initial response was to brush it off. Later some of the reasons behind it came to my notice—they did not want to consciously invite additional work and some of the issues I had highlighted were part of some strategic mistakes they made that they wanted to cover up. They didn't do anything unethical or against the policies, but they just made some wrong decisions which triggered those issues. But they would rather have their teams do additional work than own their mistakes.

When you probe into such instances, you will realize that people tend to cover up their mistakes up when they are in environments where failures and mistakes are not tolerated. If the employees have observed severe repercussions in responsibilities, pay or promotion after owning up to a mistake, it is natural for them to guard themselves by covering things up. This happens in children too if they are often punished or blamed for their mistakes. Instead, if we create a culture, both at home and in the workplace, where failures and mistakes are considered part of the efforts and focus on how to make each failure a successful failure, you will find people thriving after a failure.

In the case of ISRO, Prof Dhawan took ownership of the failure publicly. So, does it mean that we need to talk about our failure to others? It differs from situation to situation. For example, if you made a mistake on social media, then it makes sense to acknowledge and accept your mistake to your followers if it makes sense. When you realize you have made a mistake, it makes sense to go to the person who was impacted the most by that mistake, own the mistake, share what happened and apologize. And for a fact, many people do that. But, if you would like to enhance its effect even more, sincerely offer them solutions to recover from the situation. Even if you don't get a chance to apply the solution, you will be leaving a mark in the mind of that person.

We have seen how Prof Dhawan took the blame on himself. Does it mean that we need to take the blame for the mistakes other people make? Absolutely not, if you don't have a hand in it. In the case of SLV-3 failure, Prof Dhawan considered himself responsible for the strategic decisions he made as the head of the organization.

Many times, owning a mistake or a failure is accompanied by self-blaming. So, let us get it right—accepting ownership does not mean self-blaming. It just means telling yourself the actual story without judgements, from a neutral standpoint—as the storyteller of an incident in your life. You can develop the courage for that from many of the Secret Codes we discuss in this part of the book, such as believing in your purpose, developing an unbeatable self-identity, seeking feedback and practicing self-reflection and self-compassion.

Sometimes we give excuses such as 'I was expecting this' or deny the failure as 'this is nothing'. Every blame, excuse, and denial that we devise has the tendency to lead our minds to believe that it is an irrecoverable failure. However, if your true intention is to fail forward, that is bounce back from a failure and breakthrough to success, kick in that success by owning the failure.

2. Discover the core of the failure

Understanding the reason for the failure helps us bring perspective and plan our next course of action. We can use the power of mindfulness to identify and acknowledge the emotions we are feeling after a failure. Once you get a picture of your thoughts and emotions, mentally revisit the events that led to the failure or mistake. This is an important step because an error could have happened at any stage while you were pursuing a goal. For instance, there will be situations where you might even come to realize that your entire purpose or goal itself doesn't work. Then there will be situations where you learn that your purpose or goal is achievable, but the strategy you followed for fulfilling that is what led to the failure. And in some other situations, you may conclude that you had a great goal and strategy, but the execution was flawed and that led to the failure. Put some time to bring perspective and clarify in which of these stages the failure occurred. This crucial step guides you to conscientiously decide whether it is a good idea to quit something if you are considering that.

What was the goal that you were trying to achieve when the event that led to the failure happened? I recently had an interesting conversation with Edwin, a young professional in a digital marketing agency. He is a great team player and puts a lot of effort into conceptualizing the ideas the team comes up with. This was his dream job, and he has further dreams to lead a world-renowned agency one day. He said, 'One of my strategies is to learn the nuts and bolts of this industry, by contributing in every way.' However, Edwin is not happy working in the agency. He feels that since he has shown the initiative to pick up all tasks that come on his way, people are dumping all their boring tasks on him. Now he is disappointed that he is always busy doing irrelevant tasks that might not lead him to his true purpose. Being a junior copywriter, he is also scared of the repercussions of saying 'No' to people who are senior to him. He started doubting his credibility in becoming a leader, and he is contemplating looking for another job where he can just focus on his own tasks.

It is plain to understand that Edwin is at a stage where he doubts both his purpose and strategy. Though he had a well-thought-out purpose and a commendable strategy, it was the effort or the ambiguity regarding the effort that led to the current state. In his enthusiasm to learn about the industry, he unintentionally gave out the message that he is willing to take every task that comes on his way. Does that justify his need to doubt his ability to lead an agency one day? Does that justify his need to abandon his dream? Is his strategy of volunteering for tasks wrong? Does he need to change his strategy?

The answer to all these questions is an obvious 'No' if we look at Edwin's situation from the outside. Furthermore, we get the feeling that he has the right purpose, and that his strategy is useful at this stage in his career. Edwin couldn't think like us because he was invested in his emotions. But, practicing mindfulness encouraged him to look at it from a different perspective, just like us, but with more details.

Once clarity and objectivity set in, Edwin felt that he does not need to abandon his purpose or the strategy. He identified that what he needs to do is make some changes in the efforts he put to carry out his strategy. He came up with a plan to exercise a priority based approach when volunteering for tasks. He volunteered only for those tasks that provided him with learning opportunities. He decided to focus on his communication skills to let his seniors know of his schedule conflicts with confidence and diplomacy. It is not unusual for people to doubt their strategy and purpose when they come across failures. There are so many people who crush their dreams just because they do not take the time to identify the core of their failure. Taking time to identify the core of the failure gives you clarity and objectivity. Furthermore, it helps you discover your next course of action and update your Development Plan with new skills and behaviors wherever applicable.

Failing at effort or strategy stages does not usually warrant abandoning your purpose or goal. You might just have to re-evaluate, re-imagine, and re-prioritize your strategy or efforts or both.

3. Keep your self-identity intact

We have already discussed the importance of self-identity in Chapter 3. However, being able to own oneself is as important in failure as it is in success.

One of the qualities that help stalwarts like Thomas Edison and Colonel Sanders to stay motivated even after failing a thousand times is their self-identity. They do not define and identify themselves as failures. Each thought we harbour in our mind is an instruction to our brain, to create plasticity and to work towards that. When you label yourself a failure, every time you make a mistake if you have the tendency to say, 'I knew it', this label is going to become part of your self-identity.

Years ago, I founded a magazine for children. The magazine was the culmination of my passion for helping children develop creativity and a growth mindset and be ready for innovation. However, after a few years, it became difficult to sustain it as I needed to support it with revenue from other business streams. When the effort and returns didn't balance, I had to make a heartbreaking decision to wind up the magazine. Since the project was too close to my personal passion, the initial self-response was to blame myself and call myself a failure. Every night I went to bed blaming myself for not stepping up to my expectations and every morning I woke up thinking what a failure I was.

Things started changing when I broadened my perspective. I could do that only when I spoke to others. I learned from others about how that magazine acted as a catalyst for many children, and how it gave a platform for many children and adults to come out of their comfort zone and showcase their talent to a captive audience. The self-reflection and feedback from others helped me develop a stronger and more positive self-identity. I acknowledged the failure of the magazine, owned it, but stopped calling myself a failure. And this enhanced self-identity emerged as a result of my learnings from that failure.

There are people who think that their self-identity would shrink after owning a failure or making a serious mistake. When you are brave to own your mistakes and failures, you are emerging as a stronger person. Use reframing to infuse positivity in your mind and strengthen your self-identity. We have seen the steps for reframing in the context of negative feedback in Chapter 10. You may follow the relevant steps from there to reframe any self-blaming tendencies you may have. With the reframed thoughts, you may update your Development Plan with new skills and behaviours.

4. Excavate opportunities to learn and develop

Personally, running the magazine helped me boost my confidence in taking on initiatives in areas that are totally unfamiliar to me. However, I also came to realize that passion itself cannot sustain an initiative. Two of the main areas I identified for giving more focus are marketing and effective partnerships. Since I consciously identified my strengths and areas of improvement, I was able to make it in the form of a checklist and use that checklist wherever I want to use it—be it when I start a new project or giving a speech. And since then, I keep on adding things to the list and it gradually took shape to become my own Development Plan—my personal repository of skill and behaviour upgrades.

There are certain lessons that we intuitively learn and realize as part of a failure. It will help if you excavate more insights out of those lessons. Then there are learnings that we need to arrive at by delving more into the experience. You can use self-reflection and feedback to look at failures from various perspectives, and that helps in excavating opportunities for your further development. We have already explored the Drivers of self-reflection and feedback when we discussed self-awareness earlier in Chapter 5.

When we talk about learning from failures, people always inevitably consider the subject matter expertise and the way the situation was handled. However, the area that is less consciously considered is the behaviour. Take note of all areas for improvement—competence, habits, and essential skills for developing yourself further in the area you failed as well as your personality. Once you have identified your learning goals from the failure, keep your mind open to adapting changes, incorporate it as part of your Development Plan, and learn the skills and behaviours identified.

5. Re-plan and execute your solution

Prof Dhawan had devised a plan to do another launch in a year, to achieve the success that eluded him in his first try. However, not every failure gets a second chance, but that does not mean devastation. A failure is devastating only when there is no follow-up action. Some examples of effective follow-up actions are rectifying the mistake in a similar undertaking in the future or applying the learning in other areas of your life or work, or teaching the lessons from your failure to others, just like the way Dr Kalam did it. For instance, if a person doesn't get selected for a job interview, it is not entirely a lost opportunity. If they contact the interviewer again and ask for their feedback, they might provide some insights that otherwise the candidate would have missed to consider. Based on the feedback, if the candidate includes certain skills and attitude to develop in their Development Plan and attend the next interview with those additional attitudes and skills, they will be at a place to give a better performance.

6. Rebuild your personal brand

One of the side effects of a public failure or a mistake is a possible fall in personal brand. When you acknowledge the mistake and take ownership, you are letting people know that you are aware of the seriousness of the situation. That helps in assuring others what kind of a person you are. However, people might still have their doubts. When you apply your learning and execute your new solution, you are giving assurance to people that you are still serious about rectifying the mistake and applying the lessons from it. You may still come across people who are doubtful about your ability and sincerity. Your network skills will be of tremendous value here. If you have trustworthy people at work or in the family, you can ask for feedback from them regarding how others are perceiving you. You will learn more about trust when we explore the Secret Codes to People Gate in Pat 3 of the book.

Apart from that, your belief in your purpose, self-identity, self-awareness, value system, focus-all these attributes will be of tremendous help to you at this stage. And above all, the conviction with which you bravely owned your mistake and are working hard towards it should stay as a catalyst for you to build your grit at this stage.

At this stage, it doesn't matter whether you decide to quit or stay, because if you have taken the help of all these Drivers, then that will be an informed decision. Failures, rejections and mistakes remain a roadblock only when you allow them to be so. Instead, if you use a systematic approach to acknowledge them as what they are and work on upskilling yourself based on the learnings from it, you will be surprised to find yourself thanking those 'roadblocks' for your future progress.

Chapter 14

Yet, why do we quit?

The ways to strengthen your willpower

So far in this book we have come across many Secret Codes to lead our minds to unlock our hidden potential. However, we have also experienced situations where we set on achieving a goal or purpose and end up quitting or not starting at all. Why do we do that even when we are sure about our purpose? What can we do about it?

My friend Cheryl was determined to make her New Year's resolution work this year. For years, living a healthy life has been on her new year's resolution list. However, by the end of March, she either ignores it, quits it, or holds on to the resolution without making much progress. Fed up with this repeating trend, Cheryl wrote down a plan at the end of last year. The plan was to go for daily jogging at 6 a.m. and do aerobic exercises three times a week. To feel invested in executing her plan, she invested in some jogging gear from a top brand and early on New Year's morning, she excitedly got up and went for jogging. She admired the chill in the air and the soft rays of the morning sun. She felt good and told herself, 'I'm on a good start to the new year.'

Cheryl was consistent throughout the first week. But by the middle of the second week, she realized that she was getting drained. Cheryl leads a very hectic lifestyle. She is the head of product management in a manufacturing company and her days are packed with meetings with various teams around the world. Often, she needs to attend late-night calls with her boss who is based in another part of the world. Now, when the alarm rings in the morning, she feels lethargic. But she does not want to give up, so she drags herself out of her bed and continues with her plan. By the end of February, Cheryl lost her commitment to it, and she quit.

We know that Cheryl is not the only person who does it. We all know one such Cheryl, if not, it is we ourselves. If you google 'popular new year resolutions', you will see that almost all of that are personal change resolutions. Some want to lose weight, some want to spend more time with family, some want to commit to a weekly date night with their significant other, some want to quit smoking or substance abuse, some want to quit social media addiction. These are all good intentions, and they surely suggest that people generally want to see positive changes in themselves. The repetition of the same failed resolutions year after year also shows their genuine wish to see that change in themselves, like in the case of Cheryl. Yet only a few people are able to stay on it and cultivate a habit out of it.

If the wishes are so genuine, why don't people stick to practicing it? If we ask for help from others, the normal response we get is a knowing smile and the advice 'Don't give up. Step up your willpower.'

The truth about willpower

So, what exactly is willpower? And how do we step up our willpower? Does it work?

Willpower is our ability to will our mind to do things. But, we have all come across situations where we will our mind, we plead with our mind, we try to scare our mind with all possible consequences of not doing something, but in the end the mind wins and we give up.

The Marshmallow test outlines the relationship between our mind and success. It is a social science research initially designed and administered by Stanford psychologist Walter Mischel. This test is probably the most famous and repeated psychological test in the world. As part of this experiment, Mischel tested over 900 children in the four to five-year age group in the 1960s and later in the 1970s. The children were brought into a room one by one where a tester was seated. The tester places a marshmallow in front of the child on a table and offers a deal to the child. The deal is that the tester needs to step out of the room for a short while and if the child does not eat the marshmallow until they come back, they will get one more marshmallow, which means they will get two marshmallows in total. But, if they eat the marshmallow before the tester comes back, they won't get a second marshmallow.

Some children ate the marshmallow as soon as the researcher stepped out of the room. Some waited for some time, tried to control their impulse, but ended up losing their self-control and ate the marshmallow. Some children looked away from it, touched it, some even licked it and kept it back. In the end, a few children managed to control their impulse and wait till the tester came back fifteen minutes later.

As these children were growing up, Mischel and the team followed up with them and conducted studies on them and tracked their progress for over forty years and they found something surprising about these children. They found that the children that resisted their impulses and got delayed gratification with two marshmallows were doing better in several areas of life compared to the children who didn't wait. The children who resisted the temptation performed well academically, scored well on college admission tests, were able to control their frustrations and impulses better and were able to manage their stress in their adolescence. And they were having better health and better relationships later in their thirties and forties.

Delayed gratification is about resisting our temptations for the sake of achieving something grander later. That begs the question, is this self-control genetic or can it be learned? Although our genes and environment play a huge role in the initial years of our life, like most things about our brain, the sustainability of this trait depends on how well we practice and make it a habit.

This takes us back to the same question we had before. Can we just instruct our mind to listen and obey? Apparently, it does not always work. The reason is that exercising willpower requires energy and as per studies, we have only a finite amount of willpower available to spend each day. In the first half of the day when we feel fresh and agile, we are able to exercise better self-control. That is why we can say no to food and addictions more willingly in the first half of the day. In the second half of the day, after we have already used up parts of our willpower for many things, it becomes difficult for us to expend more of it. But giving up is also not a solution.

Now, what happens if we force ourselves to follow our plans without quitting even when our mind opposes it? A study at the Northwestern University found that it creates stress as our system falls into a state of conflict, which could lead to physical complications in the long-term.

Dopamine spikes

Many people consider motivation and willpower as things that are intangible. However, if you peek into your brain, you will see that these are physical phenomenon happening in our brain, with the play of neurochemicals. Dopamine is a neurochemical in the brain, and this one chemical is a part of almost everything that happens or does not happen in our lives. Dopamine is generally associated with pleasure and addiction. However, this chemical is responsible for our motivation and drive as well. Dopamine is a neuromodulator. Neuromodulators influence the communication between neurons inside our brain and hence it affects the rest of the body too. Depending on the pathway it takes inside our brain, dopamine can result in various feelings including lust, love, attention, addiction and motivation too. It is this chemical that prompts us to act, towards achieving something good or avoiding something bad.

A team of scientists from Vanderbilt University performed a study in which they did the brain mapping of go-getters and slackers. They monitored the dopamine spikes at different parts of the brain for these two groups of people. Go-getters, being willing to work hard towards their goals and rewards, had spikes in dopamine in areas of the brain associated with reward and motivation—the striatum and ventromedial prefrontal cortex. That shows a positive relationship between dopamine and the willingness to work. Whereas slackers, being less enthusiastic about working towards their goals and rewards, had spikes in dopamine at entirely different areas of the brain—anterior insula which is associated with emotions and risk perception. That shows a negative relationship between dopamine and the willingness to work. So, dopamine has completely different purposes when it is at different parts of the brain. What if we control the spike in dopamine and use it for driving our motivation? Is that possible?

Drivers to strengthen willpower

Having learned about the truth of willpower and how tangible it is, a question that begs is, 'So, what can we do to improve our willpower in a positive way and enhance the probability of us sticking to our plans?' You can use the Drivers listed in the section below to influence your motivation positively with dopamine spikes.

1. Live a purposeful life

We have learned about the importance of identifying and clarifying our purpose in Chapter 4. Living life in alignment with your purpose removes ambiguity when you face perplexing dilemmas.

A purpose is like the big scheme of things, and the goals are like the projects you undertake to achieve that purpose. You can undertake several different goals concurrently or in succession to fulfil your purpose. Make your goals and purposes SMART. As we have seen earlier in this part of the book, SMART stands for specific, measurable, achievable, realistic and time-bound. If your goal is to lose weight, without making it specific, you will never know what you are trying to achieve. The clearer and more specific your goal is, it is more likely for you to work towards it. How do you know whether you have achieved it? A measurable goal passes clearer instructions to your mind. So 'I want to lose ten kilograms' is better than 'I want to lose weight'. But 'I want to lose ten kilograms with aerobic exercise' is clearer. However, it becomes even clearer when you make it timebound, 'I want to lose ten kilograms in three months doing aerobic exercises four times a week.' This creates a good enough and clear enough goal for you. Now, is that realistic and achievable? Are you really able to exercise four times a week? Does your schedule allow that? You do not want to lose momentum later if it is not realistic to spend that much time. Based on your current medical condition and history, is setting the goal to shed ten kilograms realistic for you? Having a SMART goal means you will spend less willpower on this goal compared to a non-SMART goal. Basically, make your plans in a such way that they are clear and easy to follow and that they are connected to your purpose one way or the other.

2. Try to avoid crowding your willpower with multiple goals

If you look at new year's resolutions, you will see a list of goals. You may want to start exercising, quit smoking, take up a new online course and get organized. When you try to do all that together, your willpower depletes very fast, and you might find it difficult to stay committed to all that. What studies show is, if you don't start all of that together, you will be able to incorporate more of that as time goes by. For example, you may start first with exercising. If you are able to do it consistently, within the next few months, you might have developed a decent amount of neuroplasticity with that activity and hence you need less willpower to spend on it. At that time, you may start the new online course or start working on going smoke-free. With this step-by-step willpower building approach, it is easier to develop and improve your willpower in many different areas of your life in a healthy and sustainable fashion.

Another way to space out your resolutions or goals is to break it down into smaller chunks. Suppose you want to lose ten kilograms, split that goal into two chunks—lose five kilograms in the first three months and another five kilograms in the next three months. Now, since you are pursuing manageable chunks, the scepticism of achieving the big goal goes down. Also, chunking provides us with the opportunity to celebrate small wins and keep our motivation high.

3. Practice social emotions such as gratitude, compassion and pride

Dr David DeSteno and his research team ran an adult version of the marshmallow test in his lab. However, instead of marshmallows they used money, as marshmallows do not tempt the adults the same way it does children. As part of the test, the researchers asked, 'Do you want $35 now or $70 in three weeks?' People who were practicing gratitude in their daily lives were more willing to work for a bigger reward than the others.

Gratitude works with positive results in the workplace too. It is found that people want to work more for managers who acknowledged their efforts and expressed their gratitude. I personally have found immense mental strength by practicing gratitude over the past many years. Having a daily practice of writing a gratitude journal has helped me discover more about myself and others. It has helped me acknowledge the willpower I exercise in many situations, while appreciating the beauty of life. Though I have been doing the practice of gratitude for many years, during the time of the Covid-19 lockdown I saw its immense power in bringing perspective and resetting our emotional balance. Some of my close friends who do gratitude journaling and gratitude meditation have also shared the extraordinary benefits they reaped from their practice. And I have observed the way it has transformed their personality and overall life satisfaction positively. The results I witnessed were so compelling that I wanted to share the beauty of that with others, and that is how my book *30-Day Gratitude System* was born.

Practicing compassion towards yourself and others is a great way to strengthen your willpower muscles. Studies have also found that healthy pride is another tool that helps strengthen our willpower. What is healthy pride? It is pride without arrogance. For example, if you are generally considered competent in an area, your pride in being good at it may lead you to deliver that work on time and in high quality with personal commitment. However, if you are arrogant about it, it may result in depleting your willpower as well. Studies have also found that when there are people with healthy pride in teams, other team members respect them for their competence in that area.

By practicing these social emotions, you don't need to force yourself to do things, instead your mind will lead you to pursue your goals and your brain will release dopamine to make it a pleasurable experience for you.

4. Practice mindfulness and meditation

Knowing what is going on in our minds is a great way to exert control over our impulses. We have discussed meditation and mindfulness at length in Chapter 9. The Drivers of mindfulness and meditation can support us with a better focus on our goals and purpose. In addition, these Drivers provide great help in improving our emotional intelligence, which we will discuss in Chapter 15, and enhancing our ability to willingly pursue our plans and goals.

5. Develop deep passion for learning, unlearning and relearning

As we learn the Secret Codes for unlocking the Three Gates to our hidden potential, we come across situations where we feel that we need to learn and equip ourselves with more. We have already learnt about the neuroscience perspective that we can learn at any point in our life, irrespective of our age. Still, why do we get stuck in life?

Freya, a bright technology manager recently got promoted to take care of the sales of the technology she had been working on for many years. She knows the in and out of the technology and she had been in direct contact with the senior executives of the clients she had been serving. However, after taking up the new role she realized that her previous experiences, though useful, are not enough to acquire new customers or upsell to the existing customers. She also came to know that she had been explaining more about the technical details of the product rather than influencing the buyers from the prospective client organizations. Freya acknowledged that she needed to give a break to oversharing technical details and learn more about sales talks, persuasion techniques and relationship building. However, she is concerned about the viability of picking up and mastering these skills in her forties.

As we have seen in Chapter 2, building neuroplasticity is a result of consciously helping the brain release the right neurochemicals. When we repeatedly try the difficult part of a new skill, the brain releases the neurochemicals responsible to create solid neural pathways which initiate neuroplasticity. And while we are at it, if we think positively about the task itself, such as how we are progressing towards achieving our goal by learning this task, the brain releases dopamine and which will provide us with the motivation to prolong the learning for a little more time to enable the brain to establish that neuroplasticity. The more we learn and adapt to new and challenging situations, the more our mind gets willingly expend willpower. Developing a habit of learning new skills and behaviours and thereby encouraging your brain to build neuroplasticity on a regular basis, will help to engage your willpower to be a willing participant in your pursuits.

6. Stay true to your values when you pursue your goals

When we do something that is against our ideals and personal values, that creates tremendous mental resistance and stress. So, choosing goals and path that is in sync with your personal values will save you from unnecessarily wasting your willpower.

Willpower is all about personal care. When you nurture your mind with the right emotions and practices, your mind builds up its capability to do those tasks willingly without using much of willpower. It's a stress-free way to make this work out for us— Isn't that we all want from life?

Humans are not just intelligent beings; we are beings with emotions and a conscience too. The trick to apply willpower is to employee all the Drivers we discussed here based on the context to create the willingness to work on your pursuits. When you work on your pursuits with willingness, you are creating the perfect environment to propagate the seeds of your purpose.

Part 3

The Secret Codes to People Gate

Chapter 15

Emotional Intelligence and the 21st century
Your cheat sheet to understanding others

I came across Sarah and Mina during the initial years of my career in consulting. Both were working on the same IT project. Mina was an analyst; her responsibility was to gather the requirement from the client and Sarah worked on the software program development. When it was time for the client to test the program, it so happened that some of the functionalities weren't working the way the client had wanted and, the tester from the client sent a tasteless email to Mina copying the senior project management team. Mina felt miserable reading the letter blaming her for all the issues. She was scared that she will be punished by her management

Mina told Sarah that her programs were not working as expected and that is the reason for the humiliation she suffered. Upon hearing that Sarah burst out, 'I developed those programs based on the requirement you passed on to me. You could have been more precise about what the client needed. Why am I even surprised about this? This is not the first time you have done this. You can't blame me for what happened here.' Mina's pride was hurt, and she felt that Sarah was not taking the responsibility for her mistake, and instead blaming her for that. The tic for tac blame game went on. The next day when Sarah came to the office, Mina started talking to their other colleagues in a language Sarah didn't speak or understand. But, from some of the familiar words they used, and their looks and body language, Sarah knew that Mina was spreading malice and ridiculing her. Sarah felt upset and she sent an email to their manager about how humiliated and hurt she felt.

If you know about the software development industry, you might also know that it is not uncommon for the software developers and clients to misunderstand each other, especially in the absence of meticulous requirement analysis. And because of that reputed companies have policies to bring the discrepancy as much as they can through various checkpoints incorporated in the plan.

What Sarah and Mina could have done was to accept the situation and focus on how they can solve the issue and save their company's face instead of focusing blaming each other. They could have also formulated a strategy to prevent such situations in the future. To add fuel to the tense situation, Mina ridiculed Sarah and it got further escalated because of the official complaint from Sarah to their manager. An issue that could have got solved between two people has affected the psyche of the whole team.

The reactions of Mina and Sarah were led by their emotions. One felt frustrated and burst out, while the other lost her face and some people would classify her reaction as office bullying.

Isn't it natural for people to feel frustrated or ridiculed in such situations? Yes, emotions are part and parcel of life. But did Mina and Sarah really know what their emotions were? Based on several studies, being able to understand our own emotions, and regulating our responses to those emotions could place us in a much better place professionally, personally, and psychologically. Psychologists call this trait emotional intelligence. In fact, emotional intelligence is found to be a major predictor when it comes to corporate success. There are many people who climb the ladder of success demonstrating many leadership qualities. However, it is the emotional intelligence that determines who picks up the big position. It is not just that, there are surveys where employees have shared that they are ready to leave their current work to join another employer who will take care of their wellbeing better, even for lower pay.

If Mina and Sarah took a moment to think about how their words or actions could affect the other person negatively and themselves, they probably might not have acted in the way they did. However, there are many people who do not realize when they are happy or sad or angry. Being able to identify emotions and the reason behind the emotion is important in responding to people and situations. If we consciously observe our feelings and emotions and identify those emotions as it happens, it will make the relationships between people, organizations, and countries more peaceful and productive.

Emotions are psychological states that are created by neurotransmitters and hormones. These neurotransmitters and hormones are released in response to certain triggers, and they alert us to be prepared to take the next step. We adjust our behaviours as a response to this emotional state. If you were to take a peek into the business world a decade ago, you would see what bad press it had. Professionals were told that emotions had no place in business and hence people were conscious of displaying any emotions, irrespective of how horribly they felt in certain situations. So, many people suppressed their emotions and that resulted in frustration, anxiety and other mental health-related issues. But today, as we understand more about emotions, we are learning more about how to manage them for our benefit, rather than suppressing them. And that is where we need emotional intelligence.

The case for emotional intelligence

When humans were hunter-gatherers, they were bombarded with a lot of existential threats, from animals and nature. When the amygdala, which is the part of the brain that is located near the base of the brain, senses danger, it signals the brain to pump cortisol, a hormone that prepares our body to fight or flight. Depending on how they were fit for the situation, they either stayed there and fought the enemy or ran away from the enemy. Amygdala is the part of brain that regulates our emotion. Depending on whether it is a threat or an opportunity, it releases different hormones and takes control over our emotions and response. The word 'Amygdala Hijack' is used to define our state in such situations.

Cortisol is also known as the 'stress hormone', as it introduces stress into our system. The more cortisol is released into the system, the more the stress is, and the better we are prepared for fight or flight. High cortisol levels is also associated with a quicker heart rate, and it adversely affects digestion and the production of reproductive and growth hormones. The entire energy of the body is focused on a physical fight or flight response.

Today in the modern world, we don't face as many threats and dangers as the hunter-gatherers did. However, internally we haven't evolved as quickly as we transformed our lifestyle. As a result, we are still prone to act in a fight or flight fashion in response to a symptomatic trigger such as someone jumping in our way or hearing a loud noise or any other trigger that causes fear or anxiety. As a result, amygdala hijack happens even in situations where it is not required. This is the reason we are not able to think clearly and act accordingly when we are stressed or anxious. The antidote for that is to manage our emotions and regulate our responses. An important distinction you need to make here is, managing emotions is different from suppressing emotions. When we practice emotional intelligence we acknowledge the emotion, we get into a mental state where we are able to think clearly and then respond to the trigger with self-awareness.

We feel various negative emotions such as anger, anxiety, jealousy, sadness, hatred etc. when there is an imbalance of chemicals that contribute to our emotions. Just like we have 'stress hormones' in our system, there are 'happy hormones' too. There are five happy hormones: serotonin, dopamine, oxytocin, and endorphins. These chemicals are responsible for regulating positive and social emotions such as happiness, bonding, trust, generosity, love, gratitude, memory, decision-making, motor control, attention, pain relieving, physical healing and sleep stimulation among many other beneficial effects. When the body is in a balanced state, where stress and happy hormones are in balance, we feel true to ourselves and more in control. Since the happy hormones oversee thinking, decision-making, and memory, in our natural state, we don't come across any difficulties with thinking and decision-making, and we are able to make use of our memory while doing those activities. Hence, it is important for us to regulate our system to think and make informed decisions when we are in an elevated stress state, which is caused by negative emotions.

Emotional intelligence is not just a nice-to-have trait anymore, it is a must-have, at home and at the workplace, amidst the triggers that escalate the mental health crisis the world is facing today. Contrary to the situation in 2020, when many people were losing jobs due to the pandemic, the job landscape in 2021 is very different. We are witnessing the Great Resignation since 2021; mental health is a major factor contributing to that, among other reasons. A whopping fifty per cent of the forty-seven million people who left the workforce in the United States in 2021 reported mental health issues as the reason for their quitting. A study in the United States found an overwhelming eighty-four percent of the employees reported having their mental health affected by workplace factors.

More than half of the employees reported that their manager does not understand their problems and needs.

Furthermore, the physical boundaries between home and work are disappearing due to many people working from home, and this is a trend that is going to stay. This seems to cause work-related stress and burn out affecting personal life and relationships even more today.

In the example we saw at the beginning of this chapter, let us assume that what Sarah said about Mina was right, that she does not pass the requirements correctly or in full. Mina was disturbed because of the email and blamed Sarah, led by her emotion, and Sarah too reacted emotionally. This is a case where both people felt an emotion different from their baseline, but without acknowledging that situation, they reacted by letting their amygdala take control and make impulsive decisions, rather than taking control of their emotion and responding. We see the need for emotional intelligence in our homes too. Incidentally, that is something many of us often overlook. A home environment does not need to be particularly emotionally or verbally abusive for a person to feel not valued.

This reminds me of a discussion I had with a child who attended the International Youth Leadership and Innovation Forum (IYLIF) which I founded. Jay has loving parents who are devoted to bringing up their child with the right values, leadership strengths and academic skills. If you ask Jay's parents, they will say they want to lead their child in the right path, supporting him in learning and practicing skills that would help him develop better. One such skill they identified was interpersonal skills, they felt that Jay could take more initiative in making new friends. However, they tend to be over-analyzing and over-criticizing at times. When ten-year-old Jay did not get invited to a birthday party, they analyzed the situation and suggested that perhaps picking up and practicing some aspects of interpersonal skills will help Jay strengthen his networking skills. Jay became frustrated with his parents finding fault in him whenever they found something did not happen the way they thought was in his favour. As a result, he stopped sharing about his personal life with them. Jay's parents had all good intentions, but they were always in a problem-solving approach without considering how it was emotionally affecting their child. Moreover, they didn't try to find out from Jay whether he was ok with their constant meddling.

Stress and burn out is becoming a norm—workers are stressed, leaders are stressed, students and parents like Jay and his family are stressed, caretakers are stressed. All this points to the fact that, the lack of knowledge about how to read the emotions of other people and act accordingly, impacts us personally, emotionally as well as financially.

If we go back to the incident between Mina and Sarah you read in the beginning of this chapter, we can observe that both failed in understanding the other person as well as in controlling their response to the other person. Let's examine how they could have approached the situation in another way.

What could have Sarah done differently? Even when a person is at fault, they go to a defensive attitude when someone bursts out at them and put them on the spot. What if Sarah had understood that the trigger for Mina's response came from the client's email and responded, 'Mina, looks like the client was not happy. Shall we go through the requirements and see where we went wrong?' This would have made Mina feel that Sarah was with her and that they are together on solving the current challenge. This might have helped her feel calm.

What could have Mina done differently? Mina could have approached Sarah with a collaborative approach rather than pointing fingers at her work and competence. She missed realizing why Sarah reacted the way she did even after the incident and further escalated it by badmouthing Sarah to their colleagues.

As they discuss it, they might come across points about where Mina could be more careful about gathering the requirements from the client and communicating that to Sarah. Sarah might also come across areas to improve such as how she could ask more questions to Mina to clarify the requirement or to show how the programs work to Mina and get her feedback before asking the client to test it.

Drivers of emotional intelligence

An emotionally intelligent person knows how to unlock their potential and at the same time bring out the best in the people around them. They make other people feel psychologically safe without sabotaging their own self-confidence.

As you go higher up in the organization, emotional intelligence takes a much higher rating than IQ. Reputed psychologist and leading researcher on emotional intelligence Daniel Goleman, conducted a study on the Competence Modeling of 200 companies. The Competency Modeling traces the qualities companies identified as important for their staff. He found that eighty to ninety per cent of the competencies identified by these company for their top management staff are related to emotional intelligence. If emotional intelligence and relationship building are the predictors of success, that makes it important to pick up emotional intelligence skills irrespective of our age and position. So here are the four Drivers that are essential to develop emotional intelligence.

1. Identify your emotions and feelings

My friend Sandra had her child yelling in the house, and she answered a call with an edge in her voice. That was a call from a headhunter and later she wondered why the caller sounded unfriendly. We come across so many stressful situations on a day-to-day basis. Deadlines, conflicting personal and professional priorities, nagging spouses, financial issues and the list goes on. Since there are so many things to worry about, sometimes we do not even realize we are on edge.

Knowing our own emotions is the first step to understanding other people's emotions. If we know how we are feeling, why we are feeling so, how we want to deal with that emotion, it will help us to be the one in control of the situation. Many of our emotions hold us from expanding our horizon. Fear and anxiety hold us from dreaming big, taking action and responding to certain people and situations. When we face such predicaments, all the certificates and degrees we accumulated take a back seat.

Others might find it difficult to trust a person who doesn't know themself well enough, so they might doubt whether you are capable of handling certain roles and positions that require critical decision making or managing major clients or departments. Leadership starts with self-leadership, and self-leadership starts with self-awareness. To learn more about self-awareness, you may revisit self-awareness and the Drivers of this Secret Code in Chapter 5.

Teaching children and teenagers about identifying and naming their feelings can go a great way in their development as emotionally intelligent children and adults. Encourage them to speak out about their feelings, giving due respect to the fact that they as individuals are feeling what they are sharing and hence not to lighten it. Listening to children while they are expressing their emotions and feelings will help them express themselves better. Help them with the right words when they talk. 'Are you feeling slightly anxious after hearing about Joe?' or 'What did you feel when Ceyda say that to you?'

When your child shares that they are sad that their friend is leaving the school and you respond, 'You will get used to it, I have had friends who had left as well', the child might not share similar feelings in the future as they might feel that such feelings do not have much stand.

Another effective way to make children understand their emotions is by asking them which part of the body they are feeling it, and this is a good tool adults can also use to get in touch with their own emotions. Many people feel a fluttering sensation in their tummy when they are stressed, faster heart beat when they are afraid and rapid breathing or churning stomach when sad. Listen to the child when they share their feelings without reprimanding or judging or lightening the intensity of their emotion or feeling. I personally feel many of these physical symptoms based on my emotional state. One of the ways I use that awareness is while sending emails on difficult topics. Even when my mind tells me that I am doing ok, if my physical response gives me a different picture, I avoid sending out that email at that time and instead try to understand the emotion and the reason behind it. That helps me to self-regulate my response to that emotion and update the email if necessary, before sending it out.

2. Self-regulation

Have you ever felt angry after reading an email? My friend Jyoti narrated an incident recently. Jyoti has been helping a colleague of hers with some doubts he had, related to an upcoming presentation for a knowledge transfer session. She willingly helped him get clarity on even those areas that she was familiar with but not responsible for. Then one day suddenly she receives a meeting invite from this colleague, which he had addressed to a large group of people in the organization, in which he mentioned that Jyoti will be doing the knowledge-sharing presentation the next morning. She said, 'I was seething with anger upon reading that email. He didn't ask me whether I could do the presentation. Suddenly my goodwill backfired straight on my face. He didn't even bother to enquire whether I had the time to prepare.' Jyoti knew she was angry, so she went for a short walk inside the office which helped her to face her emotion head-on.

Jyoti said, 'There was no way I wanted to do that presentation, I didn't have the time as I was busy with a critical project, and it was not even my responsibility to do that. He might have felt that I would agree to what he said if he sends out my name in that email, but I didn't want him to take me for granted. He behaved in an immature way, but I didn't want to follow his suit and make him feel slighted by sending a reply to everyone, challenging him. I decided to come up front and tell him that this is not happening.' So, instead of making it an email blame-game, Jyoti called him up and shared her disappointment about how unprofessional he had behaved in handling the whole situation. He told Jyoti, 'I know it is not your responsibility, but you know the concept better and you will do a better job with it.' However, he didn't give a satisfactory answer for why he didn't inform Jyoti first. Jyoti calmly told him that though she now understands his perspective, she would appreciate professionalism and clear communication in the future. She told him that she neither has the time nor the responsibility to do what he thought she would do and that it is up to him to pick up the necessary knowledge and do the presentation. Her colleague came to know how his actions came across as provoking and, he rescheduled the session and did the presentation himself after researching and learning more about the topic. He also made sure that he invited Jyoti to give her views as an expert based on her knowledge of the topic.

Self-regulation is the ability to manage our responses and behaviours, acknowledging the emotional state we are in. Though Jyoti was taken aback by the original email, she mindfully took the time to consider the situation, acknowledge her emotion, think from the other person's perspective, and regulate her response without causing any damage to the reputation of her colleague or her own. Her self-regulated, but timely response helped diffuse a tense situation and calmly resolved a conflict while gaining the respect of not only the person who offended her but also her other colleagues.

Albert Einstein practiced an effective way to self-regulate his response when he felt angry. Whenever he felt angry with someone, he would write a letter to that person. But he wouldn't post that letter until the next day. The next day, when he looked at it with a calmer mind, he would decide not to send many of those letters as he was then able to recognize that his emotion-packed letter was not going to do any good, or he would rewrite the letter with better comprehension of the situation.

Let's take a step-by-step look at self-regulation. The first step is to identify the trigger. The trigger in Mina's case was the email, in Sarah's case it was Mina's reactions and in Jyoti's case, it was the email from her colleague. Pausing and identifying the trigger is a crucial step in self-regulation. Once a trigger hits, the emotion surfaces. This is where you take a mental pause to acknowledge the trigger and identify the emotion, which we have already covered that in the previous Driver. The next step is to come up with a strategy to consciously respond to the trigger. You might have come across advice such as count to ten before responding, do not send difficult emails right after drafting them and so on. These are all techniques that help you to deliberately reach the pause state. Jyoti's technique to reach the pause state was to take a stroll and get to know her thoughts and feelings to regulate her response. Self-regulation is used not only in difficult situations, but also in professional negotiations, interviews, crowd management, classroom management and so on.

Some people use self-talk to acknowledge their feelings and thoughts and to coach themselves to respond to the situation objectively, as opposed to reacting to the situation emotionally. Serena Williams, one of the greatest tennis players of all time, uses self-talk very effectively. Though she has the best coaches and counsellors available for her, at the time of action on court, she has only herself to rely on. And she uses self-talk to effectively regulate her emotional state for better outcomes in her matches.

When you start practicing self-regulation, you might feel that you are still reacting emotionally many times. In addition, many people find it difficult to pause and control their emotions in response to a trigger. If you feel that, it is normal because your brain has not developed the right level of neuroplasticity yet for you to use pause as an automatic response. There are a few skills that you can practice on a day-to-day basis that would help you with self-regulation whenever that is needed.

Practicing mindfulness is a great way to consciously intercept our thoughts and pause. In fact, this is one of the main reasons people practice mindfulness. Personally, meditation has helped me tremendously in practicing mindfulness and looking at emotional situations with an objective mind. Journaling is a handy tool that helps you understand your emotions and yourself better to regulate your responses. You may revisit Chapter 9 to learn more about the Drivers of meditation and mindfulness.

Self-regulation is a very useful Driver that children and teenagers can also learn to express how they are feeling when they face difficult situations or emotions. Developing the self-regulation at an early age provides a kickstart to the art of channeling their internal resources productively in the face of adverse situations. As part of my work, I have seen how several children, teenagers and adults successfully use metacognition and mindfulness to come to face with their thoughts and emotions, and to strategize their next move. If you need, you may revisit the metacognition techniques discussed in Chapter 12, under Drivers of Focus.

3. Social awareness

While self-awareness helps us to know our emotions, thoughts, and feelings better, social awareness helps us to understand the emotions, thoughts, and feelings of others better. It is through empathy that one develops social awareness.

I came across Melvin and Roshni at one of the organizations I consulted for. They were peers in the organizational hierarchy taking care of special projects. Melvin had the responsibility of warehousing related projects and Roshni took care of finance. They worked in a matrix management structure, where they did not have permanent teams but drew people from the region based on the projects they worked on. They often saw that Melvin's teams responded to his requests well and always strived to finish their tasks on time. Meanwhile, Roshni's team members often challenged her during project meetings and she found it difficult to motivate her team to deliver things on time. She used to wishfully remark, 'Melvin is lucky, he doesn't need to deal with the tricky finance people.'

During one such project, due to medical reasons, Roshni had to be away from work for three weeks and temporarily Melvin took over Roshni's responsibilities as well. Melvin was a little apprehensive in the beginning fearing what he will do if the finance team was going to be difficult. Though he faced some challenges in the beginning, as time went on, he felt that they were cooperating. And he started receiving responses the same way he used to get it from his own team—most of the people in the finance team were enthusiastic about doing their work and finishing it on time. Melvin trusted people with their work, gave them the ownership of their work, but was always there to support them whenever they needed. He listened actively to understand them better and always gave a listening ear and facilitated problem solving whenever they faced difficulties in carrying out their tasks or meeting deadlines. His efforts were paid off when several people from the finance team mentioned to him that they were working hard towards meeting the deadline since they wanted to help him finish the project on time as he made them feel part of the team.

That was very different from the way Roshni handled the team, she was focused only on the outcome. If someone didn't do the work, she didn't try to ask for the reason, instead she made assumptions. She didn't observe when someone was feeling low or was unusually quiet during the project meeting or when someone's body language clearly showed that they were opposed to her views. People saw her as a taskmaster with little interest in the team's wellbeing. The management noticed that Melvin reported no issues about the finance team during the steering committee meetings and that the work was progressing on time. This became a major reason for Melvin's promotion within the next few months.

Organizations, teams, friendships, and families are all made up of people. When the team members see that they are being treated as individual human beings rather than a herd, they feel that they are being taken care of. Listening and observing are big boosters of social awareness. If you go beyond verbal communication and genuinely try to understand people through their body language, facial expressions and non-verbal communication, and sense their needs empathetically, the social awareness you are developing, will pave way to fulfilling long-lasting relationships. That is why Microsoft CEO Satya Nadella considers empathy as a tool to fulfil the unarticulated needs of customers and to inspire innovation in his company. A parent who understands a child, a person who understands the emotional state of their aged parents, a friend who is always there through thick and thin, and a leader who provides a psychologically safe environment for their staff, all of them possess social awareness.

Then there are prisoners of their own emotions that neither they get to know themselves and their potential nor they notice how their emotions restrict others from expressing their true self and opinions and expanding their true potential. This gets even worse when it is done by managers and parents. As we have already seen before, developing good self-awareness helps us to understand others better. A well-nurtured neuroplasticity to observe our own feelings and thoughts automatically helps us to observe others for their emotions and imagine what they would be thinking and feeling.

Bob works in an investment bank. He climbed the career ladder from a human resources assistant to a human resources manager, after taking many evening courses, with diligent work and willpower. However, after landing the position of HR manager, he is finding it difficult to get things done. He felt he needed to step up the game and attended online courses on his discipline, started putting in more hours at work, and tried to cultivate more positive thoughts. However, he found that the people who work for him did not complete the tasks he assigned to them.

After trying everything he could, he sought his manager's advice to tackle the situation. The manager made some enquiries and told Bob that there was nothing wrong with his staff's listening skill or attitude. From that discussion he had with his manager, he came to realize that the staff think that he makes it all about himself. He talks to the staff only about work, he always talks from his side about what he needs and that he doesn't listen to their suggestions. This was an eye opener for Bob. He wanted his manager to tell the staff to listen to him, but now she was asking him to listen to the staff.

Listening is a major trait that decides how socially aware you are. We come across people like Bob in many areas of our life. Some people have spouses or partners who see the world only from their perspective. Some people have teenage children who need everything they ask for without considering the alternatives the parent is suggesting or the length at which the parents go to fulfil their wishes. Some people work for bosses like Bob who need work to be done only in their own way.

The good thing Bob did in this situation is, he asked for feedback. And what he learned is, the strategies that helped him to reach where he is now is not adequate enough to perform in the current level or to go to the next level. He found it overwhelming to transform himself over all of a sudden, yet he wanted to give it a try. The first thing he tried to do was to focus on taking notes during meetings, which helped him to engage with the topic and not to respond. He used a mental self-talk phrase, 'Do I need to say this now or can I say it later?' when he found himself pining to talk. When he found himself drifting to patronizing, he changed the way he spoke. Instead of chastising an employee for laziness, he would ask them for the reason behind the delay and try to understand their point of view. Bob said, 'Initially I wanted to use various techniques all at once. But then I realized that I was getting overwhelmed, and people were getting confused. So, I decided to try one thing at a time, which helped me to observe what works and what doesn't and improve the same technique or use another technique or add one more technique. It took me a whole year to get comfortable with it and to notice how my efforts were changing the psyche of the whole team for the better.'

Another way you can effectively develop your social awareness is by using your observation skills to read the room. An ex-boss of mine KK had this uncanny ability to do so. He was the first one to observe someone in his team or in the client team feel stressed or moody. He would cheer them up with snacks and small talk first. If that didn't solve the problem, he would talk to them to uplift their mood. Even when we were burned out, we never felt that it was his fault since we knew that he genuinely cared about our wellbeing.

Observing other people's body language is a great way to gauge their feeling. You don't need to be a body language expert to do this. If someone is not fidgeting or crossing arms or legs while you are talking, it may simply mean they are not interested in what you are talking, or they are bored. If someone spots furrowed eyebrows, the person might be annoyed or confused.

Observing gestures, behaviour and emotions in others is a great trait you can develop in children too. Storytelling and movies are great ways to develop these skills. Make a game to spot the gestures, voice modulation and body language to guess what the character on screen is feeling. Modulate your voice or change your body language and gestures to suit the emotional background when you read stories to your child.

4. Relationship Management

Building genuine relationships in the personal and professional space is a significant determinator of our overall life satisfaction. Walking into a home where you can talk openly without being judged or muted, being amongst friends who are there to support you through thick and thin, and working amongst a group of people with whom you spend time with—these are some of the indicators of maintaining good relationships though we often take it for granted.

Relationship management not only helps in enriching our personal lives, but it also helps us to progress in our careers and to develop lasting relationships with our friends and partners. This is one of the reasons why you will see an increased focus on relationship management at the workplace.

Observing how people around you treat you, self-reflecting on your finding and seeking feedback from others can help you find your blind spots in forming or maintaining relationships. There are many ways to find out how other people value their relationship with you. A simple exercise is to observe the following.

- Do you notice how people react to your presence, comments and actions?

- Are they happy when you talk to them? Or do they seem uncomfortable?
- Do they respond to your requests and instructions because they feel empowered to follow or forced to do so?

If we overwhelm others with our instructions and suggestions, like the way Jay did, without considering their emotions or asking their opinion on the matter, they do not see any advantage in your connection unless it is mandatory for them to follow. In a cohesive relationship, claiming your own space and giving space to the other party are equally important. When you establish that space, everybody in it gets the opportunity to communicate their feelings and views without the fear of being reprimanded by others.

Emotional intelligence and relationship management go hand in hand. Emotional intelligence helps us maintain stronger relationships, while relationships help us understand other people's emotions better. You will find that almost all Secret Codes we discuss in this book under People Gate are associated with building stronger relationships with people, and consciously practicing the underlying Drivers of these Secret Codes could give rise to boosting your emotional intelligence.

People with high levels of emotional intelligence are the flagbearers of collaboration and cooperation in any setting. And, practicing this Secret Code puts them at an advantage of getting considered for any position or role that requires direct or indirect people interaction and people management, including leadership roles. In a world that looks out for opportunities to automate more and more tasks with artificial intelligence, people with heightened emotional intelligence set themselves apart with a skill that, at present, is considered the final frontier of AI.

Chapter 16

The importance of trust

The most important code to unlock your People Gate

'Dogs never bite me. Just humans,' Marilyn Monroe said once. And there are many other quotes that talk about how dogs are more trustworthy compared to humans. Why are we so obsessed with trust? Why do we care about trust so much? Are we not able to live without it?

Trust builds the unspoken foundation for any relationship. 'Can I trust you?' This is the question that goes on in our mind whenever we want to make a new association with another person or organization—romantic relationship, friendship, work relationship, business relationship, every aspect of human interaction is built on trust. You place an order online upon seeing the photo of shoes, you trust that you are going to get a pair of shoes as you saw in the picture, in the right size, at the promised time. You visit your hairdresser for a haircut, you expect that your hair will be dressed or styled the way you explained it to them. When you decide to marry a person, you expect that that person is going to be your life partner through thick and thin. When you go to a doctor, you expect that the doctor makes the right diagnosis and gives you the right treatment. Would you want a colleague you struggle to trust as a lunch buddy? It is very unlikely, right?

Trust is the basis of all relationships and the lack of it is the root cause of almost all issues. If you examine some of the biggest financial scandals we had in the last few decades, such as Enron scandal, Lehman Brothers' collapse and the Asian financial crisis, we know that the fundamental problem is people and organizations taking advantage of the trust that others have put in them. It is no coincidence that trust and cheating are the main themes of many bestselling books and blockbuster films. Nowadays we also come across many online games that focus on these themes. We love trustworthy people and hate being cheated on because it is not just about cutting all contact with the person you were cheated by, it is also about reestablishing your mind where you made several plans, goals and happy memories associated with that person and more importantly the beliefs you let your mind build around this person.

If cheating is so prevalent then, why is trust important? Why are we still looking for trust? In other words, how important is trust for us to lead a successful life?

To start with, collaboration is one of the main pillars of success. In this book itself, we have discussed several roles others play in making us successful, such as that of a coach, a mentor, a feedbacker, and so on. On the work front too, we need to collaborate with our bosses, subordinates, peers, clients, customers, vendors and so on. On the personal front, we need to collaborate with many others, most of them go unnoticed by us. Likewise, we play these roles to make other people successful. Collaboration makes certain parts of our life happy, certain parts of our work easy, certain learning of ours faster and certain goals of ours a reality. So, it is impossible to shirk off other people in our life and say, 'Thank you I have figured it all out'.

Secondly, employee engagement is considered a major trait that leads to the effectiveness of both organizations as well as individuals. Higher employee engagement in an organization leads to a surge in productivity, improvement in sales offerings and an increase in profits.

We have seen that other people are crucial in order for us to be successful, but for us to be more important in their lives, so they would want to share with us and collaborate with us, they need to trust us.

A culture based on trust provides a feel-good factor to people who are part of it. We feel safe spending time with people we can trust without worrying about whether they will talk behind our back or backstab us. This helps to save a lot of mental effort and willpower as you don't need to take your mind through the additional effort of speculating what exactly this person's motive is. This means that you are most likely in a better mood than otherwise when you are working or spending time leisurely with that person. Hanging about in a trust-based culture helps us enhance our mood.

A trust based environment is also an environment where people do not feel afraid to admit their fears and own up to their mistakes. Both individuals and organizations gain a lot of learning opportunities from these disclosures and plan constructively for the future.

We often see children holding their parents' hand when they are uncertain about something or feel threatened about a person, animal or situation. Similarly, a trust based environment is a safe environment where you feel protected so that you can share your views. This encourages people to be braver and take risks. An environment where people share more of their ideas without having the fear of reprimand, ridicule or disregard is also an environment where seeds of creativity and innovation are sawn.

For example, if you have a trusted mentor at work, you might find yourself more encouraged to share an issue about your boss that really bothers you, without worrying that your mentor is going to share that with your boss. At the same time, you will also feel encouraged to share the insecurities or incompetencies you feel at work without fearing that it will negatively affect your performance rating. This environment also provides you with the right conditions to seek help and advice. A trust based environment enhances leadership skills as it boosts self-confidence, communication skills, initiative skills and collaboration skills. It also empowers people to take ownership of their responsibilities, successes and failures.

What are the factors that affect our trustworthiness and how can we develop our trustworthiness?

When you learn what happened to Ben, a high-performing business development manager in a semiconductor firm, you will understand the first of those factors. Ben and Philip have been friends before they became colleagues. In fact, it was Ben who recommended Philip to his manager Carrie when there was an opening in the team. Once Philip settled well in the organization, they realized that their personal chemistry is helping them pursue new accounts together. But the good days didn't prolong as they had expected. Within a few months, Ben came to a sudden realization that Philip got promoted. This was a role Ben had been earmarked for, much before Philip joined the firm, and Philip knew very well about it. Ben didn't even know Philip had applied for it. He felt cheated, but he didn't want to leave it at it. He decided to have a word with his manager. Afterall, it was she who had been telling him in not-so-vague terms that she was considering him for that position.

Carrie said, 'Philip has brought in several new accounts. Ben, I am quite impressed with your collaboration skills, Philip said you have been a great help in speeding up the account acquisition.' Ben told her that both he and Philip had pursued those accounts together and had been working on them together as a team. But it fell on deaf ears as Carrie had already made her impressions. In the next few days, Ben came to know that Philip had been dropping subtle hints to Carrie that he was the main salesperson among the two and that he was also mentoring Ben to help him improve his sales skills.

Ben knew that Philip was ambitious, but he could not believe that Philip would cheat him by providing misleading information to Carrie. He was shaken and felt awful that Philip didn't care about his intentions and dream, and that his trust was betrayed. He is usually conscious of the competition at the work front and, having been working in the same field for a decade he knew he needed to be careful about the vultures that prey on other people's ideas, accounts, and positions. But he let his guards down when it came to Philip because he trusted him.

When someone feels that we don't care about their intentions and dreams, our trustworthiness in their mind drops. When trust is betrayed, we feel cheated. And the associated emotions run deep and heightened. Furthermore, we question the moral values we uphold. Most of us might have dealt with untrustworthy people at some point in our personal or professional life.

In a study at Northeastern University, the researchers found that ninety per cent people cheat. However, when the same people observed another person cheating in the exact same way they did it, they reported it as unfair and that the action of cheating is against moral values. Do we have separate standards of morality for ourselves and for others? Apparently there is, this is because the person who cheats always has a reason to rationalize their actions which they fail to see when they get cheated. Philip felt that since it was a new job for him, he had to demonstrate to Carrie how indispensable he was. So, he decided to exaggerate his efforts. But he ignored how this would affect Ben's job and life. Nevertheless, to say that the once beautiful friendship they shared on and off work disappeared from their life.

Today, it is fashionable for people to say 'I care about you' or 'Don't you see I care about you?' People 'see' that you care more when you try to understand their thoughts, feel their emotions and empathize with their dreams, and make them known you value all that with your words and actions.

Studies show that we generally tend to rate our trustworthiness higher than other people's trustworthiness. So trust is an area we need to consciously build for ourselves and for others.

How do you show you are caring?

Priscilla, a young marketing professional, shared her frustration towards her colleague Matt with me. Priscilla is hardworking and she tries her best to keep the deadlines and the promises she makes. Matt is her colleague, working with her on the same project. Matt has made a tremendous network in the office, and he is friendly with all the senior-level executives in the firm. He provides free advice for other projects during those conversations and hence gets included in those projects too. However, he neglects his primary project amid all the voluntary work he does for other projects. Priscilla told me, 'I think he is trying to make an impression with the bosses. I am ok with it, but I am the one who suffers as I end up doing the work he neglects. Even my immediate manager doesn't do much about this as he doesn't want to disturb Matt since he was assigned to the other projects by the big boss herself.'

This is not the first time Priscilla got thrown under the wheels because of Matt's overcommitment. She doesn't trust Matt's words anymore and was getting stressed with overwork. She discussed her concerns with her immediate manager when a new project was in the planning stage of which Matt was also a part. Her manager ensured her that he was going to have a talk with Matt before he finalizes the manpower commitments for the project.

When the manager talked to Matt, he observed that Matt had high ambition, but he was unaware of the full extent of the problems his overcommitment causes. His lack of self-awareness resulted in him not considering the efforts that he needed to commit to fulfil all his commitments. And his lack of social awareness resulted in him not reading how it was impacting the mental and professional space of other people in his team.

How reliable are you? If you feel that other people do not trust you with your commitment or reliability, the first thing you could do is to look inward and find out more about yourself by following the Drivers of self-awareness we discussed in Part 2 of the book.

Sometimes, do you feel that you are not keeping your promises?

Sometimes, it is not the lack of self-awareness that causes untrustworthiness in people. Georgiana is an administrative assistant, and she is genuinely interested in helping others and becoming part of the big picture in her organization. She genuinely works towards it too. However, due to her helping nature, people approach her for more, and she picks it all up. She knows when she is not able to handle all that comes her way. But she feels that she will disappoint and in the case of some people, even offend them. So she draws it all into her bucket. However, even after burning the midnight oil every single day of the week, she is not able to finish a lot of her work. Her supervisor has already warned her a few times about getting organized and working smart. She feels very disappointed with herself for not acting true to her words. But her problem is that she does not know how to say 'No'.

We have a limited number of hours in a day and a limited supply of willpower to focus on work. We sometimes forget this fact and would feel bad about our lack of focus. If you are losing focus due to overworking and that is causing people to not trust you, it is time for you to review if you are saying 'No' where it is needed. If you find it difficult to say 'No', you may want to focus on improving your communication skills. For example, instead of picking up everything that comes your way, you may say, 'I can do this and this, but I won't be able to finish the other thing on time as I have a leadership survey report due', or 'I won't be able to do it now, but my schedule is sort of relaxed for next week. If it is not urgent, I can do it at that time.'

When you adopt a style of communication that does not undermine the oncoming work and at the same time respect everything that you have already committed to, you will be able to find a common ground with the other party. This type of communication will help them to understand your workload and be mindful of that next time.

Is it possible for you to be reliable one hundred per cent of the time? There are unexpected situations where we might be out of our control, there are times we forget something or make a bad judgement about time or tasks. Having open and objective communication helps in handling similar situations without impacting your credibility or reputation.

In fact, people show more understanding when we communicate honestly about our misjudgement or inability to meet our promises. Yet, many people fear that their competence and credibility will be in question if they communicate their inability to multitask and overdeliver. This is where we need to flex our vulnerability muscles and communicate our situation openly without demeaning ourselves or our confidence. I am a huge fan of Dr Brené Brown, who educated us about the importance of vulnerability through her speeches and books. What impressed me even beyond that was how vulnerable she is in her podcasts. I have found her voluntarily admitting the areas she needs to improve herself, in the topics her guests shares about.

What Priscilla said in the earlier example, summarizes the point about open communication, 'He could have told us about all the commitments he had made outside earlier. That would have helped us plan and organize our tasks and life better.'

Be brave enough to show your vulnerability to communicate honestly and effectively about your inability to uphold your promise. This will help the other person to understand how much you uphold your promises and that in turn will help you to uphold your self-identity as a person who strives to deliver their promises.

There are many surveys done by various organizations that show the importance of trust in the workplace. It helps to promote a workplace culture of honesty, mutual respect and psychological safety. With the home office concept that became prevalent with the onset of Covid, we have seen several changes in the workplace. While many companies focus on investing thousands of dollars in monitoring the online work ethics of employees, some are investing in creating a trust based culture where people feel empowered to deliver their tasks and promises rather than using the absence of physical monitoring as an opportunity to deceive.

Are you all talk and no action?

Cindy is a busy data scientist. She lives in the suburbs with her husband Dave and their pre-adolescent children. Her husband is a luxury property agent. There are days when Cindy needs to work long hours due to client meetings and overseas calls, whereas her husband has a flexible schedule. Cindy is finding it difficult to manage everything she has on her plate. Dave has all good intentions, and very high expectations from himself and from Cindy to provide the best environment for their kids to thrive in life. She and her husband communicate with each other about the best support they can give to their children. However, she feels burnt out when it comes to implementing those ideas. Dave doesn't think that it is his responsibility to put the ideas into action and he expects Cindy to do it. So, Dave does not deal with the challenges of the practical aspects of these ideas he is convinced of. He is always ready to shell out his criticism for everything that Cindy does. Cindy feels the burnout, and she feels that she cannot trust Dave on giving her the support to bring up the children or run the household effectively. Cindy has tried to talk to Dave about this many times, but Dave is quite happy and proud of what he does and is not willing to agree with Cindy on this.

Cindy is emotionally hurt; she feels that Dave is not emotionally invested in the relationship as much as he intellectually is. She lost her trust in Dave to support the family with his timely presence and involvement in their busy life? And as a result, she adopted a coping mechanism by avoiding sharing any new ideas with Dave anymore.

In our offices also, we come across people who like to dominate meetings, throw ideas and assurances, but fail to take the next step on that. Though others admire these ideas initially, gradually they lose their trust in those people as the downside of inaction take over the upside of ideas.

So, do we totally lose our trust in people if they show any of the above traits? Not necessary. I have a friend who is very knowledgeable about gardening and plants. If I come across dark spots or discolouration on the leaves of my plants, I know whom to approach as he will be more than happy to provide me with all sorts of solutions for this. But I wouldn't leave my plants with him when I am going on a holiday, because I don't trust his discipline when it comes to timely care of my plants as they deserve. Likewise, you might be competent in some areas and people might trust you in that area, but not in other areas. If you identify an area to strengthen your trustworthiness, there are many ways to do so.

Drivers of trustworthiness

In the section below, we will explore various Drivers that you can leverage on to strengthen your trustworthiness.

1. Communicate effectively and openly

As we have seen above, a lack of proper communication may result in conveying wrong impressions about yourself to other people. We will learn about the Drivers of effective communication in the next chapter. Honest and open communication is an effective tool in making other people feel less threatened by you and more impressed with you.

If you are a team lead, keep people informed of your plans and your expectations. I once listened to a speech by a much-respected education minister of a country at an event where the community organization that invited him had presented a petition for adding a new language to the school curriculum. He acknowledged the petition and said that he understood the reasons outlined by the organization and the feelings of the community, and that he would review it. And he said, 'But, no promises.' He didn't make any empty promises, and neither did he outrightly reject the plea. His open communication proved much more effective and trust-building than any empty promise he could have dished out on that platform.

2. Be a good listener

American writer and author of bestselling self-help books and training programs, Dale Carnegie said, 'Nobody is more persuasive than a good listener.' Listen actively, ask the right questions, make eye contact, express true emotions and be empathetic to the speaker. This will encourage the speaker, irrespective of whether it is a family member or a work colleague, to feel valued. When you show that you care about them and are eager to know what they share, you are conveying to them that 'I value you, I understand you and I am here to support and help if you need it.' We will learn more about listening when we discuss communication in the next chapter.

3. Make self-reflection a part of your everyday life

We have read about self-reflection and the various Drivers to practice that in Part 2 of this book. Listed below are some self-reflective questions that will help us to understand our trustworthiness better.

- 'Am I taking up more than what I can chew? What can I do to limit or avoid it?'
- 'Are my organizational skills causing me to overcommit? How can I prioritize and plan all the stuff I took on my plate?'
- 'Do I follow through on the support and promises I offered to other people? What are some recent examples? What were my recent promises and how did I fare with following those through?'
- 'Do I honour other people's dreams, goals and intentions? Did I falter in any? What steps can I take to improve my credibility?'
- 'Why am I feeling guilty about not delivering on promises? Am I overcommitting and unable to find more time? What is stopping me from saying 'No'?'

- 'Am I communicating my schedule constraints clearly and openly with others? What can I do to share it with honesty and at the same time uphold my credibility?'
- 'Do I inform people well in time if I find it difficult to keep my promises? Or are they getting the feeling that I am sweeping those under the rug?'

You may use these self-reflection questions in a personal or professional setting. At the same time, you will see that consistently practicing it in one setting helps the other settings as well. Ultimately you are training your brain to know more about yourself in the pursuit of self-development.

You can combine these questions with the self-reflection Drivers we have discussed earlier in Personal Gate to enjoy a productive self-reflection session.

4. Ask for feedback

You may voluntarily ask other people about your trustworthiness. Trust is not a trait that comes up as a standalone skill in a formal feedback session. It is an essential trait to boost many other skills such as collaboration, mentoring, commitment and so on. Still, if you ask someone 'Am I trustworthy?' they might not be able to give you an immediate answer. So, you may want to pick up some of the traits which require trust to elicit feedback from your colleagues or family members, such as

- 'When you give me a task, how confident are you that I will be delivering this work?'
- 'What are the types of work or responsibility that you are most confident to give me?'
- 'What are the areas where you find I need more commitment? How can I work on that?'
- 'If I am facing difficulties doing something, how confident are you about me sharing it with you?'

- 'Have you seen me giving false promises? Can you tell me some situations where I have done that?'

These are preliminary questions which you can start with to explore further. However, keep in mind that you need to create an environment of trust, for that person to give you genuine feedback, especially in an informal setting.

5. Do not be too rigid in getting things done the way you want to

Have you seen parents who insist that their children do things exactly the way they want them to do, study exactly the subjects they want them to study, and sign up for exactly those afterschool programs they want them to pursue? Though these parents might be insisting on these things based on their worldview and their own experience, it puts their children in a confused state all the time. Inside their mind, these children feel dissatisfaction because they feel that their parents are not respecting their choices and dreams. This may result in these children not sharing their aspirations with their parents once they reach adolescence as they fear their parents are going to shoot their dreams down.

It is not just in personal relationships that we see such rigidity in letting others use their own ideas. There are leaders and managers who insist that their team do things exactly the way they want them to do it.

If you are too controlling of other people, the message you are conveying to them is you don't trust their intelligence, sensibilities, and competencies. Set standards and give the liberty for them to choose their path to reach the destination, irrespective of whether it is your child or your team.

Lack of knowledge of our own core values and character strengths as well as of others is another roadblock in trusting other people's ideas and choices. You may revisit Chapter 4, to explore more about your core values and character strengths.

Investing in developing a trust based culture in and around you will draw people to you. People who exercise and benefit from the art of trusting develop the skills, to identify whom to trust and how to trust with patient observation and practice. Furthermore, they know that trust is a two-way road and prove their trustworthiness to others. And, with the trust and support from others, they unlock their Three Gates towards success and achievements.

Chapter 17

Effective communication and bigger possibilities
Make yourself visible with the power of your speech

Immediately after Nitin joined the new workplace as the regional head of a department, he had a meeting with the regional director, to whom he would be reporting. The regional director told Nitin that one of the critical tasks he immediately entrusted him with was a major project they have just started. He told Nitin that the regional head of another department is also involved in that project and that she would be managing the project. Nitin started joining the project meetings, but the project manager did not pay any attention to Nitin. This was a new experience for Nitin. So far in all the projects that he had been part of, the project managers welcome the new member, give them an overview of the project, and a briefing their roles and responsibilities. Nitin also felt that the project manager was rude to him whenever he initiated a conversation with her and there were instances where she ridiculed him in team meetings. After a few days, Nitin raised the issue formerly with two of his seniors, including the regional director. As part of that discussion, it was revealed that Nitin and the other manager were having similar roles in the project and that the other manager was never informed about Nitin by the regional director. We can see several different layers of communication errors and mishaps in this incident. First, there was wrong communication from the regional director about the project manager role and then there was a lack of communication between Nitin and his colleague. These communication mishaps had given rise to confusion, disruption of the team environment and loss of productive hours. There is also the 'rude' behaviour Nitin experienced from his colleague due to which he didn't feel encouraged to communicate with her further. Nevertheless, Nitin felt poor leadership and hostility in the new environment.

In any unit—home or work or society—communication is the soul that binds the people in it together. An environment where proper communication is not cultivated is a barrier to great ideas. It is a field of ambiguity as only confusion and resentment can grow in such an environment. Such a place does not foster trust, engagement, and motivation. Ineffective or lack of communication results in people in the unit operating with unclear objectives, inefficient strategies, and a general lack of motivation. Such an environment fosters disengaged team members and workplace conflicts. It would be hard to cultivate creativity and innovation in such environments.

On an individual level, communication is the window through which the world around us gets a glimpse of who we are. Your opinions and viewpoints reflect your values and character strengths. Your way of communication, or the lack of it, reflects your personality, confidence level, emotional intelligence and your interpersonal acumen. The way other people perceive your communication is a combination of your verbal and non-verbal communication.

Effective communication is one of the most important foundations of teams. We say we have an interconnected world now. In fact, interconnectedness had been the core of civilizations since the time humans evolved as social creatures. As the Covid-19 pandemic unleashed the adaptation of rapid changes in the workplace culture, an increasing number of firms are adapting leadership models that have the potential to position the organization as well as the employees to be more agile in anticipating and responding to changes.

Many people around us burn their great ideas in the fire of self-doubt and the fear of getting ridiculed. Some people do not communicate much due to prior experience such as the one Nitin faced. Limiting thoughts and beliefs prevent many people from sharing their great ideas with others. Imagine how different our society and workplaces would be if we don't doubt our ideas or don't fear ridicule.

Drivers of effective communication

You can learn more about the Drivers that you can use to improve your communication effectiveness in the section below.

1. Set your intention to communicate

When I was a young professional, communication was a skill I struggled with. I saw people charismatically speaking and sharing their ideas in meetings while I sat there as a silent spectator. I saw people sharing the great ideas I shared with them one on one as their own ideas and taking credit for that. I saw myself going invisible in the multitude of necessary and unnecessary conversations around. As a result, I could only sit there and lament on my misfortune when I saw others riding their career ladder at an accelerated pace compared to me. The biggest lesson I learnt early on in my career, sitting there as a silent witness of all these was that I would not be able to live up to my dream career success if I remained silent. Yet, I struggled to figure out a way to get out of the rut I was in and to act on that lesson.

That was the time I changed my job; I took that as an opportunity to change my image to someone who would resemble my future focused self-identity. The first thing I did was to set an intention to work on my communication skills. However, I was still combating all the limiting beliefs I had nurtured about myself, my abilities, and my language skills. Limiting beliefs create comfort zones which are usually fenced off by doubts and fears about how to behave outside the comfort zone. I thought about changing my behavior straight away—but that thought itself felt frightening and it was an impractical mission to undertake. That brought me to the conclusion that raising my confidence level, taking simple steps one at a time is the most realistic solution I would be able to sustain. So, I decided to start my make over with some well-planned steps which I was sure how to act on but was slightly outside my comfort level.

I chose my morning routine at work as the first step to effect this change. Instead of following my previous habit of walking to my seat and start working, I decided to make eye contact with people and greet them. Though it was difficult at first, with consistent practice and the self-reflection thereafter, this became a habit. Once I did that, I came to realize that people were initiating conversations with me, that made it easier for me to move to the next level—communicating to make connections. Indirectly this gave a message to people that I was a person who was willing to connect and communicate with them. After achieving a certain level of confidence in each step, I set forth new steps. That gradually gave way to speaking in small teams with familiar people. The realization that people were willing to listen to my ideas and give them a thought provided me with the confidence to share more. Before a meeting, I meticulously planned what and how to communicate in it and worked on gathering all the necessary details for it even if I was not a speaker. This preparation helped to boost my confidence in communicating. However, as I got more confident about sharing ideas, I faced disagreements and criticism too. I could move forward from there only when I decided to be more vulnerable.

2. Vulnerability opens new doors to be an effective communicator

After taking the initiative to talk to others at work, gradually I developed the courage to share about myself, my ideas, viewpoints, likes and dislikes with others. However, that resulted in coming across disagreements and criticism for some of my ideas and views. That is a natural consequence of becoming vulnerable. In fact, the meaning of the word 'vulnerability' itself is being open to attack or damage. Here we are talking about emotional vulnerability. According to Dr Brene Brown, the leading researcher and author on vulnerability, shame, empathy, courage and leadership, vulnerability is about identifying and owning our imperfections.

In my case although these disagreements and criticism were the natural outcome of communication, I was stressed out. It was all a new scenery for me. Speaking out itself was a newly developed trait, and hence the disagreements and criticisms that ensued were also novel to me. The very fact that I spent hours learning new things to fill my knowledge gap in order to share my views had resulted in creating the feeling of an imposter, a person who rightfully doesn't belong where they are with the merit of their natural talents.

The disagreements felt like public humiliation and my initial response was to defend my view at any cost. However, after a few failed attempts at defending some of the lost causes, I realized that many of those criticisms were right to the point. At that time, I started doubting myself again, I felt that I was trying to lift up something I was incapable of carrying. The imposter feeling inside me started asking myself, 'What is the use of speaking out if you are not even proficient in what you are talking about?'

The way forward was to be mindful and separate myself from the topic I was communicating. Furthermore, openly talking about some of my feelings also helped me navigate through self-doubt, fear and imposter syndrome. So, a week before a major presentation, I told some of my colleagues, 'Next week is the first time I am giving a presentation to such a huge audience. It is stressing me out.' My colleagues filled me with confidence and volunteered to sit through my mock presentation and gave me feedback which otherwise I would have failed to catch. That one moment of vulnerability helped me see things from a different perspective too. Not all people are there to sabotage your progress and people do not expect you to be 100 per cent perfect and they do tolerate some mistakes. There are many people who would genuinely help us once they get to know that we need help.

When trying to figure out a new skill or testing unchartered waters, not all of us would be making all the right moves. If you make yourself vulnerable at this point to learn more about other people's views on the topic, the reason for their disagreement, and clarification for their criticism, you are positioning yourself to improve your self-confidence and expand your skill as an active and effective communicator.

Dr Brene Brown has detailed the effects of vulnerability in our life and work very well in her book *Dare to Lead*. In it, she has highlighted the three advantages of being vulnerable— approachability, likeability and respectability.

Exposing our vulnerable side does not make people consider us incompetent, in fact they would see that we are real and authentic. When we try to show we are perfect in every aspect, others fail to relate to us, and they would consider us outside their league. Consequently, this has the potential to lower our likeability. Furthermore, the pursuit of perfection put us in a constant state of stress and that could negatively affect our mental health and relationships.

At this stage it is natural to wonder whether vulnerability is about revealing everything about us including our flaws, fears and mistakes to others. The answer is no. Vulnerability is not about seeking sympathy nor attention, it is about owning up to your real self in as many details as it is sufficient for others to understand and identify with you.

If you observe people who are both respected and liked, you will see them often balancing both curiosity and vulnerability. Moreover, vulnerable people often get admiration from their professional and personal circles. Other people would describe them as 'warm', 'friendly', 'humble' and 'non-threatening'. In addition, people feel safe to connect with them and approach them for conversations. Many well admired leaders embody the mix of approachability, likeability and respectability, with their choice to remain vulnerable.

Yet, when it comes to our own behaviour, why are we resistant to vulnerability? The answer lies in our risk tolerance. When we see vulnerability in others, we are not concerned about the risk associated with it. However, when it comes to revealing our emotions, flaws and insecurities, we normally worry about its unwanted repercussions. In such situations, focus on how showing the right amount of vulnerability in that situation will be of benefit to you, bring in some positive emotions associated with it and pick the necessary courage to demonstrate your vulnerability from it.

Vulnerability helps us to build authenticity, lasting relationships and sound leadership skills. So, when you communicate with vulnerability, it is more likely for you to gather appreciation, connection and support from your audience.

3. Clarity leads to connection

In 1948, former U.S. President Harry S. Truman said that his political opponents' strategy is 'If you can't convince them, confuse them.' Obviously, Truman was not speaking in favour of confusing the audience, though many people unknowingly use the now popular phrase citing it as Truman's recommendation.

Have you listened to speeches and presentations which you feel have been going on forever, but are still unable to grasp the idea around it? Lack of clarity in communication is a major reason behind many speakers' losing their audience, teachers failing to impart knowledge to students and leaders failing to gain support from their followers. Clarity is subjective, it depends on the audience.

Simplicity is the one of the most important factors that determine the clarity of communication. This is the reason why orators and writers look for ways to make their messages memorable for the audience. This is where people introduce models, acronyms, bullet points and linguistic devices to help the audience easily stick the message in their minds. Examples, stories and anecdotes are great tools to help your audience remember the message.

There is a famous Winnie the Pooh quote, 'It is more fun to talk with someone who doesn't use long, difficult words but rather short, easy words like, "What about lunch?"' Using jargon and incomprehensible words in one-on-one conversations and speeches could damage the receptivity of the message and the communicator. Sharing the speech with someone who doesn't know much about the topic is a great way for you to infer whether your speech is simple and comprehensible enough. ·

Sustaining the attention of people for a prolonged time is not an easy job in today's world where easy distractions and busy affairs are in abundance. Hence, concise communication is another factor that determines the clarity of your speech. Simple presentation in a concise form is the pill for clarity in communication. Again, the word 'simple' in the above sentence means simple enough for your target audience. A doctor explaining the symptoms and treatments of a newly diagnosed disease, rich with medical jargon could be considered 'simple' for an audience of medical professionals, while it might not be considered 'simple' if they deliver the same discourse to the public. Effective communicators strategize to achieve more with short but effective communication.

Paying attention to your body language and non-verbal communication is another strategy you can adopt to make your thoughts clear to the audience and at the same time engage them. Dr Alfred Mehrabian is Professor Emeritus of psychology at the University of California, Los Angeles. He has conducted pioneering research on communication since the 1960s and is well known for his groundbreaking theories on verbal and non-verbal communication. According to his 7-38-55 communication model, fifty-five per cent of our communication is non-verbal, thirty-eight per cent is related to our voice and only seven per cent is verbal. This means that ninety-three per cent of our communication is not the words that we speak, but our body language and voice. Doesn't this give you the right scientific base to focus more on your voice modulation and body language?

4. Use empathy to engage and convince

Many leaders, professionals and children attend our various public speaking workshops under the brands of *As Many Minds* and *International Youth Leadership and Innovation Forum*. These workshops were all developed under the leadership of leading experts in the domain. One of the objectives most participants state when they join the program is that they want to engage the audience with their speeches. The best way to engage the audience is to be empathetic towards who they are and what they want to achieve from your communication. In fact, this is true in all modes and all types of communication irrespective of whether you are communicating with one person or many. People feel connected to what you are communicating with them if they feel that you are addressing their needs and their problems.

One of the lessons I learned from learning, doing and coaching public speaking and communication skills is to ask myself, 'What does this audience expect from this communication?' Once you have the answer to that, the next step is to impart the information on the topic attuning it to their profile. For instance, the language and speaking style you use to share how to differentiate fake news from truth to middle schoolers would be different from the way you share the same information to a group of public policymakers. When you understand the needs of your audience with empathy and customize your communication for their profile and needs, you are preparing yourself to engage your audience.

5. Listen mindfully to communicate better

My friend Selena is a social media entrepreneur. She started her professional life by working with a newspaper and then moved on to become a successful television executive. Later she started her own business in media and marketing. Between running her businesses in multiple countries, organizing international conferences, taking part regularly in marathons and bringing up her teenage boys, she enjoys an active social life too. Selena is a people magnet and I have hardly seen her sulking on anything. She is everybody's friend and people love to be with her for her smooth conversation and fun nature.

Selena is highly energetic and the life and soul of every party. She laughs out loud at jokes and takes turns talking to everyone. But if you observe Selena, you will observe two things. To start with, although she is known for her excellent communication and networking skills, she is not the one who dominates conversations by sharing her life and achievements. Secondly, she is not a silent spectator either. She uses her communication skills to encourage others to talk and understand more about their point of view. When others share their disappointments and bad experiences, she empathizes with them. She enquires about their feelings, how they are coping with it, and what they are planning to do about it and offers her genuine support. When someone shares a happy episode from their life, she shares their joy with sincerity. When someone is confused, she provides sound advice and support. The last time I met her, she surprised me by sharing certain things I told her during our first meeting over twelve years ago. Selena listens with an intention to remember, not to find an opportunity to talk. It is hardly surprising that many of her friends have invited her to be part of their business ventures because of her empathetic nature and resourcefulness.

Communication is a two-way road. But in most cases, people just try to use that road to negotiate their own path without giving way to others, by trying to dominate conversations. Experts recommend listening as one the most important tools of effective communication. Many people advise nurturing 'active listening' skills. However, from what I have learned, experienced and observed, my recommendation is to practice 'mindful listening' skills. When you listen mindfully, you are listening to understand the message and identify the emotions that the words, voice and the body language convey, as we learned from the 7-38-55 model earlier. Together the message and the emotion help you relate to the speaker and respond constructively.

People like Selena use their listening skills to build relationships and form closer bonds. Some learn it from their background, some from working in an environment that fosters it, and some from actively identifying this as an area for improvement and develop it consciously. But the good thing is, it is a learnable skill. And it is simple. Set your mind to observe yourself in conversations, and identify areas for improvement. Be present in interactions, look out for body language clues and ask relevant questions to engage the speaker and to encourage them to share more about the topic they are talking about.

I have been a fairly good listener since young. But one of the issues I identified in my own listening habit was that I encouraged the other party to talk too much giving them little opportunity to know anything about me. This may come to you as a contradiction to what I have been talking about listening so far in this section. However, this happens in several situations, especially when the other party loves to talk and share about themselves. But, think about it, you would want to give them some information about yourself so that they can remember you, right? So, it is important to find a balance too. If you face such situations, the best way to strike a balance is to share briefly something from your experience to align with what they are saying. And if you want to disagree with them, express your disagreement with context and confidence, but with empathy. That will give the other person a glimpse of your character strength and knowledge, while admiring your communication and listening skills.

Communication is an art, but it is an art you can develop with mindful practice. If you find it difficult to sustain the passion to persevere, it is quite possible that you might need to strengthen one or more of the Secret Codes associated with your Personal Gate. In such situations, revisit the Personal Gate and check whether you need to work more on any of those Secret Codes to help you unlock your potential for effective communication.

Chapter 18

Collaboration and co-creation to fuel your growth

Expand your reach in the company of others

Arthur Fry used to work as a scientist in a company called Minnesota Mining and Manufacturing Company. An enthusiastic singer, he was part of his church choir. He used paper strips to mark the pages of his workbook. But, as you can imagine, the paper strips would move around or fly off whenever he opened the workbook for singing. Fry did not want to distract himself from his singing for a problem as silly as this. He had a unique problem, and he needed a solution.

Around the same time, Spencer Silver, another scientist who worked at Minnesota Mining and Manufacturing Company, was facing a different problem. He had discovered a unique glue that would stick things together well, but could easily separate if you apply some force. But, he also had a unique problem. He could not find a real application for his product.

The situation changed for the two scientists when Fry attended a seminar by Silver on his special glue. He felt he found a solution to stick the paper strips to his workbook in Silver's unique glue. The next day, Fry got a sample of the glue. Their company was willing to try out this new concept. The rest, as they say, is history.

The company marketed the product, first as 'Press 'n Peel' in 1977 and then as 'Post-It Notes' in 1980. In 2002, Minnesota Mining and Manufacturing Company changed its legal name and today it is known as 3M.

When two or more people come together to collaborate, it could result in co-creating ground-breaking innovations. It was his everyday challenge that inspired Fry to come up with the idea of Post-It notes. And, it was the collaboration of Fry and Silver that led to its invention. The collaboration helped the duo to think much more creatively than how they originally did, expand each other's creative confidence and innovate something that was beyond their initial needs. It also helped them to get a third collaborator, that too a powerful one, their company, 3M. Today Post-it, the product they co-created, is sold in over one hundred countries, and 3M has won several awards for it. Good collaborations can make the smartest ones even smarter, just like how Fry and Silver helped 3M with one more feather in its cap.

My not-for-profit book *Breakthrough* was released in 2018, the book was the product of the collaborative power of seventeen women thought leaders from around the world sharing their experiences and knowledge to help other women discover their own breakthroughs. Post-release, many people mentioned to me they wanted to collaborate with me to write books. A young man approached me asking "Why don't you curate a book co-authored by men?" Another gentleman wanted to co-create a book with me on innovation. Many women wanted me to mentor them in their writing journey. These are people who have established their credibility in various fields and have proven themselves with inspiring actions and out-of-the-box thinking. What makes these highly accomplished people reach out? To find the answer to that, we need to look into the power of collaboration.

What exactly is effective collaboration?

Collaboration happens when two or more people come together to co-create a common goal. If you understand what makes an effective collaboration, you can use that skill to expand your People Gate, increase your circle of influence and unlock another layer of your potential.

What leads to the co-creation of great ideas from an effective collaboration is collective intelligence. Collective intelligence, as the term suggests, is the intelligence that surfaces from collaboration. In simple terms, collective intelligence encompasses collective efforts for giving birth to a common objective, with the aid of healthy competition for improving the contribution of each member in the group, and robust mechanisms for making collective decisions. In such groups, it is not the cult mentality, but it is the respect and acceptance that each member cultivates towards other members of the group, that takes the group towards its common objective.

The traditional definition of teams has vastly changed now. In the past, in most organizations, people were vertically organized under one manager and the reporting and collaboration were much more linear. However, today with the matrix structures adopted by businesses, people are grouped under several teams. And these team structures change based on the goals or projects they are working for. And this has an effect on the psychology of the team and the team members.

In 1965, psychologist Bruce Tuckman introduced the Four Stages of Group Development—Forming, Norming, Storming and Performing. Forming is the stage where the team members come together, understand the objective and try to make connections with other members of the group. In the next stage, Norming, each member is assigned their roles and responsibilities.

This is the time you would find many teams falling apart due to interpersonal conflicts and judgemental behaviours. The third stage, Storming, happens when the individuals start working together, establishing trust and work dynamics with other members of the group. In the fourth stage—Performing—the team begins to bring excellence, keeps the differences at bay for the larger purpose of the group, finds passion and motivation in working towards achieving the objective of the team and identifies closely with the group.

Whenever a new member joins the team, the team dynamics need some changes and the team goes through the four stages again in response to that. The success of the final stage depends on the success of all the stages. For example, if some members of the team make their competitions visible externally, it may result in less cohesion among all the group members and subsequently less connection to the objective.

In today's business climate, where organizations are innovation-focused, they are expecting more from teams rather than just working with each other to achieve the set objectives. They are looking for more meaningful interactions within the group to enhance the innovation potential of the team. Effective collaborations give rise to blooming good ideas into great ideas and eventually into some amazing products or services.

Good collaborations are part of our personal life too. An instance where we see effective collaboration at play in personal life is parent-teacher collaboration. Recently my friend Shiba got a call from her high schooler's teacher. The teacher told her about some behavioural issues he had been observing in the child. At first Shiba did not believe it, but she didn't want to discount the teacher's intention too. She set up a meeting with the teacher to understand more about his perspective. When she understood where the teacher was coming from, she not only understood the teacher's earnest intention but also sought his help to collaborate in helping the child. As both of them worked together, and shared with each other the progress of their strategy and adjusted it accordingly, they established a continuity which turned out to work well for their objective—to help the child succeed. Shiba was happy that within a few weeks, they were able to help the child realize his areas for improvement and adjust his behaviour accordingly. Shiba could have chosen to disbelieve the teacher even before the first stage of their collaboration started. Both of them understood the objective and foresaw how it would benefit them individually and that paved way for helping each other and achieving success in their chosen collaboration.

In the 1970s, Tuckman and psychologist Mary Ann Jensen added one more stage to the Four Stages of Group Development—Adjourning. Adjourning is the process of ending the collaboration. This fifth stage is even more relevant in today's matrix reporting structures. We usually see team celebrations at the end of a project to mark the end of the collaboration for that particular objective. At the end of an effective collaboration, it is not uncommon to see the same team getting assigned to a new project or the team members embarking on founding some initiative together. You can find many such repeated collaborations in movie industries, where the stakes are high, a director trying to repeat some of their cast and crew to establish the team dynamics faster. There are many ways to integrate collaboration in our lives to achieve much more than what we individually can achieve.

Drivers of collaboration

In this section, we will explore the Drivers that can help us form effective and long-lasting collaborations.

1. Conflicts are the path to collaboration

Conflicts are part of every endeavour that involves two or more parties. Given the fact that we are all unique individuals with our own opinions about various topics and situations, it is difficult to avoid conflicts. But what differentiates a good group from a not-so-good group is not the absence of conflict, but the management of those conflicts. There are people who avoid expressing their conflicts in opinion with others because they don't want to create discord in the group. Conflict of opinion in a group shows us the diversity of thoughts within the group. However, having a proper mechanism to acknowledge the conflict and deal with it is important for the collaboration to work and deliver its objectives.

There are studies that show that a certain amount of competition is good for people to feel motivated, sharpen their skills and deliver better performances. However, unhealthy competition can be detrimental to the performance and morale of the group. You can observe many common features in groups where unhealthy competition prevail. In such groups, what matters the most to the members is to show themselves and others who is the winner. If individuals in the group are competing with each other or have formed camps that support competing individuals, the benefits of the collaboration will no longer exist and the group's focus shifts from its purpose and the group fails to deliver the quality it could have delivered if there was effective collaboration. In addition, the individuals also get stuck in their strategies as they don't share their special knowledge and strategies, because of their fear of others learning and using their strategies to come out as winners before them. Productivity, problem solving, co-creation and innovation suffer in such environments. As more people in the group get more competitive with others, the group starts looking more like a collection of silos rather than a collective endeavour. The group will be forming most of their time and energy in Forming and Norming. As a result, they fail to smoothly transition to the subsequent stages and this may even lead to the disintegration of the group.

Social awareness and emotional intelligence of the people in the group have a big hand in determining how the group handles conflict of opinion. In a study by MIT Sloan School of Management, researchers analysed the difference in efficacy of remotely in comparison to working face-to-face. From the results they obtained from over 5,000 participants from more than 1,300 groups, the researchers found that the efficacy of working remotely can be as effective as working face-to-face. However, they also found that there are certain conditions that help remote working flourish as effectively as face-to-face. They found that collective intelligence is what predicts the success of a collaboration.

The groups in which collective intelligence work efficiently carry two major distinctions. Firstly, who is doing the work? These groups identify the members who are best at different tasks and assign the responsibility of those tasks to them. In addition, they need to possess good social skills as well. The researchers found that groups with members having high social skills and social awareness tend to pick up verbal and non-verbal cues from others and are able to coordinate more effectively. Secondly, such groups ensure that all tasks have been allocated to various members within the group. Strategically structuring collaborations in this manner helps in the efficient handling of conflicts and smooth functioning of the group.

2. Acknowledge and adjust your defensive behaviours

Britney and Todd have been married for over a decade. Britney feels that Todd is judgemental and he does not value her for who she is. Whenever they face any issue, Todd has a tendency to blame her for everything. When she tries to talk to him, he makes her feel guilty and condemns her character, her parenting style and her roots. He brings up past incidents in a bid to prove to her she doesn't demonstrate good manners and values. Britney feels Todd pulls a mask over his faults and exaggerates her faults, and that his defensive nature leaves each and every one of their disagreements unresolved. As a result, Britney experienced severe anxiety and she started to ignore issues, and Todd's retorts.

When Britney tries to defend her actions or brought the current issue into the discussion, Todd gets overly defensive and behaves as if he can never be at fault. Over the course of time, Britney's attitude changed from trying to solve the problem to preserving her peace of mind and dignity. She acknowledges that there are issues, but she does not want to deal with them as she believes that the environment was not conducive enough for problem-solving. You can see two different types of defensiveness here. You can see that Todd is defensive about acknowledging and working on the areas Britney is highlighting, at the same time you can see that Britney has developed her own defensive mechanism against getting hurt while solving problems.

A study published in the British Journal of Social Psychology identified defensiveness as a major reason behind the inability of executives to acknowledge or address problems in their own organizational culture. The study found that the problem-solving capacity of a group decreases as defensiveness increases. Defensiveness affects all kinds of groups—personal, familial and organizational. People get defensive when they see a threat in a situation. Defensive nature might also stem from their need to avoid accountability.

Defensiveness comes with the attitude of justifying our own actions and words, even when we are clearly at fault. Defensive people tend to accuse someone else for their faults and question your credibility when you give feedback to them. They start from a place of distrusting the motivation of others and that in turn fuels their tendency to stop listening to others, when they say anything against themselves or their beliefs like the way we saw in the above example of Britney and Todd.

Defensiveness stems from fear and insecurities, and as the meaning of the word 'defensive' suggests, they are trying to safeguard themselves from people and things they consider as a threat to themselves. Most of us may exhibit some of these tendencies from time to time, but that doesn't mean that we are overly defensive. However, if you exhibit many of these tendencies frequently, it is time to take a closer look at how others are responding to those behaviours.

Defensiveness is a barrier to forming effective and long-lasting collaborations. If you feel that you have a tendency to get defensive, try to identify what makes you feel threatened. Furthermore, revisit your self-identity and assess whether the other person is saying anything that contradicts your self-identity. For example, a person who identifies themselves as being thoughtful and empathetic might find it difficult to hear from someone else that they are rash and unempathetic. In either case, self-reflection and asking for feedback from trusted sources would be of help to understand the nature and reason for your defensiveness. Over-defensiveness is a reminder for us to strengthen our Personal Gate. You may use the Drivers we discussed in Part 2 of the book to boost your self-awareness and strengthen your self-identity to reduce your defensive tendencies and advance your collaboration skills to a greater degree.

On the other hand, you could also face situations where others in your group are defensive. In such a situation, it would be good to understand what makes them feel threatened. Once you have that knowledge, make them feel safe in those areas. If a person feels threatened in a situation and others keep doing things that will further strengthen the feeling, the collaboration will further decay.

There are two aspects that help to eradicate the effects of over defensiveness in a collaboration. The first is to understand your own defensive feelings and to adjust your behaviour based on that. The second is to understand other people's defensive feelings and to adjust your own behaviour to make them feel safe.

3. An open and non-judgemental culture to boost morale and innovation

In his autobiography *Long Walk to Freedom*, Nelson Mandela talks about his first trip overseas. In 1962, Mandela travelled to Ethiopia to gain support for his freedom movement in South Africa. As he was boarding the Ethiopian Airlines flight to Addis Ababa, he was taken aback by seeing a Black pilot. Mandela writes that he panicked as he had never seen a Black pilot before and wondered whether the man was capable of flying the plane and taking him to his destination safely. As he quickly captured his thoughts, he realized that though he was fighting against the apartheid to give equal rights to the Black people in South Africa, he himself had developed unconscious biases, stereotyping the very people he was fighting for. All of us are culpable to entertain certain unconscious biases.

Judgements from conscious and unconscious stereotyping of people interfere with our logical and rational thinking and impact our perceptions and actions. So rather than assuring ourselves that we are not biased or judgemental, it would be a good idea to consciously capture our thoughts and probe whether we are judging people's ideas and opinions based on our own biases. We might have biases based on multiple factors including other people's gender, race, age, religion, nationality, sexual orientation, position and so on. One of the major factors that decide the success of a collaboration is the diversity of ideas that it generates. The diverse backgrounds of people in a group increase the chances of unearthing various issues and bring in fresh perspectives and deeper insights for solving those issues. Such groups provide the fertile ground for creativity and innovation, if managed consciously.

When people who stand for a common objective come together with varying talents and skills, they are positioned well to make an impact much greater than they are individually capable of. IDEO is one of the most successful design firms in the world, with a legacy of Apple's first mouse for Apple's first personal computer. With a human-centred design, they have pioneered the art of developing out-of-the-box innovation concepts. OpenIDEO is an initiative by IDEO to solve pressing problems around the world by crowdsourcing ideas, and harnessing the power of digital connectivity. The members of the OpenIDEO community come together for a social issue, brainstorm on clarifying the problem, bring up ideas to solve the selected issue, get feedback and refine ideas and then submit the refined ideas again, working within a given timeframe. Once the sourcing of the ideas is done, OpenIDEO and the client select the best ideas and provide funding to solve the problem using those ideas. So far they have engaged hundreds of thousands of people from all around the world and leveraged 19,000 ideas to make a positive impact, by solving challenging problems that threaten the existence of our planet or of the lives on it.

When I facilitate design thinking or brainstorming, I constantly come across the power of diversity at play. Times when a marketing associate helped solve a finance department issue, an IT consultant helped solve a product packaging issue, a newcomer on her first day in an organization helped change the strategy of a project to reduce its length from six months to two weeks-there are so many examples that demonstrate the benefits of using diversity to unite people for a cause rather than divide them. So, welcome diversity rather than resisting it, share ideas and encourage others feel safe to share their ideas as well.

A characteristic of diverse groups is the presence of people with various levels of self-confidence and self-awareness within the group. You may come across people who are not confident enough to share their ideas in groups. In such situations, it will help to actively listen to them, acknowledge their ideas and appreciate and add on to those ideas wherever it is relevant. In order to reach that stage, first members of the group need to feel safe and then make others feel safe to communicate and share, using the Drivers we discussed in the last chapter.

In many groups, people are assigned a task they have expertise in. Though this builds expertise within the organization, there are chances that people become ignorant of the other areas of the business and hence in some cases affect the decisions they make. This is the reason many organizations practice job rotation programs, where employees get the opportunity to work for other areas of the business after working in a particular job in the organization for a given time. This provides the employee with an understanding of the overall business process and helps them use that knowledge to solve business problems innovatively. A well-crafted diverse environment is a breeding ground for creativity and innovation.

4. Let others shine

It is important for anyone who gets into a collaboration to understand the dynamics of such an endeavour. If one person wants to be the centre of attention in the group and expects others to treat them with distinction and reverence, the collaboration will eventually lose its objective and will cease to be sustainable. We need to let others shine where they truly deserve it.

In November 2017, McDonald's Argentina celebrated McHappy Day, a one-day fundraiser event to donate all sales from their famous Big Mac burger to children with cancer. McDonald's found an unexpected collaborator—Burger King, their rival, decided to support them for the cause. Burger King Argentina decided not to sell any Whopper on that day, and dubbed it 'A day without Whopper'. Whenever a customer visited any of their 107 outlets across the country for Whopper, the staff politely asked them to go to the nearest McDonald's outlet and get Big Mac. As the onlookers were left dumbstruck, the King, the mascot of Burger King, went to a nearby McDonald's outlet and ordered Whopper. Since Burger King kept it a top secret till the morning of the day, this unexpected support put everybody including McDonald's in shock. When McDonald's published the outcome of the event, it was revealed that they sold 73,437 more Big Mac compared to the previous year's McHappy day.

The very next morning Burger King returned to selling Whopper. According to Burger King Argentina, it was a compelling enough cause to forget the differences and support their rival. This was not an official collaboration formed together by both parties. Nevertheless, this shows that when you are in a collaboration, official or unofficial, we need to give more importance to the common objective than the personal need for accolades. At the same time, success depends also on how much the individuals in the group support other and let them shine for their efforts. A successful collaboration entails a mindset where individualist tendencies make way for a sustainable and invigorating culture. In the case of McHappy Day collaboration we discussed above, Burger King received a lot of positive media coverage and popularity among customers. Five years later, at the time of writing this book, when I googled 'McHappy Day Argentina', I found several of the top hits had the name 'Burger King' also in the title. Nonetheless, when you let others shine, it is not always mandatory that your support and praise for others will bring in accolades for you.

In a collaboration, people bring in various skill sets and mindsets. While it is not a single person to shine always, it is a place where individuals need to be appreciated for their contributions to the cause they are working on, just like what Burger King did. When you acknowledge and appreciate the contributions of someone and support them sincerely, you are inviting the support of that person and other people who notice the leadership skills you are demonstrating with that deed.

5. Don't forget to build yourself

Working in a group exposes us to people of different skills. In many groups, people are assigned a task they have expertise in. Observing and learning from others in the group helps us to enhance our skills and build new skills. When there is an exchange of knowledge and skills between people in the group, the group becomes more engaged, and people in each role gets a glimpse of the challenges and obstacles faced by other members in performing their own roles. Though this is not a new idea and has been known forever, and many people are genuinely interested in developing themselves in such a manner, a lot of them face the tough reality of not getting enough time and mental space to focus on anything other than their own tasks. Tight deadlines, multiple projects and dealing with multiple sets of people sap your energy, induce stress and hence you may feel that you are not as productive as you would want to be.

We need to take a relook at our purpose as we discussed in Personal Gate in such situations as well—the skills you want to develop and the reasons behind it. Working together to create collective intelligence is a result of using cerebral and emotional intelligence. As you take part in more collaborations and make use of the Secret Codes of the People Gate, it is common to come across productivity, self-identity and self-confidence-related issues. At this juncture, it would be a good idea to proactively review the various Secret Codes of Personal Gate we explored in Part 2 of the book, to ensure that you upskill yourself with productivity skills, and update your self-identity to support your expanding influence. You may also formulate a Development Plan for the various areas you thus identify. If you are involved in multiple groups, formulate your Development Plan separately for each of those groups, if that helps.

Throughout this chapter, we saw the importance of understanding others and collaborating with them focusing on the success of a common objective. However, many people face an obvious dilemma in group settings. Given that, groups are the settings where you get the chance to demonstrate your leadership skills, how do we know when to show our own skills and when to hold back? There are people who put a lot of effort in showing off their worth. Often that doesn't work for long, especially if it is not substantiated by their work, work ethics and emotional intelligence. Showing off might work in certain situations, but if you want to establish your collaboration skills and identity in the team, the best strategy is to cultivate your authenticity and demonstrate that in how you treat your work and your team members.

The strategies we discussed above are great ways to demonstrate your worth, and when you couple that with effective communication skills, others will notice you for your contributions and skills.

People who develop their collaboration and co-creation skills bring together the knowledge, skills and ideas to carve their path even in the midst of uncertainties and disruptions. The emergence of concepts like crowdfunding and crowdsourcing are examples of this. Those who carefully cultivate these skills emerge out victorious in enabling their ideas and viewpoints. With that, you are not only unlocking the Secret Codes of your People Gate but also accelerating your pace to unlock the Secret Codes of the next Gate—Universal Gate.

Part 4

The Secret Codes to Universal Gate

Chapter 19

Be an influential change maker
Lead the change

Nineteen-year-old Nichol Ng was at home with her mother when a policeman and a bank official called on and stuck a white paper on their door. The white paper carried the official notice of seizure of their home following the collapse of her father's multimillion-dollar business and subsequent bankruptcy, during the Asian Financial crisis of the 1990s. As they moved from the comfort of their terraced house into a rental flat, Nichol had to sacrifice her dream of living a comfortable life and studying and travelling around the world, to quickly come face-to-face some rough realities of life. She grew up in a closely knit family, and wanted to help her family in overcoming the difficult times they were passing through, so she took on several part-time jobs to make ends meet while studying at the university.

According to Nichol, an exceptional leader is one who acknowledges their fear and vulnerability and is not afraid of showing that to others. But this realization didn't come automatically. Though she had demonstrated leadership skills and was engaged in group activities right from her school days, she had a hidden side. Unbeknown to the outside world, deep down Nichol was insecure, she was extremely insecure about her body and had been suffering from eating disorders since the age of six. She also felt intellectually inferior as she studied in a top school, demonstrating below-average academic performance. As a result, Nichol had always been in search of an alter ego that didn't have any of the imperfections she believed she had. In order to bridge the gap between her alter ego and herself, and to ignore her fears and insecurities, she got busy by throwing herself into community and social causes and leading others to contribute to that.

After getting a university degree, Nichol became a marketing executive, but the family was still drowned in debt and she believed her purpose to save her family from this crisis. So, Nichol embarked on reviving the family's food distribution business, and her younger brother Nicholas joined her later. The journey was not smooth, the pair survived many storms and learned much from their failures. At the same time, they were observing another phenomenon—an increasing number of people in a first-world country such as Singapore were suffering from hunger. Having gone through a major financial blow in their own lives and still going through the repercussions of that, they knew how difficult it was for those people. Nichol and Nicholas observed one more phenomenon—many major producers of F&B were disposing of their inventory months before the expiry dates. That was an opportunity to help both parties and hence they co-founded The Food Bank Singapore, a charitable organization that provides free food to the underprivileged.

Nichol had to negotiate with many parties including government agencies, multinational conglomerates, shopping malls and community organizations to make her objective of feeding the hungry a reality. In order to handle that gigantic effort with confidence, she worked on many Secret Codes of her Personal and People Gates, to run a business and a charitable organization in parallel. People noticed her enthusiasm and commitment. She became the inspiration for many and was invited to speak at many events, many of which were at educational institutions. That is when Nichol felt the tug from within—'Am I being truthful to the people I am talking to?'

Having experienced body image issues in the past, Nichol was aware of how youngsters were feeling pressurised internally and externally about their looks, and the performance pressure they were facing in a merit-driven society. She realized that she can be true to her role as an inspiring figure not by showing others how successful and perfect she is, but by sharing her imperfections and insecurities with others. Nichol took the time to dig out what her followers needed—a person they can relate to in overcoming their internal and external struggles on their path to growth and success. Hence she decided to show her vulnerable side and started sharing her struggles with her body image issues and eating disorder and the steps she takes to overcome them, which only a handful of people knew before. All this while Nichol was in search of an alter ego, but she discovered that there is no need for finding an alter ego when she can derive her personal strength from her own vulnerabilities.

Today as the owner of a successful business and the co-founder of The Food Bank Singapore, Nichol credits her influential leadership to the strength she derived from her vulnerabilities and fears. Her staff and the community look up to her, but she does not want to portray a picture-perfect image to them. She believes that as a leader her strength is in inspiring and influencing her staff and followers, by demonstrating to them how she plans, persists and perseveres in the face of insecurities, fears and challenges.

Enlarging your circle of influence

As you advance in your professional, social and personal circles gradually unlocking your Personal and People Gates, there will come a time when you would realize that you are leading change and people are looking up to you for vision, direction and leadership. And, with and without set policies, you are influencing those people. Children get influenced by parents, social groups get influenced by prominent members of the group and employees get influenced by the team and organizational leaders. Then there are people with larger influence, such as political leaders, leaders of social media platforms and the leaders of international institutions like WHO, where they influence the behaviour and course of civilization with their vision and policies. There are cases where leadership comes with a position, and then there are situations where you assume leadership. While a parent's leadership comes with their role, a founder's leadership and the position stem from their vision.

A leader's mindset revolves not only around their own individual aspirations, but also the vision and mission of the organizational unit they are part of, and developing the people in the organizational unit to implement those vision and mission. And many such leaders are influencing people globally. Some people suddenly feel overwhelmed with the amount of attention and expectation they receive when they are perceived as leaders. When I founded As Many Minds, I wanted to spread the culture of creativity, communication, confidence and collaboration through our services and products. What startled me was the number of people and media who would come to me for my opinion and ideas. People started considering me an expert in many areas, which I didn't believe I was. Through seeking feedback from others and self-reflection, I realized I had to adjust my self-identity, acknowledge where I have reached and upskill myself. When people look up to you, you feel the responsibility to be credible and effective. Leadership is a mindset change, where a person consciously develops and expands their skills and talents to match the expectations of the role.

A leader influences the culture of the group by defining values and leading the change by working within the set values. The followers of the leader follow the cultural change by experiencing and observing which specific behaviours are appreciated and which are discouraged. At Food Bank Singapore, following Nichol's lead, the staff knows that they don't need to be perfect always, hence they feel it is okay to talk about their imperfections where it matters.

Changes warrant conscious adjustments in behaviours, habits and thoughts and it involves some element of uncertainty. So making people follow a call for change is difficult and hence, it is common to come across resistance to change. There are organizations that spend hundreds of thousands of dollars on formulating new strategies, yet additional efforts and money is spent on coaching the leadership to change their mindset to initiate and influence the change.

It is true that there are many leaders who force culture and direction on others to comply. However, it is noticeable that such an environment fails to build worthwhile relationships and to tap the full commitment, talent and creativity. As a consequence, people in such environments are not empowered enough with a personal agency to do quality work, and they develop neither the skillsets to rise up to challenging situations nor the mental agility to take on calculated risks. On the other hand, if a great leader uses their influential skills to drive culture and mindset changes, you will see a positive transformation in the morale and output of the group. Great leaders use their influence to shape the culture, disseminate their messages to others and steer others to follow certain behaviours and guide the group towards establishing efficient transformation willingly.

Drivers of your influencing skills

Let's take a look at the Drivers you can use to improve your influencing skills to effect change.

1. Acknowledge your role and share your vision

New leaders bring in new ideas and visions and, people and usually organizations expect them to bring in some cultural changes. Acknowledging this fact to yourself is the first step in infusing confidence into yourself for living up to your role. What kind of changes you need to make in your self-identity to perform confidently in your new role? We have already seen that self-identity has a direct influence on our agency and self-confidence. Many times leaders face self-doubt and a deficit of agency in carrying out certain initiatives. Many times people doubt their ability to make big decisions. Convincing yourself of your role, your responsibility and your agency to make and implement decisions helps in sharing your vision and direction with others convincingly.

When a self-doubting leader shares their vision, the team can feel the lurking confusion and indecision from the leader's words, body language and cues. Convince yourself of who you are and what you stand for, before you convince others. Strengthen your Personal Gate and People Gate to take the fast track to unlock your Universal Gate.

2. Build your team's mindset and engage their self-identity

People look for leaders who trust their strengths and build them. However, trust in leaders has seen a sharp decline over the years. According to Edelman Trust Barometer for 2022, sixty-six per cent people feel that government leaders and sixty-three per cent people feel that business leaders are trying to mislead them purposefully.

Collaboration is the backbone of a team, and in a sustainable collaboration, each member of the team should feel that they are growing and are valued in the team. Allow your team to expand their own potential by trusting them with challenging tasks. Let them navigate through the experience of stepping outside their comfort zone and expanding their comfort zones. At the same time, make sure that you are there to encourage, give constructive feedback and mentor them. People value your advice and recommendations better when they see that they are growing in your leadership.

As we saw earlier in People Gate, people like to listen to others who are trustworthy. Trusting your team is important, and making them trust you is also equally important. When you deliver your promises, when you give valid reasons when things don't work out as expected, when you embrace the values you spread, when you listen to others in the face of a discouraging incident, when you support your team, when you show interest in people as individuals rather than just part of a team—all these are instances where your team is getting the indirect message that you are a trustworthy person.

A charismatic leader actively engages their followers' self-identities in the interest of the set mission. They observe people for their talents and contributions, and are aware of the fact that the positive self-identity of the individual members of the team plays a huge role in the success of the mission. They promote the team for their collaborative contributions and individuals in the team for their mindset and efforts. They influence their team and followers not just for the outcome of their efforts, but also for the efforts and strategies they adopt to progress towards that outcome—the growth mindset way of praising the process.

3. Establish your authenticity

The circle of authenticity of an influencing leader grows deeper and wider when they demonstrate credibility, authority and personal integrity. People want to follow someone 'real', hence the authenticity of a person is something that others attribute to you. The authenticity of a person is an extension of having a strong self-identity. A person who knows how to carry their authenticity in everything they do is also a person with a healthy pride. You may take a look at Part 2 of the book to learn more about self-identity and healthy pride.

There are many leaders and influencers on social media with huge followings. They did not gain their following by blowing their own trumpet. But, what they do is share valuable content and opinion that demonstrate their mettle. Who is that person whom you regard as a great leader in your acquaintance? What is their authenticity? Think about how they project their authenticity. Now, think about the areas you can demonstrate your authenticity in your Personal, People and Universal Gates. What can you do to establish your authenticity in these areas?

4. Use socio-emotional leadership to influence sustainable transformation

Mobilizing a group for change involves demonstrating your influential skills in many different areas, including conflict management, mediation, thought leadership, and crises among others. Hence relationship management is a part and parcel of the life of a change maker and, social emotions can help you a great deal in lifting the morale of the group, getting the buy-in and negotiating positive outcomes. Additionally, it helps in managing people in authority, stakeholders, shareholders, and unions. Furthermore, it plays a big role in managing subordinates. When you make your followers feel that they are important to the success of the mission or organization, provide them support and guidance, listen to them and understand their needs, you are a problem solver.

As a leader, one of the biggest powers you can exercise is sound influencing skills. Your influencing skills determine the success of your undertaking, the people involved in it and your purpose. If you are conscious of this and include it in your Development Plan, you will realize your power in dreaming, planning and building bigger and greater things in your life and succeeding in that.

Chapter 20

Mastermind Group
The more you grow, the more diverse perspectives you need

One of the well-known leadership idioms is 'It's lonely at the top'. Many CEOs experience this feeling once they take up the role. However, this is not something that only the CEOs in top companies experience, many leaders in smaller companies and people who take up various causes also experience this. There are many factors that contribute to it. Sometimes the mere responsibility of the position itself becomes a hindrance to socializing with other people. Sometimes it becomes difficult for people at the top to come across like-minded people who have enough time to socialize. Sometimes the leaders themselves feel unprepared for the roles they are carrying and hence imposter syndrome and fear of failure pose detrimental effects on their confidence and growth.

Then, there is also the case of how other people's perceptions about leaders limit their interactions with them. For example, there are many people who put the leaders on a pedestal and look up to them because of their position, wealth and influence. They expect the leader to be perfect, decisive and know-it-all. In a nutshell, when you reach a certain stage in your professional or social life, it gets increasingly difficult for you to find people who can relate to your level of thoughts and aspirations. Also, it gets increasingly difficult to come across people who are able to help you see that there is more potential, some you haven't even realized you have, hidden inside you, and help you uncover those. As you uncover more of your potential, you will realize that there is still more to uncover. At any stage in life, when you doubt your abilities, that is a call to more learning and perhaps some unlearning. As bestselling author and two-time winner of the Thinkers 50 Award for the #1 Leadership thinker in the world, Marshall Goldsmith, said, 'What got you here won't get you there.' The kind of resources and people you need to uncover the hidden potential is different at different stages in your life, and that outlines the relevance of unlocking the Three Gates.

A mastermind group is a mentoring group where people come together to get mentored and mentor others to help them achieve their goals. You will find great sharing of knowledge and experience in the group to help each other. The group helps you to be part of a network of peers who are able to peer mentor you, and lift you to higher levels of potential. At the same time, you get the opportunity to lift and mentor others, helping them uncover their hidden potential.

It is important to note that being part of a mastermind group is beneficial for anyone who wants to excel in their life at any age or stage. Sometime you come across highly ambitious people who want to take a faster path to their goals but are unable to find likeminded people around them. No matter how many talks you listen to or how many inspirational figures you follow, nothing gives as much drive as interacting with people who can influence you, challenge you and help you perceive things you otherwise wouldn't, while being non-judgemental. In a mastermind network, the members form the synergy to raise the bar by sharing and learning distinct knowledge while being practical, building motivation and bringing clarity to ambiguous ideas and issues.

Drivers to find your mastermind group

In the case of start-ups with substantial funding, it is very common to see founders and CEOs becoming part of the exclusive mastermind groups of exceptional individuals who have found success in founding or running similar or bigger organizations. They get the opportunity to be peer-mentored because the other members of the mastermind or their organizations either have a stake in the start-up or those organizations are also funded by the same investor, and hence the success of the start-up is of everybody's interest. The important thing here is not how they entered into the mastermind group, but how much importance the business world gives to such mastermind networks.

Choosing the right mastermind group is of foremost importance to reap the rewards from it. Let's explore some Drivers that will help us understand the nuances of joining a mastermind group.

1. Set your goal

A mastermind group is neither a networking event nor it is for casual socializing, you are joining it with a specific goal. Spend some time engaging in self-reflection and if needed, soliciting feedback to clarify your goal for joining the mastermind group. Listed below are some questions you can use to set your goal.

* What do you want to achieve from the group?
* Are you looking to connect with like-minded people?
* Are you looking for special knowledge or mentoring that you won't find otherwise?
* What is the profile of the people in the mastermind group that you will benefit from?

- What is the specific objective you want to achieve? By when do you want to achieve it? If you achieve that, how is it going to directly influence your purpose?

Delve more into the details of your goal to join the group. For instance, if you are joining a speaker's mastermind group, depending on which stage you are in your speaking journey, there are many skills you can grow and polish, such as improving the body language, speech delivery, voice projection, engaging the audience, speech scripting and so on. Then there are career-specific areas such as getting referrals for speeches, introduction to speaker's bureaus and so on. Think about the areas you want to improve or get knowledge about and the people in the group who would be able to help you with that. Also consider and plan what you will do once you start getting the benefits as you envisioned. Are you able to quantify the benefit you will enjoy if you join the group? This is especially important when you join exclusive mastermind groups where the membership fees can go up to five-figure amounts.

2. Decide on the type of mastermind group

Not all mastermind groups are created equal. But, if you choose the type of group that best fulfils your goal, you will see yourself benefitting from it the best. In order to choose the group, it will be good to know the types of groups that we commonly come across. We can broadly classify three mastermind groups.

- **Mentoring-focused mastermind group:** In such groups group members help other members solve their issues by giving timely advice, resources, referrals and mentorship. There are many entrepreneur mastermind groups that fall in this category in which you will find veteran and established founders and senior executives mentor and guide upcoming young entrepreneurs.

- **Accountability infusing mastermind group:** Such groups are formed to help members achieve specific goals. For example, in a book writing accountability group, every group member might be writing their own separate book. But as a group, they set goals to achieve various milestones of book writing together. They also push and encourage each other to complete their own book. You can see such mastermind groups with goals such as course design, product conceptualization and so on.

One of the challenges I faced before I wrote my first book was that I was taking all my time for research and was not writing. Initially, I felt I was being thorough with what I was bringing on the table, but soon I nailed the actual issues I was facing. I was facing imposter syndrome which put me in a perfectionist attitude. The second issue was that I had not set a definite timeline for the book. Around that time, I came across another person who was also working on her first book. We formed an unofficial mastermind group to set timelines and to push each other to respect and accomplish that. It went very well initially. However, at some point, she started drifting away from her dreams. Her focus shifted from writing the book to developing her own courses. I felt that she could have done both together, but as we discussed earlier in this book, once your purpose wavers, it is difficult to keep your eye on it. The momentum I gained from starting the mastermind group and setting the timeline itself served me well to stay true to those timelines and complete my book. Even when you are in charge of the group, you might come across people who are not accountable. A group of two or three people, is always a slippery slope as any person leaving or not aligning with the group decisions has the potential to bring the morale of the entire group down.

- **Growth-focused mastermind group:** Such groups are focused on building the mindset of people to take the extra mile to grow in their pursuits. You will find people from diverse fields come together to get benefitted from the synergy of innovative spirit and camaraderie in the group. An example is that of a group called Vagabonds. In 1896, Henry Ford, met his childhood hero Thomas Edison briefly when he was working for Edison's company Edison Illuminating Company of Detroit. Ford at that time was working on his experimentation on developing affordable car engines. Possessing a natural spark for innovation in various fields, Edison was all support for Ford's pursuit. Ford looked up to Edison, and they stayed in touch even after he left Edison's firm to found his own car manufacturing company. In 2014, Ford visited Edison in his home state Florida with John Burroughs and together they visited the wetlands of Everglades. And that formed the roots of their mastermind group which they called the Four Vagabonds.

The four members of the Vagabonds group were visionaries from as diverse fields as you could imagine. The group had Henry Ford, the founder of Ford Motors, Harvey Firestone, the founder of the Firestone Tyre and Rubber Company, inventor Thomas Edison and naturalist John Burroughs. True to the meaning of the word Vagabonds, they travelled and camped together every summer, did many fun and adventurous activities, and invited other successful people, such as former American President Warren G. Harding, and respected agriculturist Luther Burbank, to join them and engage in some stimulating conversations. To outsiders, they were a bunch of rich and famous people who had the money and time to have fun in the summer. But, these were the people who changed the course of the history of mankind in many remarkable ways. And they believed that the luminous minds in their mastermind collaboration had a hand in invoking their innovative thoughts around various topics. Apart from having fun and engaging in stimulating conversations, the mastermind group also premeditated various ventures. For instance, in 1927, Edison, Ford and Firestone partnered together to form Edison Botanic Research Corporation, to embark on a major research project to find a domestic natural source for rubber in America, where it was imported from other countries till then.

The best-run mastermind groups are particular about benefitting the members. If members feel that the group does not have events or members that help to fulfil their objectives, the group frizzles out irrespective of who are the members in it or how promising its premise sounds.

3. Decide on the group based on factors that will help you achieve your goal

Recommended number of people in a mastermind group is about seven to eleven. However, you will be able to find mastermind groups with more people as well. You can find a mastermind group for entrepreneurs and founders. You can find groups for various industry sectors such as IT, finance, F&B, public speaking, coaching etc. You can also find various groups catering to various demographics such as women leaders, millennial entrepreneurs and so on. Many such groups also have hundreds and thousands of members in it. Find out how these groups engage the members before you single out a group. With the proliferation of social media and video calls, geographic boundaries have disappeared, and that makes it easier to create mastermind groups with participants from across the world.

As part of my career, I have created mastermind groups and enjoyed their benefits. One of the mastermind groups I run is for educational leaders, and the main criteria for joining that group is that only people who have attended my coaching programs can join this group. The reason for that is that everybody will be speaking the common vocabulary and process and hence it is easy for people to discuss and decide on certain models and processes they would follow to expand their leadership influence.

4. Frequency, accessibility and commitment are of essence

'We are the average of the five people we spend the time most with,' famous author and motivational speaker Jim Rohn said in a speech. Being part of a mastermind group is good, but having quality access to masterminds on a regular basis has a big role in determining whether the group will be of benefit to you. In a mastermind group, you do not want to fall into a situation where the hierarchy prohibits certain people to contact certain other people, or that the frequency of the meetings is too far apart to form a sustained effect on your thinking, performance and execution.

Now, what would you do if you are not able to find the mastermind group you are looking for or it is not accessible? It is simple, start your own mastermind group. If you have a good template for your mastermind group, it is easy to start one, but the difficulty is in maintaining it. It requires investing time, and effort for a long period. It requires people management skills; you need people to support you and at some point in time, the group should be able to run even in your absence. To create a successful mastermind group, ensure that the rules are well established and followed. Choose members based on how well they fit with the objective of your group, and how committed they are towards their goals and towards the group. If the members are not serious or the rules are not followed, the may lose its footing and soon become dysfunctional.

Years ago, I co-founded a mastermind group for teens and tweens named Confidence Hub. These were children who had learned the power of a growth mindset, confidence and communication in their life. The weekly mindset group meetings started with an informal 'How's life?' segment of chit-chat and activities. In the latter part of the meeting, the children set their goals for the next week, recounted how they performed in the previous week's goals, got peer-mentored by other group members and also learned something new from the coaches to develop their personality on a daily basis. As time went by we observed that these children were setting bigger goals and strategizing steps to achieve those goals. We saw how they became adept at feeling and understanding the difficulties faced by other group members and provided practical solutions empathetically. And along with that, they gained a lot of confidence in approaching life and in themselves.

A mastermind group is a great repository of strengths you can amass from other individuals in the group, as long as you are there with clear goals. This is the place where you can shorten your learning curve and accelerate your pace towards your purpose with the collective wisdom from the group. While benefitting from it, be cognizant of the fact that others are also there with their own goals. Hence be prepared to share your efforts, expertise and experience to help others achieve their goals as well. Unlocking your Universal Gate is an invitation to conceive those possibilities that perhaps no one else thinks are possible. Choosing the right mastermind group and actively contributing and benefiting from the group can provide you with the confidence, courage and competence to open that Gate.

Conclusion

Because you are worth it

Nova Spivack is the co-founder of Arch Mission Foundation. His mission is to ensure that even if we as a species manage to destroy ourselves or get destroyed by some other larger force, there will be clues and resources left behind so that someone will be able to restart our species and understand our civilization in the future. For that the Arch Mission Foundation is preserving the wisdom, culture and biology of our planet in a solar system-wide project called The Billion Year Archive™. Spivack's vision for the Billion Year Archive is, 'Wherever humanity goes, so shall go the Archive; wherever goes the Archive, so shall go humanity.' He launched the Archive sending a small library in the glove compartment on Elon Musk's Tesla Roadster that is currently orbiting the sun and expected to be continuing that for at least the next thirty million years.

Do you remember the story of the moon mission we started this book with? The time capsule that is hosting the tardigrades in the moon was sent by Nova Spivack's Arch Mission. Though the idea of this time capsule may sound quirky for some, Beresheet is also the story of the survival of Spivack's efforts to leave a mark of our tiny blue dot in this infinitely vast universe.

It is Spivack's personal mission that became part of these major global projects. It was his wide-open Personal and People

Gates that led him to the next level—the Universal Gate, which in turn steered him to organizations like SpaceX and ISIL to make his larger than life dream a reality.

With a well-established Personal, People and Universal Gates, none of your ideas will be tagged impossible. That is because at this level, the clarity of your thoughts will be at a higher plane, your conviction of your purpose will be so comprehensible, your energy to make your dreams will be unparalleled and you will have developed the traits to sprinkle the water yourself to remain imperishable no matter how adverse the situation that it leads you to. Your life is a testament of the Three Gates you unlock. You have all the rights and skills to unlock those Gates and marvel at the enormity of the hidden potential you have unlocked while exploring the still abundant potential hidden inside you. Unlock your hidden potential with the help of the Three Gates framework and enjoy your success, because you are worth it.

References

Introduction

1. 'In Depth | Beresheet.' *NASA Solar System Exploration*, https://solarsystem. nasa.gov/missions/beresheet/in-depth/.

Chapter 1

2. 'Tectonic shifts in global supply chains' BofA Global Research, https://www. bofaml.com/content/dam/boamlimages/documents/articles/ID20_0147/ Tectonic_Shifts_in_Global_Supply_Chains.pdf

3. National Population and Talent Division, Strategy Group, Prime Minister's Office, et al. *'Population in Brief 2021'*. Sept. 2021. https://www.population. gov.sg/files/media-centre/publications/population-in-brief-2021.pdf

4. *'Fostering Innovation through a Diverse Workforce'* Forbes Insights, https://www. forbes.com/forbesinsights/StudyPDFs/Innovation_Through_Diversity.pdf

5. Hewlett, Sylvia Ann, et al. 'How Diversity Can Drive Innovation.' *Harvard Business Review*, Dec. 2013, https://hbr.org/2013/12/how-diversity-can-drive-innovation

6. 'High-Skilled Immigration Increases Innovation | the Hamilton Project.' *Hamiltonproject.org*, 9 Oct. 2018, www.hamiltonproject.org/charts/ high_skilled_immigration_increases_innovation .

7. 'How We Picked the 2020 Kid of the Year.' *Time*, https://time.com/5916802/ how-time-picked-2020-kid-of-the-year/.

8. Walker, Jon. 'The Self-Driving Car Timeline—Predictions from the Top 11 Global Automakers |. Emerj - Artificial Intelligence Research and Insight.' *Emerj*, https://emerj.com/ai-adoption-timelines/self-driving-car-timeline-themselves-top-11-automakers/.

9. 'Renault-Nissan and Microsoft Partner to Deliver the Future of Connected Driving.' *Stories*, 26 Sept. 2016, https://news.microsoft.com/2016/09/26/

renault-nissan-and-microsoft-partner-to-deliver-the-future-of-connected-driving/.

10. Griffin, Matthew. 'Experts Are Starting to Agree That AI Will Replace CEO's.' *311 Institute*, 12 May 2017, www.311institute.com/experts-are-starting-to-agree-that-ai-will-replace-ceos/.

11. 'Measuring the U.S. Internet Sector: 2019 - Internet Association.' *Internet Association*, 26 Sept. 2019, http://internetassociation.org/publications/measuring-us-internet-sector-2019/.

12. '22nd Annual Global CEO Survey CEOs' Curbed Confidence Spells Caution.' *PwC*, 2019, https://pwc.com/gx/en/ceo-survey/2019/report/pwc-22nd-annual-global-ceo-survey.pdf.

13. 'Latest Nationwide Study Shows 1 in 7 People in Singapore Has Experienced a Mental Disorder in Their Lifetime.', 11 Dec. 2018, https://www.imh.com.sg/Newsroom/News-Releases/Documents/SMHS per cent 202016_Media per cent 20Release_FINAL_web per cent 20upload.pdf.

14. OECD (2013), *Education at a Glance 2013: Highlights*, OECD Publishing, Paris, https://doi.org/10.1787/eag_highlights-2013-en.

Chapter 2

15. Dweck, Carol S. *Mindset : The New Psychology of Success*. New York, Ballantine Books, 26 Dec. 2007.

16. 'Change Your BRAIN by Using These Hacks to Increase Your DOPAMINE | Dr Andrew Huberman.' *YouTube*, Tom Bilyeu, 23 Sept. 2021, www.youtube.com/watch?v=xLORsLlcT48.

17. Huberman, Andrew. 'Controlling Your Dopamine for Motivation, Focus & Satisfaction | Huberman Lab Podcast #39.' *YouTube*, 27 Sept. 2021, www.youtube.com/watch?v=QmOF0crdyRU.

18. Sindu Sreebhavan. *Great Growth Mindset Challenges*. Singapore, As Many Minds, 7 Mar. 2020.

19. Sindu Sreebhavan. *Infinite Possibilities: Unlock Your Real Potential with the Secret Recipes of Superachievers*. Singapore, As Many Minds, 5 July 2018.

20. Aggarwal, Anjali, and Sindu Sreebhavan. *Breakthrough: Secrets of Growth, Happiness and Bouncebacks from Women around the World*. Singapore, As Many Minds, 20 Apr. 2018.

21. Sreebhavan, Sindu. *30-Day Gratitude System: A Complete System to Develop a Habit of Gratitude and Enhance Your Self-Leadership and Growth Mindset*. Singapore, As Many Minds, 31 Mar. 2020.

Chapter 3

22.   Gilbert, Dan. 'The Psychology of Your Future Self.' *www.ted.com*, TED, 2014, www.ted.com/talks/dan_gilbert_the_psychology_of_your_future_self.

23.   'Mindset Expert Shows You How to Control Your Negative Thoughts | Trevor Moawad on Impact Theory.' *YouTube*, Tom Bilyeu, 3 Mar. 2020, www.youtube.com/watch?v=5lCeWtXPKko.

24.   Crocetti, Elisabetta, et al. 'Capturing the Dynamics of Identity Formation in Various Ethnic Groups: Development and Validation of a Three-Dimensional Model.' *Journal of Adolescence*, vol. 31, no. 2, Apr. 2008, pp. 207–222, 10.1016/j.adolescence.2007.09.002.

25.   Crocetti, Elisabetta, et al. 'The Utrecht-Management of Identity Commitments Scale (U-MICS).' *European Journal of Psychological Assessment*, vol. 26, no. 3, Jan. 2010, pp. 172–186, 10.1027/1015-5759/a000024.

26.   Schwartz, Seth J., et al. 'Daily Dynamics of Personal Identity and Self-Concept Clarity.' *European Journal of Personality*, vol. 25, no. 5, 9 Nov. 2010, pp. 373–385, doi.org/10.1002/per.798, 10.1002/per.798.

27.   'Personal Development Market Size, Trends, Opportunities, and Forecast.' *Verified Market Research*, Oct. 2021, www.verifiedmarketresearch.com/product/personal-development-market/.

28.   *Interview with Anil Kumar on 28 April 2022*

Chapter 4

29.   'Niravu Residents Association.' *Niravu*, www.niravu.com.

30.   Anima, P. 'It Takes a Village.' *The Hindu*, 13 June 2014, www.thehindu.com/features/metroplus/it-takes-a-village/article6111736.ece.

31.   'Warren Buffett Speaks with Florida University.' *YouTube*, www.youtube.com/watch?v=2MHIcabnjrA.

32.   Peterson, Christopher, and Martin E P Seligman. *Character Strengths and Virtues: A Handbook and Classification*, 8 Apr. 2004, Washington, American Psychological Association; New York.

33.   Epperson, Stephanie Dhue, Sharon. 'Most Workers Want Their Employer to Share Their Values — 56% Won't Even Consider a Workplace That Doesn't, Survey Finds.' *CNBC*, 1 July 2022, www.cnbc.com/2022/07/01/most-workers-want-their-employer-to-share-their-values.html. Accessed 31 July 2022.

34. 'Remote Work Improves When Companies Share Their Values with Employees.' *Columbia Business School*, 13 July 2021, www8.gsb.columbia.edu/ newsroom/newsn/11470/remote-work-improves-when-companies-share-their-values-with-employees.

35. Hsin, A., and Y. Xie. 'Explaining Asian Americans' Academic Advantage over Whites.' *Proceedings of the National Academy of Sciences*, vol. 111, no. 23, 5 May 2014, pp. 8416–8421, www.ncbi.nlm.nih.gov/pmc/articles/PMC4060715/ pdf/pnas.201406402.pdf, 10.1073/pnas.1406402111.

36. Shafer, Leah. 'The Other Achievement Gap.' *Harvard Graduate School of Education*, 17 Apr. 2017, www.gse.harvard.edu/news/uk/17/04/other-achievement-gap.

Chapter 5

37. Bryant, Adam. 'Satya Nadella, Chief of Microsoft, on His New Role.' *The New York Times*, 20 Feb. 2014, www.nytimes.com/2014/02/21/business/satya-nadella-chief-of-microsoft-on-his-new-role.html.

38. Eurich, Tasha. 'Working with People Who Aren't Self-Aware.' *Harvard Business Review*, 19 Oct. 2018, hbr.org/2018/10/working-with-people-who-arent-self-aware.

39. Dierdorff, Erich C., and Robert S. Rubin. 'Research: We're Not Very Self-Aware, Especially at Work.' *Harvard Business Review*, 12 Mar. 2015, hbr. org/2015/03/research-were-not-very-self-aware-especially-at-work.

Chapter 6

40. Baikie, Karen A., and Kay Wilhelm. 'Emotional and Physical Health Benefits of Expressive Writing.' *Advances in Psychiatric Treatment*, vol. 11, no. 5, 2 Jan. 2018, pp. 338–346, www.cambridge.org/core/journals/advances-in-psychiatric-treatment/article/emotional-and-physical-health-benefits-of-expressive-writing/ED2976A61F5DE56B46F07A1CE9EA9F9F, 10.1192/ apt.11.5.338.

Chapter 7

41. Lembke, Anna. *Dopamine Nation : Resetting Your Brain in the Age of Cheap Pleasures*. New York, Dutton, 24 Aug. 2021.

42. Chowdhury, Madhuleena Roy. 'The Neuroscience of Gratitude and How It Affects Anxiety & Grief.' *PositivePsychology.com*, 9 Apr. 2019, positivepsychology. com/neuroscience-of-gratitude/.

Chapter 8

43. Zhang, Huaiyu, et al. 'Self-Criticism and Depressive Symptoms: Mediating Role of Self-Compassion.' *OMEGA - Journal of Death and Dying*, vol. 80, no. 2, 8 Sept. 2017, pp. 202–223, doi.org/10.1177/0030222817729609, 10.1177/0030222817729609.

44. Cash, Thomas F. *Encyclopedia of Body Image and Human Appearance*. Amsterdam, Elsevier, 23 May 2012.

45. Neff, Kristin D. 'Self-Compassion, Self-Esteem, and Well-Being.' *Social and Personality Psychology Compass*, vol. 5, no. 1, Jan. 2011, pp. 1–12, doi.org/10.1111/j.1751-9004.2010.00330.x, 10.1111/j.1751-9004.2010.00330.x.

46. Neff, Kristin. *Self-Compassion : Stop Beating Yourself up and Leave Insecurity Behind*. New York, William Morrow, 2015.

47. Twenge, Jean M. *Generation Me : Why Today's Young Americans Are More Confident, Assertive, Entitled--and More Miserable than Ever Before*. New York, Free Press, 4 Apr. 2006.

48. Enns, Murray W., and Brian J. Cox. 'Perfectionism, Stressful Life Events, and the 1-Year Outcome of Depression.' *Cognitive Therapy and Research*, vol. 29, no. 5, Oct. 2005, pp. 541–553, doi.org/10.1007/s10608-005-2414-8, 10.1007/s10608-005-2414-8.

49. Newby, Jennifer, et al. 'Neuroticism and Perfectionism as Predictors of Social Anxiety.' *Personality and Individual Differences*, vol. 106, 1 Feb. 2017, pp. 263–267, www.sciencedirect.com/science/article/abs/pii/S0191886916310947, 10.1016/j.paid.2016.10.057.

50. Egan, Sarah J., et al. 'Perfectionism as a Transdiagnostic Process: A Clinical Review.' *Clinical Psychology Review*, vol. 31, no. 2, Mar. 2011, pp. 203–212, doi.org/10.1016/j.cpr.2010.04.009, 10.1016/j.cpr.2010.04.009.

51. Ito, Tiffany A., et al. 'Negative Information Weighs More Heavily on the Brain: The Negativity Bias in Evaluative Categorizations.' *Journal of Personality and Social Psychology*, vol. 75, no. 4, 1998, pp. 887–900, 10.1037/0022-3514.75.4.887.

Chapter 9

52. Luders, Eileen, et al. 'Forever Young(Er): Potential Age-Defying Effects of Long-Term Meditation on Gray Matter Atrophy.' *Frontiers in Psychology*, vol. 5, 21 Jan. 2015, www.frontiersin.org/articles/10.3389/fpsyg.2014.01551/full, 10.3389/fpsyg.2014.01551.

53. Taren, Adrienne A., et al. 'Dispositional Mindfulness Co-Varies with Smaller Amygdala and Caudate Volumes in Community Adults.' *PLoS ONE*, vol. 8, no.

5, 22 May 2013, p. e64574, doi.org/10.1371/journal.pone.0064574, 10.1371/journal.pone.0064574.

54. Desteno, David. *How God Works*. S.L., Simon & Schuster, 14 Sept. 2021.

55. Desteno, David. *EMOTIONAL SUCCESS : The Motivational Power of Gratitude, Compassion and Pride*. Pan Macmillan, 23 Jan. 2020.

Chapter 10

56. Tseng, Julie, and Jordan Poppenk. 'Brain Meta-State Transitions Demarcate Thoughts across Task Contexts Exposing the Mental Noise of Trait Neuroticism.' *Nature Communications*, vol. 11, no. 1, 13 July 2020, p. 3480, www.nature.com/articles/s41467-020-17255-9, 10.1038/s41467-020-17255-9.

57. Pai, Hsiang-Chu. 'The Effect of a Self-Reflection and Insight Program on the Nursing Competence of Nursing Students: A Longitudinal Study.' *Journal of Professional Nursing*, vol. 31, no. 5, Sept. 2015, pp. 424–431, 10.1016/j.profnurs.2015.03.003.

Chapter 11

58. *The Reinvention of Company Culture 2022 Global Talent Trends*. LinkedIn, https://business.linkedin.com/content/dam/me/business/en-us/talent-solutions-lodestone/body/pdf/global_talent_trends_2022.pdf

59. *Interview with Pascal Bornet on 7 April 2022*

Chapter 12

60. Jha, Amishi. *Peak Mind : Find Your Focus, Own Your Attention, Invest 12 Minutes a Day*. New York, Ny, Harperone, An Imprint Of Harper Collins, Publishers, 19 Oct. 2021.

61. Csikszentmihalyi, Mihaly. *Flow: The Psychology of Optimal Experience*. New York, Harper and Row, 1 July 2008.

62. Loh, Kep Kee, and Ryota Kanai. 'Higher Media Multi-Tasking Activity Is Associated with Smaller Gray-Matter Density in the Anterior Cingulate Cortex.' *PLoS ONE*, vol. 9, no. 9, 24 Sept. 2014, p. e106698, doi.org/10.1371/journal.pone.0106698, 10.1371/journal.pone.0106698.

Chapter 13

63. Lehner, Stephan R., et al. 'Rats Benefit from Winner and Loser Effects.' *Ethology*, vol. 117, no. 11, 3 Oct. 2011, pp. 949–960, doi.org/10.1111/j.1439-0310.2011.01962.x, 10.1111/j.1439-0310.2011.01962.x.

64. Zhou, Tingting, et al. 'History of Winning Remodels Thalamo-PFC Circuit to Reinforce Social Dominance.' *Science*, vol. 357, no. 6347, 13 July 2017, pp. 162–168, doi.org/10.1126/science.aak9726, 10.1126/science.aak9726.

65. Robertson, Ian H. *The Winner Effect : The Neuroscience of Success and Failure.* New York, Thomas Dunne Books, 16 Oct. 2012.

66. Maxwell, John C. *Failing Forward.* HarperCollins Focus, 3 June 2007.

67. 'Dr A.P.J. Abdul Kalam: Former President of India: Speeches : Details.' *Dr A.P.J. Abdul Kalam*, 10 Oct. 2003, abdulkalam.nic.in/sp101003-2.html.

Chapter 14

68. Adams, Susan. 'Feeling Grateful Makes You a Better Saver and Investor, Study Shows.' *Forbes*, 1 Apr. 2014, www.forbes.com/sites/susanadams/2014/04/01/feeling-grateful-makes-you-a-better-saver-and-investor-study-shows/.

69. Mischel, Walter, et al. 'Cognitive and Attentional Mechanisms in Delay of Gratification.' *Journal of Personality and Social Psychology*, vol. 21, no. 2, 1972, pp. 204–218, ttps://doi.org/10.1037/h0032198, 10.1037/h0032198.

70. Baumeister, Roy F, and John Tierney. *Willpower : Rediscovering the Greatest Human Strength.* New York, Penguin Books, 28 Aug. 2012.

71. Miller, Gregory E., et al. 'Self-Control Forecasts Better Psychosocial Outcomes but Faster Epigenetic Aging in Low-SES Youth.' *Proceedings of the National Academy of Sciences*, vol. 112, no. 33, 13 July 2015, pp. 10325–10330, doi.org/10.1073/pnas.1505063112, 10.1073/pnas.1505063112.

72. Salisbury, David. 'Dopamine Impacts Your Willingness to Work.' *Vanderbilt University*, Vanderbilt University, May 2012, news.vanderbilt.edu/2012/05/01/dopamine-impacts-your-willingness-to-work/.

73. Treadway, Michael T., et al. 'Dopaminergic Mechanisms of Individual Differences in Human Effort-Based Decision-Making.' *The Journal of Neuroscience*, vol. 32, no. 18, 2 May 2012, pp. 6170–6176, www.ncbi.nlm.nih.gov/pmc/articles/PMC3391699/, 10.1523/JNEUROSCI.6459-11.2012. Accessed 13 May 2020.

74. DeSteno, David, et al. 'Gratitude: A Tool for Reducing Economic Impatience.' *Psychological Science*, vol. 25, no. 6, 23 Apr. 2014, pp. 1262–1267, doi.org/10.1177/0956797614529979, 10.1177/0956797614529979.

75. Dickens, Leah, and David DeSteno. 'The Grateful Are Patient: Heightened Daily Gratitude Is Associated with Attenuated Temporal Discounting.' *Emotion*, vol. 16, no. 4, 3 Feb. 2016, pp. 421–425, 10.1037/emo0000176. https://static1.squarespace.com/static/52853b8ae4b0a6c35d3f8e9d/t/56b245717da24f5a07998fd3/1454523763659/the-grateful-are-patient.pdf

76.   Sreebhavan, Sindu. *30-Day Gratitude System: A Complete System to Develop a Habit of Gratitude and Enhance Your Self-Leadership and Growth Mindset.* As Many Minds, 31 Mar. 2020.

77.   Salerno, Anthony, et al. 'Pride and Regulatory Behaviour: The Influence of Appraisal Information and Self-Regulatory Goals.' *Journal of Consumer Research,* vol. 42, no. 3, 10 July 2015, pp. 499–514, doi.org/10.1093/jcr/ucv037, 10.1093/jcr/ucv037.

78.   Williams, Lisa, and David Desteno. 'Pride Adaptive Social Emotion or Seventh Sin?' *https://static1.squarespace.com/static/52853b8ae4b0a6c35d3f8e9d/t/528d260ae 4b059766439b8d0/1384982026025/pride-adaptive-social-emotion-or-seventh-sin.pdf*

79.   'How Do Leaders Manage the Tension between Pride and Arrogance?' *HBS Working Knowledge,* 30 Nov. 2016, hbswk.hbs.edu/item/how-do-leaders-manage-the-tension-between-pride-and-arrogance.

80.   Daus, Catherine S., and Stephen R. Baumgartner. 'Ain't Too Proud to Beg! Effects of Leader's Use of Pride on Groups.' *International Journal of Environmental Research and Public Health,* vol. 17, no. 19, 29 Sept. 2020, p. 7146, 10.3390/ijerph17197146. https://doi.org/10.3390/ijerph17197146

Chapter 15

81.   Goleman, Daniel. *Emotional Intelligence.* New York, Bantam Books, 1997.

82.   'Gartner for HR | Support Well-Being in 2021 and Beyond.' *Gartner,* www.gartner.com/en/human-resources/trends/support-wellbeing-2021-and-beyond.

83.   'Half of Employees Quit Their Job for Their Mental Health in 2021.' *HRM America,* www.hcamag.com/us/specialization/benefits/half-of-employees-quit-their-job-for-their-mental-health-in-2021/326840.

84.   Daniel Goleman, Strategies to Become More Emotional Intelligent | WOBI.' *YouTube,* 20 Nov. 2017, www.youtube.com/watch?v=pt74vK9pgIA.

85.   'Microsoft's Satya Nadella on Flexible Work, the Metaverse, and the Power of Empathy.' *Harvard Business Review,* 28 Oct. 2021, hbr.org/2021/10/microsofts-satya-nadella-on-flexible-work-the-metaverse-and-the-power-of-empathy.

Chapter 16

86.   Zak, Paul. 'The Neuroscience of Trust.' *Harvard Business Review,* 19 Dec. 2016, hbr.org/2017/01/the-neuroscience-of-trust.

87. Feltman, Charles. *The Thin Book of Trust: An Essential Primer for Building Trust at Work (Edition:2)*. Thin Book Publishing, 2021.

88. Covey, Stephen R. *Trust & Inspire : How Truly Great Leaders Unleash Greatness in Others*. London, UK, Simon & Schuster, 2022.

Chapter 17

89. Brené Brown. *Dare to Lead : Brave Work, Tough Conversations, Whole Hearts*. New York, Random House, 9 Oct. 2018.

90. Brene Brown. *Power of Vulnerability: Teachings on Authenticity, Connection, and Courage*. Sounds True, Incorporated, 15 Nov. 2012.

91. Vasudevan, Manoj. *How to Become the World Champion of Public Speaking*. Singapore, As Many Minds, 30 Apr. 2019.

Chapter 18

92. Riedl, Christoph, et al. 'Quantifying Collective Intelligence in Human Groups.' *Proceedings of the National Academy of Sciences*, vol. 118, no. 21, 17 May 2021, p. e2005737118, doi.org/10.1073/pnas.2005737118, 10.1073/pnas.2005737118.

93. Wenzel, Michael, et al. 'The Effects of Moral/Social Identity Threats and Affirmations on Psychological Defensiveness Following Wrongdoing.' *British Journal of Social Psychology*, 7 Apr. 2020, doi.org/10.1111/bjso.12378, 10.1111/bjso.12378.

Chapter 19

94. 'Edelman Trust Barometer 2022.' Edelman, https://www.edelman.com/sites/g/files/aatuss191/files/2022-01/2022%20Edelman%20Trust%20Barometer%20FINAL_Jan25.pdf

95. Shamir, Boas, et al. 'The Motivational Effects of Charismatic Leadership: A Self-Concept Based Theory.' *Organization Science*, vol. 4, no. 4, 1 Nov. 1993, pp. 577–594, doi.org/10.1287/orsc.4.4.577, 10.1287/orsc.4.4.577.

96. Fisher, Roger C, et al. *Getting to Yes: Negotiating Agreement without Giving In*. New York, Penguin, 3 May 2011.

97. *Interview with Nichol Ng on 21 May 2022*

Chapter 20

98.   'The Vagabonds - the Henry Ford.' *The Henry Ford*, www.thehenryford.org/
      collections-and-research/digital-resources/popular-topics/the-vagabonds.

99.   'Thomas & Mina Edison, Henry & Clara Ford.' *Edison and Ford Winter Estates*,
      www.edisonfordwinterestates.org/about/historical-people-places/.

Conclusion

100. 'Arch Mission Foundation - Preserving Humanity Forever, in Space and on
      Earth.' *Arch Mission Foundation - Preserving Humanity Forever, in Space and on
      Earth.*, archmission.org.

Acknowledgements

It was late in the night when I received a message from Nora Abu Bakar of Penguin Random House enquiring about writing a book. In the discussions ensued in the days following, Nora told me that my experience in multiple industries as part of my consulting and coaching career, my experience with youth as well as educators as an entrepreneur and my exposure to various countries places me at a unique position to write a book addressing various demographics. Unlike my previous books, this book took rather long time to finish, you will read more about that in Chapter 9. During those times, Nora listened to me with empathy and waited patiently for me to finish the book. Nora has my gratitude for her boundless trust and confidence in me.

Amberdawn Manaois, the editor, proved to be exceptionally helpful, particularly with her quick comprehension and smart questions on approach and style. My sincere gratitude to her and to the entire team from Penguin Random House that worked hard to make this book a reality.

I am grateful to my husband Manoj for motivating me and giving his feedback on several chapters from time to time. My son Advaith and Aditi are my biggest cheerleaders. Though teenagers, with their well-grounded and mature nature, they analyzed many concepts in this book, and gave straight yet compassionate feedbacks that helped me take a relook at various parts of this book with a fresh perspective. Without the immeasurable support of these three people, this book would not have been possible.

As a young child, I learnt about perseverance and duty from my parents Ramesh and Prabhavati Pillai, who took the role of running a joint family which had its own politics, challenges and struggles, with great courage, pride and ownership. I learnt the virtues of selfless service from their lives. Though my dad did not live to read any of my books, the habits of reading and analyzing books and newspaper editorials he instilled in me, had been a shining light throughout my writing career.

My three sisters-in-law Suchetha, Manju and Shilpa, and my dear friend Hima, who are exceptional women with extraordinary strength, love and compassion, were always there to listen to my ideas and frustrations and cheer me up during the journey of writing this book.

My friend Anoop Kumar's creativity is something I have great trust on. He has been my go-to person for analyzing the cover designs of many books written by Manoj, Advaith and me. His insights on the proposed cover designs driven by his senior executive outlook and his creative mind have helped me in the case of this book too. I am much grateful to him for his advice and suggestions.

There are several people I have had interviews and discussions with while writing this book. I have used anecdotes from many of their lives to establish many concepts discussed in this book. Some among them are senior executives, some are mid-level executives, some are entrepreneurs and some are students. Some gave me the permission to reveal their identities and stories, some gave me the permission to reveal their stories but not their identities and some though shared their stories with me I could not include those because of several reasons. Nevertheless, these are brave people who have been kind to share many intimate details of their lives with me for this book and I am immensely grateful to them for that.

The endorsers of a book are generally busy individuals. People approach them for endorsements because they have proved with their lives and deeds that they are champions in their games. I am truly grateful to all those amazing stalwarts for taking the time to read and synthesize this book, and pen down their genuine thoughts.

There are countless people I am grateful to, for directly or indirectly being a part of my learning journey. That includes people I worked with, people I have coached, children who have taken part in the workshops I organized and the audiences of my keynotes and training programs. All these experiences have contributed to questioning my knowledge and beliefs and shaping my perspectives about human potential and its expansibility.